LEGAL ENGLISH

'This is a much needed text and should be on the reading list of all students who need to get to grips with language issues.'

Dr Sharon Hanson, PhD, Senior Lecturer in Law,
Department of Law and Criminal Justice Studies, Canterbury Christ Church University

'I would recommend this book to students who intend to study law and need to learn legal language.'

Alison Chisholm, Sussex Centre for Language Studies, Sussex University

'This book fills a very important gap and will be gratefully appreciated by both students and teachers of legal English. It is an authoritative introduction to a field which is becoming more and more significant internationally.'

David Rowson, MBE, Head of English, Bellerbys College, London

PEARSON

We work with leading authors to develop the strongest educational materials in law, bringing cutting-edge thinking and best learning practice to a global market.

Under a range of well-known imprints, including Longman, we craft high quality print and electronic publications which help readers to understand and apply their content, whether studying or at work.

To find out more about the complete range of our publishing, please visit us on the World Wide Web at:
www.pearsoned.co.uk

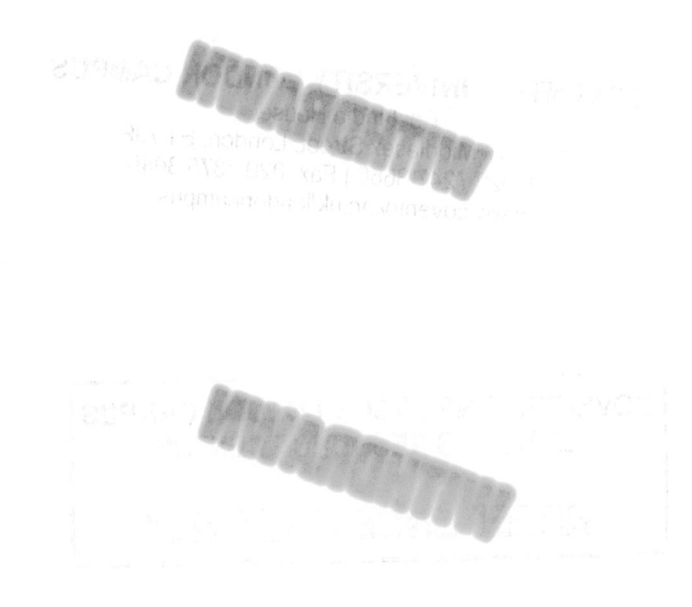

Second Edition

LEGAL ENGLISH

How to understand and master the language of law

William R. McKay, Helen E. Charlton and Grant Barsoum

Harlow, England • London • New York • Boston • San Francisco • Toronto
Sydney • Tokyo • Singapore • Hong Kong • Seoul • Taipei • New Delhi
Cape Town • Madrid • Mexico City • Amsterdam • Munich • Paris • Milan

Pearson Education Limited
Edinburgh Gate
Harlow
Essex CM20 2JE
England

and Associated Companies throughout the world

Visit us on the World Wide Web at:
www.pearsoned.co.uk

First published 2005
Second edition published 2011

ISBN: 978-1-4082-2610-0

British Library Cataloguing-in-Publication Data
A catalogue record for this book is available from the British Library

Library of Congress Cataloging-in-Publication Data
McKay, William R. (William Robert), 1959-
Legal English : how to understand and master the law of language /
William R. McKay, Helen E. Charlton, and Grant Barsoum. — 2nd ed.
p. cm.
Includes index.
ISBN 978-1-4082-2610-0 (pbk.)
1. Law—Great Britain—Terminology. 2. English language—Conversation and phrase books (for lawyers) I. Charlton, Helen E. II. Barsoum, Grant. III. Title.
KD313.M35 2011
340'.14—dc22

2011011020

10 9 8 7 6 5 4 3 2 1
12 11 10 11

Typeset in 9/12 LinoLetter by 73
Printed in Great Britain by Henry Ling Ltd, at the Dorset Press, Dorchester, Dorset

Contents

Acknowledgements

The publishers and authors would like to acknowledge the following for granting permission to reproduce copyright material:

Introductory paragraph of a chapter entitled '*Mens Rea*' (on p. 21) from *The New Oxford Companion to Law*, edited by Peter Cane and Joanne Conghan (2008) Oxford University Press

Figure 6.1 (on p. 145) and Figure 6.2 (on p. 146) adapted from Smith and Keenan's *English Law*, 15th edition (2007), Pearson Education.

Excerpts from the Articles of Association are taken from LRM Europe Limited. Reproduced with permission.

While every care has been taken to establish and acknowledge copyright and to contact the copyright owners, the publishers tender their apologies for any accidental infringement. They would be pleased to come to a suitable arrangement with the rightful owners in each case.

Preface

English is the predominant language of international legal practice and its importance to students, lawyers and business professionals cannot be overemphasised. A good command of language is crucial to professional success, particularly in the legal field. Yet legal English includes some vocabulary virtually exclusive to the legal domain and some common English words even have different or special meanings when used in a legal context. Modern legal English is further complicated by words stemming from Latin and Norman French as well as Old English and going back some one thousand years.

This book has been written to assist those wishing to become more conversant in English within a legal context, whether for the purposes of:

- undergraduate legal study;
- vocational preparation, such as for a legal practice course (LPC), a Bar professional training course (BPTC), the Bar aptitude test or the English language test element of the Qualified Lawyers' Transfer Scheme;
- study for courses of other professional bodies with legal content;
- legal practice or other professional work involving legal issues.

This second edition therefore also explores the language of law for undergraduate students, as well as for those studying other professional courses. This includes additional features in academic writing and reading skills.

The book is of particular relevance to those using English as a second or foreign language, but it will also be of assistance to native English speakers. It is indeed for anyone who wishes to build confidence and enhance their English language skills for legal academic or practical purposes. It is therefore intended to serve as a resource for a variety of individuals, including those:

- aiming to study or presently studying law within an English language jurisdiction (whether for academic or vocational training purposes);
- presently involved in the legal or business domain whose work brings them into contact with legal practice.

With the benefit of feedback on the first edition, the overall structure and approach of the book has been improved in this second edition. The text is divided into two parts: the first part focuses on reading and writing for law; the second part covers speaking and listening skills for both students and professionals. The chapter headings now relate directly to particular areas of legal language usage, so that the reader can quickly identify relevant sections of the book for guidance on topics including:

- the study of law and academic writing;
- legal writing in practice;
- drafting of legal documents for business, commerce and court;

- presentation skills;
- interviewing and advising;
- negotiation;
- advocacy.

The text can be quickly referenced to check the correct use of English in a particular situation, or it can be worked through methodically to build competence in all areas through the course of a structured programme of study. The reader therefore has the flexibility to use the book over time for any number of purposes, for example for help with legal study, assistance in writing for a particular purpose, preparing for a mooting competition or a presentation, drafting legal documents, negotiating on behalf of a client or acting as an advocate in court.

Legal English can be used by readers with or without any prior legal training. Core legal topics are explored using realistic legal materials through exercises and case studies for specific linguistic purposes. Looking first at the use of language in academic legal study, including writing for academic purposes and reading and researching legal texts, the book then further develops those linguistic concepts for effective legal practice. Thus the book offers readers a valuable learning resource designed progressively to enhance relevant and meaningful communication skills in both written and oral legal English. The material is arranged in a logical sequence of increasing complexity to allow the reader to build upon their learning step by step as concepts are reinforced throughout the book. The exercises in this text can be used either for self-study or in a group or classroom setting. By working through the exercises and learning from the examples given in the text, the reader can develop his or her potential for effective communication and successful academic and professional development.

The accompanying companion website, **www.mylawchamber.co.uk/mckay**, offers further language guidance, including audio files to demonstrate oral language skills in realistic legal scenarios.

Finally, please note that all documents contained in this work are for illustration purposes only and should not be regarded as having any precedent value whatsoever.

In addition, we would like to acknowledge colleagues and users of the first edition who have provided valuable feedback, all of which we have tried to take on board in terms of the content and structure of this new edition. We would also like to acknowledge the sterling efforts of Carole Drummond at Pearson Education for her final editing of the book and for ensuring that everything 'came together' in the final stages of production. Lastly, but certainly not least, our sincere thanks go to our editor, Christine Statham, whose calm and mature guidance has been of fundamental help in consolidating and bringing to fruition this second edition.

William R. McKay
Helen Charlton
Grant Barsoum
June 2011

Part 1

Written communication skills

Chapter 1

Academic writing

Learning objectives

This chapter will help you to:

- understand the conventions of academic writing for law exams and coursework;
- improve your writing style;
- achieve higher grades for your written assignments;
- practise writing a wide range of sentences;
- develop your skills in paragraph writing and text organisation;
- use linking words accurately;
- understand how punctuation marks work and practise using them correctly;
- realise the importance of acknowledging the source in your writing.

INTRODUCTION

While studying for your law degree, you will be asked to write essays, answer problem questions and submit other written coursework. The main purpose of this chapter is to help you understand the requirements for high marks through exploring the essential elements of English language usage needed to improve your writing style. Addressing points of law and developing logical argument in essays and problem questions will also be discussed in this chapter. The examples and explanations given in this chapter will help you gain confidence in expressing your ideas clearly and logically. Once you have finished studying this chapter, you will need to continue writing as the more you practise writing, the better your writing style will get. Improving your academic writing style will in turn help you improve your grades.

The starting point is learning to understand the conventions of academic writing; the focus then will be on the grammar of various types of sentence as well as developing your skills in using punctuation marks. This chapter will also provide guidance and practice for linking ideas in order to develop your skills in paragraph writing.

Guidance for referencing and warning notes about plagiarising are given at the end of the chapter.

ACADEMIC WRITING STYLE

The vocabulary you use, the way you arrange words and the length of the sentences you write form your writing style. Style varies according to the purpose of writing, even for the same subject matter. For instance, you will find that the style used for a law essay is different from that for legal documents and correspondence. It is therefore important to use the appropriate style.

Features of academic writing

In order to understand what we mean by features of writing style for studying law at university, we need to examine the difference between writing for academic and professional purposes and other forms of writing. Thus, before you start writing, your first step is to develop your ability and skills in using different degrees of formality in English.

Informal and semi-formal English

In everyday communication – both oral and written – we generally use informal and semi-formal English, as shown in the following examples. Read these sentences carefully and note how English is used:

1. Police in the dock over evidence to foreign courts.
2. You reckon to finish the essay by next Friday?
3. You mustn't drive through a red light, it's an offence.
4. He's been pinching money from the till for donkey's years, but when his boss caught him he knew he was in hot water.
5. The Chairman stepped down as boss of BP with a bitter sideswipe at critics.
6. We can't make head or tail of this report.
7. If you can identify any of the yobs call Crimestoppers anonymously on 0110 222 333.
8. A tax dodger buried £140,000 in his aunt's grave in a bid to fool the Inland Revenue.
9. I wouldn't believe a word he says, he's a conman.
10. She thought she could get away with it but she was nicked for shoplifting.

Use of vocabulary

The following table refers to the above examples and provides the informal and semi-formal words and phrases and their standard English equivalent.

Sentence number	Informal/semi-formal usage		Meaning/standard English usage
1	in the dock	(colloquial)	on trial
2	reckon	(colloquial)	expect
3	musn't	(colloquial)	must not
4	pinch	(colloquial)	steal
	for donkey's years	(colloquial)	for a long time
	in hot water	(colloquial)	in trouble
5	step down	(phrasal verb)	resign
6	can't make head or tail of this report	(idiom)	cannot understand it at all
7	yobs	(slang)	rude, noisy, aggressive youths
8	dodger	(slang)	elusive; a person who evades paying taxes by trickery
	in a bid to	(colloquial)	in an attempt to

(*continued*)

Sentence number	Informal/semi-formal usage		Meaning/standard English usage
9	conman	(slang)	swindler
10	get away with it	(phrasal verb)	do it without being caught/ punished
	nicked	(slang)	arrested

In spoken, informal English, we often use chunks of the language, in other words phrases and parts of sentences. This point is illustrated in sentence 2 in the above examples; it is not acceptable in standard English but totally acceptable in informal speaking. When you are chatting with friends, most people would not worry much about the grammatical correctness of your sentences so long as you can get the message across. This is not the case, however, in academic and legal English.

Formal or standard English

Note that colloquial and slang words are not used in formal English and neither are informal idioms. Standard English is used and each sentence should be grammatically correct.

Understanding the difference between informal and semi-formal English and formal or standard English will help us change informal writing into the more formal academic style, as shown in the following examples taken from the sentences above:

Informal (sentence 4): He's been pinching money from the till for donkey's years, but when his boss caught him he knew he was in hot water.

Formal: He has been stealing money from the till for a long time, but when the manager caught him, he realised that he was in trouble.

Informal (sentence 8): A tax dodger buried £140,000 in his aunt's grave in a bid to fool the Inland Revenue.

Formal: In order to evade paying taxes, a man buried £140,000 in his aunt's grave in an attempt to deceive the Inland Revenue.

Good practice tip

When writing for academic or legal purposes **do not** use slang words or colloquial English. Always use standard English.

Exercise 1.1

Rewrite the following sentences, changing them into formal/standard English:

1. Sorry we can't offer you a place on this course.
2. University fees have gone up a lot lately.
3. This department was set up to help students out.
4. Think I've got some typos in my essay.

→

5. Prices have been slashed.
6. Lots of small businesses went bust last year.
7. They've got to put the meeting off till our mate comes back from the conference.

Using legal English in academic writing

The following sentences are examples of written English in a legal context. Read them carefully and pay particular attention to the use of vocabulary, punctuation, sentence structure and length of sentences:

1. No person shall intentionally or recklessly interfere with or misuse anything provided in the interests of health, safety or welfare in pursuance of any of the relevant statutory provisions.
2. Consideration must be given at the time of the contract or at some point after the contract is made.
3. The courts have always recognised certain situations where a promise made subsequent to the performance of an act may nevertheless be enforceable.
4. The classification of offences as indictable and summary broadly reflects a distinction between serious and minor crimes.
5. If the landlord fails to carry out his/her duties or cannot be traced, the court may appoint a receiver to undertake the landlord's duties under s.37(1) of the Supreme Court Act 1981.
6. In principle, private persons may institute prosecutions in English law for any criminal offence unless by statute this has been excluded.
7. The protection of human rights cannot be confined within national boundaries.
8. A full list of shareholders is required with the first and every third Annual Return thereafter.
9. Directors are legally responsible for filing their company's annual accounts and annual return on time, and all companies that deliver accounts late receive a late filing penalty.
10. Prior to the Homicide Act 1957, all persons convicted of murder were automatically sentenced to death.

Legal vocabulary and terminology

Look at the following words given in the above examples:

in pursuance of (sentence 1) (or pursuant to) in accordance with.

provisions (sentence 1) legal statements.

promise (sentence 3) term used in the law of contract.

indictable and summary (sentence 4) terms used in criminal law.

persons (sentence 6) In general English the word 'people' is commonly used, but in formal and legal English the word 'persons' is used instead.

You might notice that some of this vocabulary is not used in everyday speech but is particular to legal English (e.g. 'persons'). You might also notice that some common English words can have different or special meaning in a legal context (e.g. 'promise').

For legal terms such as 'indictable offences' in sentence 4 above, you will need a law dictionary. You might find 'indictable offence' in some dictionaries, but not in others. So, look for the noun, i.e. indictment, and you should find the word 'indictable'.

Punctuation

Correct punctuation is important in legal writing. Incorrect or insufficient punctuation can entirely alter the meaning of the information you are conveying. This can have very serious consequences, particularly in legal practice where it is crucial to ensure that what you write is concise in meaning.

Brackets ( )

These can be useful for academic writing, to add information while avoiding confusion as to meaning. For instance:

> If Mrs Jones was driving while using her mobile telephone (which she denies) then the court is likely to decide that she was driving negligently.

Apostrophe

The way in which an apostrophe (') is used can make a big difference to the meaning expressed. Consider for instance the following sentences:

1. Both the partner's legal assistants are called Gordon.
2. Both the partners' legal assistants are called Gordon.

The placement of the apostrophe in the first sentence tells us that one partner has two assistants and both of them are called Gordon. In the second sentence it tells us that there are two partners who each have an assistant called Gordon. That's a big difference in meaning and it depends on the placement of the apostrophe!

The apostrophe is used for:

- *Contractions*: Contracted forms are widely used in informal and semi-formal English, as demonstrated in the set of examples on page 4. In sentence 3 'mustn't' is the contracted form of 'must not'. Other examples of contractions: 'He's been' (sentence 4), 'can't' (sentence 6), and 'wouldn't' and 'he's' (sentence 9). Note that in the contracted form the apostrophe replaces the missing letters.
- *Possession*: In sentence 5 of the examples on page 6 the apostrophe in 'landlord's duties' refers to the duties of the landlord. Similarly, in sentence 9 'their company's annual accounts and annual return' means the annual accounts and annual return of their company.

  Possession indicates that something/someone belongs to something/someone; this simply means that we put the apostrophe followed by the letter 's' to replace the word 'of'. So, instead of 'the recklessness of the defendant', we write 'the defendant's recklessness'.

  If the noun is in the plural form and ending in 's', we just add the apostrophe at the end of the word, e.g. 'the defendants' recklessness', or 'the partners' assistants'.
- *Plural*: In some short words ending in a vowel, the apostrophe is used for the plural form, for example 'do's'.

Remember:

- When dealing with plural nouns the apostrophe should be placed after the 's'. You will see for instance that this is where the apostrophe is placed with 'directors' meetings' and 'shareholders' meetings'.
- The apostrophe is also placed after the possessive 's' when a singular noun ends in 's', e.g. 'James's case'. With singular nouns, however, the apostrophe should be placed before the possessive 's', e.g. 'the expert's report', 'Gordon's witness statement'. This is also the correct position for the apostrophe with irregular plural nouns, e.g. 'women's court attire'.

Good practice tip

Do not use contracted forms in academic essays.

Confusing words

'whose' and 'who's'

'Whose' is a relative pronoun, i.e. a word to replace 'her', 'his' or 'its' in a complex sentence as in 'The witness whose shop is very close to the scene of the crime has given evidence in court.' (Note: complex sentences will be explained later in this chapter.)

'Who's' is the contracted form of 'who is' or 'who has'.

'its' and 'it's'

'Its' is a possessive adjective, i.e. a word to indicate that something belongs to something else. For example: 'Your essay is within the word limit, but its introductory paragraph is very long.'

'It's' is the contracted form of either 'it is' or 'it has' (see p. 7 for an explanation of contractions).

Full stop

A full stop (known in the US as a 'period') indicates the end of a sentence. Remember to then start every new sentence with a capital letter.

Comma

These punctuation marks are used to separate different parts or clauses of a sentence. They are particularly useful for longer, complex sentences (see p. 16 below). You will also see how commas are important in drafting legal documents in Chapter 4.

Hyphen (-)

- Notice the use of the hyphen in the following words: 'semi-formal', 'ex-world championship contestant'. The hyphen is used here because we added a part ('semi-' and 'ex-') at the beginning of each word; this part is called a **prefix**. Prefixes are added at the beginning of a word in order to change the meaning of the word.

- Notice the use of the hyphen in the following words: 'her brain-damaged son', '30-month prison term'. We can shorten complicated descriptions, such as when talking about the woman's son 'whose brain was damaged', by rephrasing the description as 'her brain-damaged son'. The same applies to '30-month prison term'.

Exercise 1.2

Rephrase the following using a hyphen:

1. a trial that lasted 12 days
2. there are five members of the committee
3. deliberation that took four hours
4. a point that was made in a good way
5. the jury consists of 12 men and women
6. the law made by judges

Semicolon (;)

Read the following text and notice the use of the semicolon:

> Lord Denning in *Bulmer* v *Bollinger* provided some guidance for lower courts. He said that the following facts should be taken into account:
>
> 1. the facts should be decided first;
> 2. the reference to Luxembourg would cause delay and therefore add to the costs of the parties, so the lower court should deal with the case and leave it to an appeal court to decide whether or not to make a reference;
> 3. the wishes of the parties should be taken into account although it was the court's decision whether to make a reference or not;
> 4. the need to avoid overloading the European Court of Justice (ECJ).

You will have noticed that the comma is used since it has many functions and serves us well in numerous instances. The semicolon, unlike the comma, has limited functions, so it is rarely used in informal/semi-formal English. However, semicolons are used in academic and legal English mainly to provide a list of factors or items, as shown above. We also use semicolons when we have some short sentences which all have one complete meaning. If you write these parts as separate sentences, the reader might lose parts of your message.

Exercise 1.3

Some of the commas in the following paragraph are incorrectly placed, others are missing. Rewrite the paragraph and put the commas in the right places:

In 1972 the Parliament passed the European Communities Act 1972 (ECA), in order to enable the UK to become a member of the European Community, thus avoiding further legislation. One of the many impacts of European legislation, was the introduction of laws written for a civil law interpretation. Subsequently the introduction of the Human Rights Act 1998 (HRA) required all statutes to be compatible whenever possible. As a result of these two Acts we have seen a change in statutory interpretation.

Exercise 1.4

The following text is about studying law at university and lacks punctuation. Rewrite it, putting the appropriate punctuation and dividing it into paragraphs:

A full time law degree course lasts for three years and you are expected to study on average four modules each semester some modules are compulsory while others are optional it is useful for academic study to look at one way of classification of law under such classification there is a distinction between public and private law the main focus of public law is the role of law and government in society in other words it deals with the relationship between the state and its citizens and so this includes constitutional law administrative law and criminal law you might find that constitutional and administrative law is counted as one module private law is mainly concerned with the relationship between individuals and business as well as the duties and rights of individuals towards each other thus private law covers a wide range of modules such as law of contract law of tort land law family law company law employment law etc in addition to the above classification when you study the English legal system you will find that law is divided into two areas namely civil law i.e. private law and criminal law.

Quotation marks (inverted commas)

When quoting exactly what someone has stated use *double* quotation marks (" ") to indicate that you are quoting the actual words, for example:

"I admit that my advice was negligent on that occasion."

Double quotation marks are widely used in the UK.

When quoting from a text, *single* quotation marks are used to indicate that the material has been copied. Double quotation marks are then used to indicate the words actually spoken or stated in the text. For example:

'The defendant gave his evidence and said "I admit that my advice was negligent on that occasion."'

The single quotation marks indicate that this sentence is copied from a source, and the double quotation marks indicate that these are the actual words of the defendant.

As a general rule, place commas and full stops *inside* quotation marks. Colons (:) and semi-colons (;), however, should be placed *outside* the quotation marks. For instance:

The Purchaser hereby agrees to purchase the "machinery"; delivery is to be made within fourteen days.

Question marks

These are not commonly used in academic legal writing, but if you are stating a direct question then a question mark should be used. For instance:

Was it reasonably foreseeable that Jennifer's negligence would cause such serious injury?

Exclamation marks

These are not commonly used in academic legal writing, but may be used to place emphasis on what is being stated. For instance:

> John established liability in court and was awarded one million dollars compensation!

An exclamation mark can be used to express surprise or to convey the impression that what is being stated is extraordinary. It is normally placed at the end of the sentence or statement, as with a full stop.

Capital letters

Rules about using capital letters are basic but very important in any academic or professional writing. Here is a brief list of instances where you should always use a capital letter:

- At the beginning of every sentence:

  There must be valid offer and acceptance for an enforceable contract to exist.

- For the names of individuals and places as well as titles of individuals:

  Mrs Jones lives in Washington, USA and her son is presently studying in Australia, where many of his fellow students are unsurprisingly Australian.

- For days in the week, names of months, historical eras, and cultural as well as religious events and festivals:

  Wednesday August Christmas the Middle Ages

- For the titles of publications:

  I bought a copy of a book entitled *Business Law* yesterday.

- For abbreviations (see the Glossary for a range of typical abbreviations and their meanings):

  CPS; NB; PTO.

In order to expand your vocabulary you are strongly advised to use a general English dictionary and a thesaurus in addition to a law dictionary.

An English dictionary provides the pronunciation of a word whereas law dictionaries do not. Most English dictionaries indicate the difference between British and American spelling and whether the word is formal, slang, dated, etc. They also tell you the grammar of the word – verb, noun, adjective, etc. Some also provide some synonyms, i.e. other words of similar meaning.

A thesaurus is a helpful tool for most writers since it provides synonyms and, in addition, antonyms, i.e. words of opposite meaning. To illustrate the advantages of using a dictionary and a thesaurus, let us look up the word 'intentionally' which appeared in the first example under 'Academic and Legal English' above. In most dictionaries you will find 'intentionally' adv. and 'intentional' adj. with sentences by way of examples, but the meaning is explained under the noun 'intention'. Now, if we look up the word 'intentionally' in a thesaurus, we can find other words with similar meanings, such as 'deliberately', 'on purpose', 'wilfully', etc.

Good practice tip

When writing an essay or answering a question, use a wide range of vocabulary. Use standard, formal or academic words, or legal terms. It is essential to use an English dictionary and a thesaurus in addition to a law dictionary in order to enrich your vocabulary.

Be careful also to use correct legal terminology. Read the following text to familiarise yourself with some legal terminology commonly used in academic writing as well as in legal practice.

- A case is *overruled* when a *higher* (*superior*) court decides that the decision in the original case should not be followed.
- A decision is *reversed* when the case is appealed to a higher court (an appeal court) which decides that the original court (the lower court) either: applied the law wrongly or decided a question of fact which could not rationally be supported by the evidence.
- English courts must follow (i.e. are *bound by*) decisions made by superior courts on cases involving similar circumstances. This is known as the *doctrine of precedent*.
- To avoid being bound by such an earlier decision it is necessary to *distinguish* the case being considered from the earlier superior decision.
- A court decision made without regard to applicable earlier binding precedent from a higher court or statutory provision is known as a decision given *per incuriam*.
- Several judges usually sit in the appeal courts. If the decisions of all those judges agree then there is a *unanimous* judgment.
- If there are conflicting decisions then the case is decided by *majority* decision. The decision of the majority is known as the *majority judgment*.
- The decision of a judge who disagrees with the majority judgment is known as a *dissenting* judgment.
- The reason or principle behind the decision in a law case is termed the *ratio decidendi* (*'ratio'* being Latin for *the reason* and *'decidendi'* meaning *for the decision*). This is often abbreviated to the *ratio*. Always look for the *ratio* when reading a case and apply it to the question you are dealing with.

Active and passive voice

In developing an academic argument or applying a point of law to a specific case, writing is not a personal matter. For this reason the passive voice is frequently used, as shown in some of the earlier examples:

'...cannot be traced...'

'...has been excluded...'

'...is required...'

Academic English is thus conventionally written in the third person. As a general rule for essay writing you should avoid writing in the first or second person. This differs from writing in practice (such as when writing a letter to a client), when you should normally write in the first person. The passive voice helps to convey objectivity. On the other hand, the use of active verbs can achieve an impact on the reader or listener by delivering the message directly and concisely.

Active: The barrister presented the defendant's case to the court.

Passive: The defendant's case was presented to the court by his barrister.

Use of the passive voice will be covered in more detail in Chapter 4.

It is also good practice to get into the habit now of ensuring that you do not express your own feelings on an issue when essay writing. For instance, avoid comments in the first person such as 'I feel' and 'I believe.' Judges don't usually like these expressions, taking the view that you should be presenting your legal arguments based on the law, not on what you personally think or believe. For example, 'Harry's dismissal from Herbert and Co. is probably an unfair dismissal' is preferable to 'I think Harry's dismissal from Herbert and Co. is probably unfair.' However, you may use the first person in a reflective piece of writing if asked to state your personal position or to relate a personal experience.

SENTENCE STRUCTURE

Sentences in formal academic and/or legal writing tend to be longer than those used in everyday English. However, it is good to use a variety of sentences in your writing. In this section we'll look at three types of sentence that you can use: simple sentences, compound sentences, and complex sentences.

Good practice tip

Use a wide range of sentences: some simple and short; others long, compound or complex.

Simple sentences

Look at the structure of the following sentences:

1. The Crime and Disorder Act 1998 removed the requirement for committal proceedings for offences triable only on indictment.
2. Everyone has the right to freedom of expression. This Article shall not prevent States from requiring the licensing of broadcasting, television or cinema enterprises [Human Rights Act 1988, Article 10].
3. Mere circumstances, however provocative, do not constitute a defence to murder.
4. A negligent misstatement is a false statement made without reasonable grounds for believing it to be true.
5. Constitutional law is mainly concerned with the legal structure of the government and its relations with its citizens.

In each of the above sentences there is a subject and a verb.

Sentence number	Subject	Verb
1	The Crime and Disorder Act 1998	removed
2	Everyone This Article	has shall not prevent
3	Mere circumstances	do not constitute
4	A negligent misstatement	is
5	Constitutional law	is concerned

Good practice tip

Make sure that each sentence you write has a subject and a verb.

Sentence structure and connectives

Keep in mind as you write that just as your overall written work should address each topic and issue in a logical order, each sentence should also follow a logical structure. Take for instance the following example:

> A defence to a claim form must, within fourteen days from the date the defendant receives the claim form accompanied with the particulars of claim, be filed at court.

The same information can be conveyed in a clearer way by revising the structure of the sentence to place the subject and verb closer together and placing the intervening words at the end of the sentence, e.g.

> A defence must be filed at court within fourteen days from the date on which the claim form accompanied with the particulars of claim are received by the defendant.

Compound sentences

A compound sentence is formed by joining two simple sentences. The two sentences can be simply joined by a comma (,):

> The evidential burden is to satisfy the judge, the burden of proof is to satisfy the jury.

The two parts can also be joined by a linking word, such as 'but', 'and' or 'as'. Look at the following examples and read the comments given at the end of each sentence on the use of the comma:

A. The doctrine of transferred malice applies to secondary parties as it does to principals. Here the comma is not needed because both parts refer to the same subject, namely 'the doctrine'.

B. 1. The Court of Criminal Appeal allowed the appeal.
   2. The Court of Criminal Appeal quashed the conviction.

These two sentences can be joined together:

The Court of Criminal Appeal allowed the appeal and quashed the conviction. If the two parts refer to the same subject, here 'The Court of Criminal Appeal', a comma should not be inserted.

C. The accused admitted having the necessary recklessness and so the involuntary intoxication could only be relevant to mitigation. The comma is optional in this example, i.e. we can put commas before and after 'so'.

Adding information to a sentence

Look at this sentence:

Mr Justice Sales said that issues of contract law, legitimate expectation and application of general rules of tax law all arose in this case.

If we want to add additional information to this sentence to clarify the issues of contract law and legitimate expectation, we can put this additional information *between commas* following the words we want to clarify, as shown below:

Mr Justice Sales said that issues of contract law, under rules of general private law, legitimate expectation, under rules of general public law, and application of general rules of tax law all arose in this case.

Notice that the additional information has been inserted between two sets of two commas.

Now read the following extract from a law report that appeared in *The Times* newspaper on 17 March 2010, paying attention to the use of the commas:

Lord Justice Hooper said that the defendant, involved in a traffic accident, was asked by the police who he was and he produced a Czech driving licence which, on investigation, proved to be false although stating his true name.

The charge against him, under section 25 of the 2006 Act, was that he was knowingly in possession of a false document with the intention of using it for establishing a registrable fact.

The parts shown between commas are additional information in the sentence.

We can do the same with *brackets* ( ). Brackets can be useful in academic writing when you want to add information to a sentence without confusing its meaning. For instance:

If Mrs Jones was driving while using her mobile telephone (which she denies) then the court is likely to decide that she was driving negligently.

Notice that the information in brackets lets us know some additional information, i.e. that Mrs Jones *denies* that she was using her mobile phone while she was driving, without distracting from the main idea of the sentence.

Good practice tip

To add information to a sentence without changing its grammatical structure or confusing meaning, you can put the additional information between two commas or enclose it in brackets.

Complex sentences

In order to understand the structure of a complex sentence, we need to be familiar with clauses (main and subordinate). You will find that each of the following two sentences has a complete meaning:

> This principle has been widely accepted.
>
> There has been much dispute over what the term 'harm' means.

Here there is a contradiction, and we can use the word 'although' to link them:

> Although this principle has been widely accepted, there has been much dispute over what the term 'harm' means.

The second part of the above sentence has a complete meaning and can stand alone, so it is the **main clause**. The first part 'Although this principle has been widely accepted' does not give a complete meaning; it is the **subordinate clause** in this sentence.

Good practice tip

Make sure that every sentence you write is grammatically correct.

Linking words and phrases

Expressing contrast

The following linking words are used to express contrast:

> although but despite even though however in spite of nevertheless nonetheless though whereas while yet

Now, let us examine the structure of the first part of the above complex sentence:

> Although this principle has been widely accepted, there has been much dispute over what the term 'harm' means.

'*Although*' is followed by the subject ('*this principle*') and a verb ('*has been accepted*'). When we use '*despite*' or '*in spite of*', the first part becomes a **phrase**, i.e. it has no subject or verb, as follows:

> Despite the wide acceptance of this principle, there has been much dispute over what the term 'harm' means.

'*Despite*' or '*In spite of*' should be followed by a noun or -ing form (verbal noun/gerund).

Note: the sentences above start with a subordinate clause, i.e. 'Although this principle...' and 'Despite the wide...' The **comma** is used before introducing the second part of the sentence (the main clause).

Look at another example and notice the position of the comma:

> Although murder is generally regarded as the most serious crime, it has not been defined by statute.

This sentence can be rewritten as follows:

> Murder has not been defined by statute although it is generally regarded as the most serious crime.

Good practice tip

If you start a sentence with a linking word, such as 'although', 'despite' or 'if', a comma is needed, but if you use the linking word in the middle of the sentence the comma is not needed.

Exercise 1.5

Linking words

The following linking words and phrases are widely used in academic writing; they are arranged in alphabetical order.

accordingly	consequently	moreover
additionally	due to	on condition that
as a result	even if	owing to
as long as	for this reason	provided that
assuming	furthermore	since
as well as	hence	so
because	if	therefore
because of	in addition	thus
besides	in case of	unless

Rearrange the above words/phrases in three groups according to their function:

1. **Addition**
2. **Cause (reason) and effect (result)**
3. **Conditional clauses**

Relative clauses

Two or three simple sentences can be joined together, through the use of relative pronouns, to form a complex sentence. This type of sentence is widely used in academic textbooks and legal documents.

For example, look at the following two sentences:

1. The first year of a law degree helps you understand the essential elements and doctrines of English law.
2. In the first year you are expected to study constitutional law, contract law, criminal law and one or two optional modules.

These two sentences can be joined together as follows:

> The first year of a law degree, in which you are expected to study constitutional law, contract law, criminal law and one or two optional modules, helps you understand the essential elements and doctrines of English law.

As 'the first year' is repeated, it has been replaced by 'which', which is a relative pronoun. This part of the sentence, 'in which you are ... modules', is called a relative clause.

Here is another example:

1. The student has just left the room.
2. This student's book is lying on the floor.

These sentences can be joined together as follows:

> The student whose book is lying on the floor has just left the room.

> *Note*: Words such as *'which'*, *'who'*, *'whose'*, *'whom'*, *'that'* are called **relative pronouns**; they replace a word or part of a sentence to link a relative clause.

Here is a further example:

1. It is quite possible for a harm to be caused by two or even more people.
2. Each of them contributed significantly to the creation of the harm.

By joining these two sentences together, the new sentence reads:

> It is quite possible for a harm to be caused by two or even more people each of whom contributed significantly to the creation of the harm.

> *Note*: The relative pronoun 'whom' is used in academic, formal and legal English to replace the object of the sentence – in the above example it replaces 'them'. 'Whom' is not used in informal English.

Exercise 1.6

Form one sentence for each set of two sentences:

1. (a) A person cannot be bound by a contract.
   (b) He was not a party to this contract.
2. (a) A mother was found guilty of murder.
   (b) She had injected her brain-damaged son with a lethal dose of heroin to end his suffering.
3. (a) The directors of some hospitals will be prosecuted under new manslaughter laws.
   (b) Patients in those hospitals have died from superbug infections because of failures by senior management.
4. (a) Lord Judge, the Lord Chief of Justice, said that he was commuting Carlos Khumala's 30-month prison term to a suspended sentence as an 'act of mercy'.
   (b) Lord Judge comes from the ranks of criminal barristers and judges.
5. (a) The Limitation Act 1980 imposes time limits.
   (b) An action for breach of contract must be brought within the time limits.
6. (a) An ex-world championship bridge contestant was jailed for life for killing his wife.
   (b) He constantly belittled his wife's card-playing abilities.

We can also join three or more sentences to form one long complex sentence, as shown in the following example:

1. The first Parliament was assembled by Simon de Montfort in 1265 to give counsel to Henry III.
2. This parliament included, for the first time, representatives from the shires, cities and boroughs of England.
3. It also included the feudal barons.

The first two sentences can be joined together as follows:

> The first Parliament, which included, for the first time, representatives from the shires, cities and boroughs of England, was assembled by Simon de Montfort in 1265 to give counsel to Henry III.

Now we can add the third sentence, but the clause, i.e. subject ('it') and verb ('included'), needs to be changed to a phrase to improve the style; the third part can be rephrased 'as well as the feudal barons'. So, the new sentence reads:

> The first Parliament, which included, for the first time, representatives from the shires, cities and boroughs of England as well as the feudal barons, was assembled by Simon de Montfort in 1265 to give counsel to Henry III.

Note: The relative pronoun 'which' refers to 'the first Parliament', and because it is already specified we put a comma before 'which'. This is called a **non-defining clause**. A non-defining clause includes information which can be omitted from the sentence without destroying the meaning of the sentence.

Here is another example:

1. The burden of proof is on the Crown.
2. As a result, evidence is sufficient.
3. This evidence might leave a reasonable jury in reasonable doubt whether or not the defendant was provoked.

One sentence can be formed:

> Since the proof of burden is on the Crown, evidence which might leave a reasonable jury in reasonable doubt whether or not the defendant was provoked is sufficient.

Note: In the above sentence the relative pronoun 'which' refers to 'evidence', but 'evidence' here is not in the general sense and in order to tell the reader what kind of evidence it is we need to be specific. So, we cannot put commas here. This is called a **defining clause**. The information in a defining clause cannot be omitted since the sentence would not make sense without it.

Good practice tip

Commas are needed in a non-defining clause, but they are not needed in a defining clause.

Exercise 1.7

Join the following three sentences, forming one complex sentence:

1. The Clearstream trial in France had five defendants and some forty civil claimants (or plaintiffs).
2. The defendants were accused of involvement in a smear campaign.
3. The names of the claimants had been linked to fake bank accounts supposedly holding the proceeds of bribes from an arms deal.

SPELLING

The origins of many words in the English language stem from and retain influences from other languages, including for instance Anglo-Saxon (or Old English). Consequently, the way in which some English words are spelt does not always conform with conventional rules. There are, however, some basic maxims to keep in mind, for example, that well-known rule: 'i' before 'e' except after 'c'.

Exercise 1.8

The words in **bold** in each of the following sentences are commonly used in legal writing. Write the correct letters in the blank spaces in each of those words in bold in order to spell each of those words correctly.

1. It is **appar__nt** from the facts provided that John drove his car negligently.
2. Jennifer is the sole **ben__ficiary** of her uncle's will.
3. The judgment of the court was that the **defend__nt** was liable for having caused the accident.
4. The client **rec__ __ved** a cheque from her solicitor this morning.
5. My legal **practi__e** does not include providing advice on corporation tax and I therefore **refe__ __ __d** Mr Anderson to another lawyer who does **speciali__ __** in that area of work.

You can refer to the correct spelling and meaning of other words commonly encountered in a legal context in the Glossary at the end of this book.

While many software programs have a 'spellcheck' facility (which should be used with caution), keep in mind that many of these programs use American spelling for words and that American and British spelling sometimes differs, as for example in the following table:

British	American
programme	program
centre	center
colour	color
recognise	recognize
familiarise	familiarize

Note how American spelling typically uses 'ize' in a word whereas British spelling often uses 'ise'.

PARAGRAPH WRITING

Paragraph organisation and text flow

So far, we have examined the vocabulary and grammar of different types of sentence in order to develop our skills in writing clear, correct and concise sentences. Now let us look at the way we arrange the sentences and organise the text to help the reader follow our ideas, thoughts and arguments easily, i.e. the flow between sentences.

The following text is the introductory paragraph of a chapter entitled '*Mens Rea*' in a criminal law textbook. Read the text and notice how the writer links and connects sentences to each other. (Highlighting has been added to assist you.)

> Criminal liability depends upon responsibility. Responsibility, presumptively, depends upon proof of fault. A traditional legal synonym for 'fault' is 'guilty mind'. *Mens rea* is a synonym for 'guilty mind'. Modern usage, however, restricts the meaning of *mens rea* to the mental state provided expressly or impliedly in the definition of the offence. By convention this is held to include negligence, which is the fault requirement for some offences but is not strictly a 'mental attitude'. Responsibility may sometimes be assigned and punishment may occur in the absence of negligence or any mental attitude. In such cases liability is termed 'strict'.

The flow of the first few sentences in the above text can be illustrated as follows:

Criminal liability → responsibility → proof of fault → guilty mind → *mens rea*
Mens Rea (modern usage) → limited to → mental state

Good practice tip

Sentences should be arranged in logical order to help the reader follow your discussion easily.

Exercise 1.9

Here are five jumbled sentences. Put them in the right order to form a passage about 'Separation of powers':

1. Judicial separation, or independence, from the other powers is crucial; otherwise courts might discriminate when they apply laws – to the advantage of the government and against its opponents.
2. The separation of powers is an important principle of liberal constitutionalism.
3. A pure separation of powers is observed in France, where ministers may not sit in the National Assembly and the ordinary courts may not interfere with decisions of the executive or declare laws invalid.

4. The point of the latter is easy to grasp: it would be dangerous for the legislative and executive powers to be controlled by the same body, for it might enforce its own laws tyrannically.
5. In its classic formulation by Montesquieu in *L'Esprit des lois* (1748), it asserts that there are three different functions of government, which should be discharged by distinct institutions; the principle requires both a separation of functions and a separation of persons discharging them.

Read the following paragraphs, paying attention to sentence structure, punctuation and content of each paragraph:

> For a profession that is obsessed, indeed comforted, by detail and process, the imminent upheaval in regulation will mean a big shock.
>
> From October 2011, the 110,000 solicitors in England and Wales will be governed by what is called outcomes focused regulation (OFR). They will no longer have a thick, prescriptive code of conduct to comply with; instead there will be ten core principles and a relatively short series of 'outcomes' for the client that solicitors have to achieve. Three years since launching the present code of conduct, itself much shorter than what came before, the Solicitors Regulation Authority (SRA) is touring England and Wales to introduce solicitors to OFR as part of its radical shake-up of regulation.
>
> It is timed to coincide with the liberalisation of business rules under the Legal Services Act 2007 and the arrival of alternative business structures.
>
> Neil Rose, *The Times*, 17 June 2010

You have noticed that paragraphs in the above text vary in length, but each one addresses one specific point. There are no specific rules as to the length of a paragraph; each paragraph focuses on one point/area of the discussion.

Good practice tip

Each sentence should have a complete meaning and be able stand on its own. Similarly, each paragraph should deal with only one specific issue or point.

WRITING FOR EXAMS AND COURSEWORK

We have examined the importance of text organisation and logical order in paragraph writing. Order and organisation are essential aspects of academic writing and should be seen from start to finish in your work.

Structuring your writing

A well-structured essay has a clear **introduction**, a **main part** (the 'body' of the essay) and a clear **conclusion**.

Introduction

Introduce the topic in your introductory paragraph, telling the reader what you are about to discuss and what you want to achieve with your answer. This will help you in planning the structure of your work. Particularly when writing for exams, your introductory paragraph should demonstrate that you have clearly and accurately identified the legal issues in the question. Read the question carefully and work out the legal problem and the points you are expected to cover. Do not repeat the question or the facts stated in the question.

For example, consider the following essay question:

> Mr Francovich has been dismissed from his employment as a salesman. His employer, Fabrico Limited, has told Mr Francovich that his dismissal is due to him having stolen money from the company. Mr Francovich worked at the company's British depot in Birmingham, England. Can an employer fairly dismiss an employee for this reason? Explain your answer.

You might begin your answer as follows:

> The issue in this case is contained in Section 98 of the Employment Rights Act 1996. This section sets out six acceptable reasons for which an employer can fairly dismiss an employee. The relevant reason here is clearly the employee's conduct since the reason for dismissal is theft.

Good practice tip

> Always remember to identify the legal issues raised in the question in your introductory paragraph.

Another good way of beginning your introductory paragraph is:

> The issue in this question concerns... This case also raises issues of...

Main body

Having identified the legal issues in the introductory paragraph, you can start dealing with each legal point. For each point you need to refer to the statute and state clearly the principle of law and how it applies to the facts of the case in question. When you cite any case for binding precedent purposes, you must give reasons for citing the case.

While studying law you will realise that there is often a number of qualifications or exceptions for a rule. Thus, when you answer a question think about qualifications or exceptions.

It is important to decide which issues are not relevant. A weak answer consists of 'chunks' of text on a particular topic copied out from a book or manual in the hope that some of what is being written will be relevant to the question and pick up marks. This is easily detected by a tutor. It is a common mistake and shows poor application of relevant law. You will only achieve a good result by answering the specific question which has been asked. Therefore, don't write out all you know about a particular topic or issue regardless of which aspects are relevant to the actual question. If you are answering a question on legal theory or concepts, first identify the specific factual and legal issues involved. Then explain them with reference to the particular question in a logical order.

Conclusion

In the concluding paragraph, highlight the main points you have discussed. This will help to support your answer. There should be a link between your conclusion and introduction. Demonstrate to the reader that you have discussed and addressed the issue(s) you raised in the introductory paragraph, but do not simply repeat the previous discussion.

Make sure that you answer the question in your conclusion. For instance, if you were asked whether you agree or disagree with a statement, be sure that your position is clear. Similarly, if you were asked to advise someone on a legal matter according to the facts, be sure that your advice is clear. For example, you might write,

> In conclusion, in the absence of fraud, the debts owed to Janet by Vesuvio Limited will not be recoverable from Gordon, the owner of the company.

Explaining case law clearly

It's also important for a lawyer to be capable of summarising or 'distilling' the key legal principles and findings contained within a case decision. Effective application of the relevant law to the specific facts provided in a question is even more crucial when answering problem-style questions. Problem questions are those requiring you to apply the law to a hypothetical situation with specific facts and to provide sound and practical advice. The examiner is looking for effective application of the relevant aspects of law to the particular facts and circumstances set out in the question. Keep in mind that you are not being asked to teach law but rather to answer a specific question. So when writing your answer always think: am I applying the relevant law to the facts and details contained in the question?

An easy way of remembering this approach is to keep in mind the ISA formula:

I – ***Identify*** exactly what you are being asked to do and identify the topic/legal issues.

S – ***State*** the relevant law.

A – ***Apply*** the relevant law to the specific facts and circumstances provided to you and *Advise* by arriving at clear conclusions.

Your essay should also provide an analysis of the relevant law. This requires you to reach conclusions based on an explanation of how the facts in the question relate to the law. Explain and give reasons for your answer. Key phrases from a court judgment, statute, etc., relating specifically to the issue you are discussing, can be quoted in support of your answer, but do not quote excessively. Always clearly indicate the source of your quotations.

Good practice tips

- Underline words in the question which indicate the key topics and issues.
- Write a short 'bullet style' checklist of the main issues required before writing your answer. This will help to ensure that you cover issues in an appropriate order and depth (i.e. by giving the correct 'weight' to each issue in terms of how much you write). Remember that a good answer to a problem question applies the law to the given facts in this way, explaining the answer.
- When writing coursework, review your work the following day when your mind is refreshed and proofread carefully.

Be careful to do what the question asks you to do. Look for words such as:

- compare (consider similarities and differences)
- contrast (show differences)
- discuss; describe; explain (make clear, interpret, give reasons for)
- illustrate (demonstrate with examples)
- outline (set out main features, general principles, etc.)

Analyse the relevant issues in more depth in the main body of your answer, developing your arguments with reference to the given facts. Refer to relevant law and show how the law you are referring to (whether a statute, case, etc.) supports or develops the issue or problem raised by the question. To ensure that you cover all relevant issues and details in a logical order it can be very helpful to first write a plan of the required content. Identify the relevant topic(s). Underline key words in the question to help you. Consider for instance the following essay question:

> How does English law distinguish between workers and employees? Explain how this legal distinction affects an individual's employment law rights.

By rushing into writing all you know about employment law rights, such as the law of unfair dismissal and discrimination in the workplace, you would not be answering the actual question. By thinking carefully about exactly what is being asked, however, it can be seen that this question requires discussion of the various criteria or tests for determining if someone is an employee or not (e.g. whether the person must personally provide the work, how much control is exercised over the person in the course of his work). The question also asks you to 'explain' how this affects an individual's employment law rights. So your answer should also set out how some rights are restricted to *employees*, such as the right to make an unfair dismissal claim, etc. (Note that you are *not* being asked to write everything that you know about the law on unfair dismissal.) Once you have identified the legal topics and issues which relate to the question, remember to avoid simply writing down all you know about those areas of law. Think carefully about what specific aspects of law are relevant to the question. Then apply that law to the facts and circumstances of the actual question.

Consider again, for instance, the following question:

> Mr Francovich has been dismissed from his employment as a salesman. His employer, Fabrico Limited, has told Mr Francovich that his dismissal is due to him having stolen money from the company. Mr Francovich worked at the company's British depot in Birmingham, England. Can an employer fairly dismiss an employee for this reason? Explain your answer.

The relevant law for answering this question is contained in the Employment Rights Act 1996. Section 98 of that Act sets out six acceptable reasons for which an employer can fairly dismiss an employee. The relevant one here, however, is clearly the employee's ***conduct***, since the reason for dismissal is theft. While there are other acceptable reasons for dismissal in law under this section of the Act (such as capability and redundancy) no marks are likely to be awarded for setting out or discussing those other reasons. They do not relate to the question.

Similarly, when identifying related issues raised by a question, the examiner is usually looking for evidence of good understanding. You can do this by emphasising those issues specifically relevant to the facts of the question. Do not dwell on those which are not. Consider for example a question on the law of contract requiring you to consider the issues involved in determining whether a binding contract exists. If you are specifically told in the question that an offer was made by one party to another, you will get few if any marks for discussing whether or not an offer exists.

Try to address only one topic or issue per paragraph. Link your paragraphs by showing how each paragraph relates to the preceding one. Always write in paragraphs and not simply by listing bullet points unless specifically asked to do so. By addressing the issues in a relevant order you will make it easier for the reader to follow and understand what you have written. Use headings and sub-headings appropriately to 'flag up' distinct issues.

Keep in mind any word limit imposed on your written work. (This is also good practice for your future legal career since judges also sometimes impose word limits on documents which lawyers are required to produce for court!) Analyse, comment and explain objectively rather than emotionally. This shows professionalism. So base your answer on legal grounds and not moral or emotional ones. State what the law says, not what you think it should say (unless you are asked for your opinion). Your personal feelings and bias are not usually what the tutor is looking for.

For instance:

> The claimant's case has merit since, based on the evidence, he is likely to establish on the balance of probabilities that the defendant was negligent.

This is more objective than:

> It is my feeling that the claimant's case has merit since I think that, based on the evidence, he will establish on the balance of probabilities that the defendant was negligent.

Also notice how the 'third person' is used instead of the 'first person'. Give reasons for your arguments and conclusions. For example:

> In the absence of fraud, the debts owing to Janet by Vesuvio Limited will not be recoverable from Gordon, the owner of the company. In the case of *Salomon* v *Salomon and Co. Ltd* (1897) AC, the House of Lords held that a company is a distinct legal entity. It is therefore regarded in law as having a separate legal personality.

Note how the first sentence provides a clear answer to the question as to whether Gordon, the owner of the company called Vesuvio Limited, is personally liable for the debts of the company. The second sentence then provides the legal reason as to why he is not (citing an important and relevant case which established that a company is in law a separate legal entity).

Note carefully how many marks are allocated to a question and whether the question is split up into sections (such as Question 1(a), Question 1(b), etc.). Similarly, check how many marks there are for each such section of the question. This will provide an indication of how much detail and content is required for that question or section. You will waste much valuable time in an examination or assessment if you write a four-page answer for a question worth 5 marks for instance. Conversely, if you write a half-page answer for a question worth 30 marks you will clearly not be providing sufficient content or depth of analysis to attain all the available marks.

Prioritise your arguments, emphasising the most effective and important ones. Place more emphasis, or 'weight', on the main issues. Finally, summarise your main points and reach a well-reasoned conclusion with regard to the specific issues which the question raises. This will help you to formulate clear answers and explain them logically and persuasively.

Good practice tips

- Address only one issue per paragraph.
- Prioritise your points and arguments.
- Keep paragraphs relatively short (usually no more than five or six sentences per paragraph).

You will also demonstrate more effectively that you genuinely understand a particular legal concept or principle by providing a straightforward and clearly understood explanation. A weak answer will merely mention statutory provisions, cases and legal principles without also saying why they help to answer the question. Always state why the statute, case or legal principle contributes to answering the question. Explain the principle, rule or main finding(s) (i.e. the *ratio decidendi*) which the case establishes. Then make clear how it applies to the facts of the question you are answering. If there are several relevant cases (precedents), ask yourself whether they are consistent. Discuss the main findings of each case if they are important to the question. Compare those cases with each other, indicating how they are consistent as well as how they differ from each other. State clearly what cause(s) of action and issues each case raises, as well as how each case contributes to the points you are making. Consider for instance: does one case support the other? Does the later case overrule earlier ones?

Critically analysing a case

When analysing a case in your answer, summarise the judge's decision and his or her reasoning in reaching that decision. How senior is the court? Remember that in many jurisdictions, including in the English legal system, less senior courts (termed lower courts) are bound by other relevant decisions made by higher courts. This is known as the doctrine of *stare decisis* (meaning 'to stand by the previous decision'). This is also sometimes referred to as the doctrine of precedent.

So consider: which authorities (cases) did the judge apply in reaching his or her decision? Which of those authorities did he or she distinguish based on the facts of the case? Look for the principles and reasons on which the decision is based.

Finally, work to become competent in these skills now and you will put yourself in a good position for providing effective professional advice and assistance whether in legal practice or business.

'The battle for copyright on YouTube'

To see how these important skills are used in actual academic writing, let's look at the text of an academic essay entitled 'The battle for copyright on YouTube' by Professor Gary Slapper of the Open University, *The Times*, 1 July 2010. (Asterisks have been added to point out examples of vocabulary.)

First, read the introductory paragraph below and notice how the author has introduced the topic.

> It was once possible to commit greater robbery with a fountain pen than with a shotgun. Today, however, using the internet and other people's creativity, online entertainment aggregators* such as video-sharing sites can cause greater loss to intellectual property owners than anyone ever could with a pen.

Vocabulary

aggregators: huge/colossal providers

Now read the main part or body of the article, paying attention to how the paragraphs are organised and the main point covered in each paragraph:

> In an important American case, Viacom alleged that YouTube, the entertainment aggregator, had systematically allowed its site to include a profusion* of copyright-infringing* clips and films. Viacom, which owns Paramount Pictures, MTV and Comedy Central, sued Google, which owns YouTube. It claimed $1 billion for the alleged online piracy. The English Premier League also sued, alleging violation of its rights. The two claims were combined in one case – and were recently rejected by the US District Court for the Southern District of New York.
>
> The decision has worrying implications for the creative industries as it permits online businesses, such as YouTube, to be less rigorous in policing their sites than copyright owners would like. Tom Frederikse, an American attorney* and digital media solicitor at Clintons, regards the decision as 'a blow for the beleaguered content industries'.

→

Frederikse, also a record producer and engineer who has worked on more than a hundred UK top 40 records, expects that 'wider policy issues may figure more prominently* in a higher court'.

The lawsuit argued that about 160,000 copyrighted clips from Viacom films and programmes were posted without authorisation on YouTube and downloaded more than 1.5 billion times without any payment accruing to copyright holders. Google counter-argued that it had complied with the law by removing any rights-infringing clips as soon as an owner identified one. It said the lawsuit threatened the way millions of people 'legitimately' exchange information, news, entertainment and political and artistic expressions.

Google's defence was based on the 'safe harbour' principle in Section 512 of the US Digital Millennium Copyright Act 1998 that protects sites such as YouTube if they do not have 'actual knowledge' of the infringing films on their site, are not aware of the 'facts or circumstances from which infringing activity is apparent', receive no financial benefit from those clips, and expeditiously* remove them once notified. Viacom and the Premier League argued that Google did have knowledge of unauthorised films, and was aware of the facts and circumstances of infringements but failed to act.

In rejecting the case, Judge Louis L. Stanton ruled that YouTube did not have actual knowledge of the specific offending films and, when alerted to 100,000 of them, removed them in one business day. The court ruled that 'mere knowledge of prevalence of such activity [unlawful uploads] in general' would not deprive a site owner of the 'safe harbour' defence.

Unlawful uploads on YouTube 'may be a small fraction of the millions of works posted' and a general knowledge of such violations does not create a duty on the site owner to discover which of their users' postings infringes copyrights.

Every 60 seconds, 24 hours of film are uploaded to YouTube, but it generally has no way of identifying new clips that breach copyright. Under the legislation, the judge ruled that the burden of policing copyright falls on copyright owners.

English protection of intellectual property began in 1709 with an Act to promote 'The encouragement of Learning' by vesting* ownership of books in their authors. It prohibited people copying authors' work 'to their great detriment* and, too often, to the ruin of them and their families'. The law has developed to accommodate new technologies and to balance interests.

In the US, a Senate committee has noted that there has to be a clear way for copyright owners to protect themselves against 'massive piracy' of the music, movies and literature that are 'the fruit of American creative genius', while the owners of the host sites need assurance that they can develop the internet without being exposed to huge liability for unintentional and unknown copyright infringements.

Creative artists and production companies will be worried by the New York ruling that YouTube was not liable for hosting films whose copyright status it simply had assumed to be lawful.

Penelope Thornton, a senior associate at Hogan Lovells, suggests an alternative strategy: 'Arguments that platforms are liable simply for turning a blind eye to infringement are not finding favour with courts. This is likely to encourage rights holders to come to agreements with platforms – for example, to share advertising revenue from infringing content rather than take action.'

Vocabulary

attorney: in the USA, a qualified lawyer who has the right of advocacy in court.
detriment: the state of being harmed or damaged.
expeditiously: quickly and efficiently; to expedite (v); to speed up or to hasten

figure more prominently: appear more important
infringing: to infringe (v); to violate; infringement (n); violation
profusion: multitude; a huge quantity
vesting...in: placing; conferring; bestowing

Now read the concluding paragraph and notice how it is linked to the introductory paragraph:

> In the internet age, a film somewhere is a film everywhere. The judgment given in New York will be similarly ubiquitous* and will affect us in two ways: first, because the court's reasoning, or the reasoning of a higher court if it is appealed, will affect judicial thinking in many jurisdictions; and second, because the behaviour of gigantic corporations such as Viacom, Google and YouTube, now guided by the New York judgment, will touch the lives of all the world's 1,802,230,457 internet users.

Vocabulary
ubiquitous: everywhere

Exercise 1.10

The following paragraphs form a text about the development of English law, but they are not in the correct order. Rearrange them:

1. Statute law can be used to abolish common law rules which have outlived their usefulness, or to amend the common law to cope with the changing circumstances and values of society. Once enacted, statutes, even if obsolete, do not cease to have the force of law, but common sense usually prevents most obsolete laws from being invoked. In addition, statutes which are no longer of practical utility are repealed from time to time by Statute Law Repeal Acts. Nevertheless, a statute stands as law until it is specifically repealed by Parliament. This may take place by implication as where an earlier Act is repealed by a later one which is inconsistent with it.
2. From the Tudor period onwards Parliament became more and more independent and the practice of law making by statute increased. Nevertheless, statutes did not become an important source of law until the past two centuries, and even now, although the bulk of legislation is large, statutes form a comparatively small part of the law as a whole. The basis of our law remains the common law, and if all statutes were repealed we should still have a legal system of sorts, whereas our statutes alone would not provide a system of law but merely a set of disjoined rules.
3. An Act of Parliament is, in general, binding on everyone within the sphere of its jurisdiction, though it may not be binding if it infringes the Treaty of Rome, as the *Factortame* case shows, but all Acts of Parliament can be repealed by the same or subsequent parliaments; and this is a further exception to the rule of the absolute sovereignty of Parliament – it cannot bind itself or its successors.
4. Parliament's increasing involvement with economic and social affairs increased the need for statutes. Some aspects of law are so complicated or so novel that they can only be laid down in this form; they would not be likely to come into existence through the submission of cases in court. A statute is the ultimate source of law, and, even if a statute is in conflict with the common law or equity, the statute must prevail. It is such an important source that it has been said 'A statute

→

can do anything except change man to woman,' although in a purely legal sense even this could be achieved. No court or other body in the UK can question the validity of an Act of Parliament.

5. In early times there were few statutes and the bulk of law was case law, though legislation in one form or another dates from AD 600. The earliest Norman legislation was by means of Royal Charter, but the first great outburst of legislation came in the reign of Henry II (1154–89). This legislation was called by various names: there were assizes, constitutions and provisions, as well as charters. Legislation at that time was generally made by the king in council, but sometimes by a kind of parliament which consisted in the main of a meeting of nobles and clergy summoned from the shires.
6. It should also be noted that the Human Rights Act 1998 permits UK courts to make declarations of incompatibility where a UK Act of Parliament is found to violate the European Convention on Human Rights. However, UK courts cannot disapply Acts of Parliament on this ground in contrast to the situation where a challenge is made on the ground of violation of EU law.
7. In the fourteenth century parliamentary legislation became more general. Parliament at first asked the king to legislate, but later it presented a bill in its own wording. The Tudor period saw the development of modern procedure, in particular the practice of giving three readings to a Bill.
8. However, the validity of an Act of Parliament can be challenged before the European Court of Justice (ECJ) on the ground that it is in conflict with the Treaty of Rome. Reference should be made to *Factortame Ltd* v *Secretary of State for Transport (No 2)* (1991) where a successful challenge to the validity of the Merchant Shipping Act 1988 in the ECJ was successful and resulted in the repeal by the UK government of certain sections of that Act.

Once you have checked your answer, read the whole text, noting sentence structure and how linking words/phrases, such as 'in addition', 'nevertheless' and 'whereas' are used.

Good practice tips

- In the introductory paragraph identify the main issues/points raised in the essay title/question. Explain clearly what you are going to discuss and why you are writing this paper. Your introductory paragraph should be relatively short and its length dependent on the overall essay length.
- You should discuss all the points you plan to deal with in the main body of the essay. Divide the main body into logically arranged paragraphs.
- Check that each sentence is grammatically correct and meaningful, i.e. it makes sense on its own.
- Check that each paragraph deals with one point/issue only.
- Use a wide range of short and long sentences: simple, compound and complex.
- In the concluding paragraph highlight the essential points discussed in the main body, linking the introductory and concluding paragraphs.
- **Do not write**: introduction, main body or conclusion.
- Do, however, use appropriate headings for separate issues.

ACKNOWLEDGING THE SOURCE IN ACADEMIC WRITING

While you are studying, whether for your first degree in law or for a postgraduate course, you will undoubtedly refer to materials for use in your written coursework. You must acknowledge all the sources and materials from which you have used texts, views, interpretation and analysis when writing academic essays, problem questions or providing a legal opinion. In academic writing it is vital to acknowledge the source and to use the proper means of referencing.

Bibliography and references

In journal articles, a list of textbooks, articles, websites and other sources is given at the end of the article. This list is generally arranged by the authors' surnames in alphabetical order.

A **bibliography** is a list of all textbooks, websites, materials and sources you have actually read and studied to understand and address the points raised in the essay title or a problem question.

You should also give **references** to all sources and materials you have mentioned, i.e. referred to, in your written coursework and essays.

Referencing systems

There are various referencing systems used in academic legal writing for referring to source material. These systems vary in the way information about the source is arranged, but they all require the following:

- author's/authors' surname and initial(s);
- title of the book (italicised), chapter or article;
- edition number (if it is not the first edition);
- year of publication;
- publisher;
- place of publication.

To illustrate the difference between one referencing system and another, the source may appear in a number of ways:

Elliot, C. and Quinn, F., *Criminal Law*, Pearson, 2010, 8th edn.

Elliot, C. and Quinn, F. (2010) *Criminal Law*, 8th edn, Harlow: Pearson.

Elliot, C. and Quinn, F. (2010) *Criminal Law*, 8th edn, Harlow, England, Pearson.

You will have noticed that in each case above we start with the author's surname and *not* with the book title, regardless of the system. As there are many referencing systems, you should ask your tutor or lecturer which system you are supposed to follow.

You might come across an **edited book**, which means that each chapter or section of the book is written by a different author and the whole book is edited by an editor. Referencing such books should be made as follows:

- Surname and initial(s) of the chapter author(s), the chapter title, surname and initial(s) of the editor(s), book title (italicised), year of publication, edition, publisher, place of publication.

When you refer to an **article from an academic journal**, you need to give the following:

- Author's surname and initial(s), title of article, journal title (italicised), year of publication, volume number, the article's page numbers.

Example:

> Herring, I. and Palser, E. (2007) 'The duty of care in gross negligence manslaughter', *Criminal Law Review* 24, 759–65.

If you use an article from a **newspaper**, the following information is needed:

- Author's surname and initial(s), the newspaper, the date.

For **electronic resources**, referencing should include:

- Full URL address, other details such as the author or the owner, date the website was last updated, date you accessed the website.

Referencing

Referencing means referring to or quoting from the source of authority within the text. When you give a quotation, you must put quotation marks and the page number. If you put many quotations in your academic essay, the essay would appear as if you have copied sentences and paragraphs and pasted them on your paper. This does not show the reader or the examiner whether you understand what you have read or not, and you would not get a good grade for your essay. You will get better marks if you paraphrase what you have read. Paraphrasing will be discussed and explained in Chapter 2.

There are two ways of citing references in the text: first, referencing is made either before or after the quotation, for example (Bradley and Ewing, 2008, pp. 165–7); the second one which is in common use for academic legal writing is the footnote system. In the case of footnotes, you give a number for each source you refer to within the text and use a footnote at the bottom of the page or an endnote at the end of the essay for the numbers of those references. You should ask your tutor which system you should follow.

Citing a case

When you refer to a case, you need to give the correct case title and source, e.g.

> *Williams* v *Roffey Bros and Nicholls (Contractors) Ltd* [1990] 1 All ER 512

'All ER' indicates a case from the All England Law Reports.

We have already seen that it is important to provide authority for the assertions you make in an essay. In legal practice you will also be expected to support legal arguments with legal authority. So get into the habit of doing so now. Consider the following statement:

> It is established law that an incorporated company has a separate legal personality with rights and liabilities of its own which are distinct from those of its owners. This provides the owners of the company with limited liability when conducting business in the name of the company.

This statement is basically correct but fails to cite the relevant legal authority. In particular, the House of Lords case of *Salomon* v *Salomon* [1897] established the principle of a company having a separate legal personality. When citing cases, include the year of the case and the names of the parties.

For coursework, a case should also be correctly referenced, which means indicating its source. When writing an essay under examination conditions, precise referencing may not be so important provided the case is named and dated correctly (e.g. *Cable & Wireless plc* v *IBM United Kingdom Ltd* [2002]). Check the policy of your particular learning institution. Most tutors and learning institutions require the use of either the Oxford or the Harvard method of citation and referencing. With the Oxford method, which is probably the most universal in the UK, the names of the parties are stated (in *italics*, in **bold** or underlined), followed by: the year in brackets; the volume number of the report the case is from; the relevant abbreviation for the law report 'source' (e.g. 'WLR' for the Weekly Law Reports); the page number in the law report, e.g.:

Williams v *Natural Life Health Foods Ltd* [1998] 1 WLR 830.

It is also fairly common for Commonwealth and US law reports to be cited in this manner.

Similarly, for citing other information sources, such as practitioner texts or journals, the layout is firstly the author's name, followed by: the author's initials; the title of the article; the year of publication; the volume or issue number; the journal abbreviation; the page number at which the article appears, e.g.

Johnson, E., 'Law for Business' (2010) 44 MLR 288, at page 125.

The Harvard method differs in that the abbreviation indicating the law report (such as WLR) is placed in a footnote or other reference section rather than in the main text, so that only the case name and date appears in the main text, (e.g. *Williams* v *Natural Life Health Foods* [1998]). For citing other information sources, the Harvard layout is, for example: Johnson, E. (2010), 'Law for Business', *Modern Law Review*, Issue No. 44, April, p. 125.

A new form of 'neutral' citation for cases reported on the internet has developed, so that cases can be easily found these. The year of the case is shown in square brackets, followed by the abbreviation indicating the particular court and then by the serial number of the case (cases start at '1' each calendar year), e.g. [2005] UKHL 1. The abbreviations used for different courts include:

UKHL – House of Lords

EWCA Civ – Court of Appeal (Civil Division)

EWCA Crim – Court of Appeal (Criminal Division)

When referring to an Act of Parliament (statute) in an essay, ensure that you include at least the 'short title' along with the year the Act was passed (e.g. the Human Rights Act 1998). An illustration of this, showing the first page of the Human Rights Act 1998, is contained in this book (p. 200).

When referring to a particular section of an Act, mention the section then the Act, for instance 'Section 2 of the Unfair Contract Terms Act 1977'. If the word 'section' is being used anywhere in the sentence other than at the beginning, then use the initial 's' ('ss' for the plural) as an abbreviation, e.g. 'It is clear from s.2 of the Unfair Contract Terms Act 1977 that a party to a contract cannot exclude civil liability for death or personal injury resulting from negligence.'

Abbreviations used in referencing

Here is a list of commonly used abbreviations:

ed. editor
eds editors
edn edition
et al. *et alii* [Latin] and others – to be used when there are more than two authors
ibid. *ibidem* [Latin] in the same source; as stated in the previous reference
loc. cit. *loco citato* [Latin] in the text already cited
op. cit. *opere citato* [Latin] in the source cited
pp. pages
vol. volume

Plagiarism

If you refer to some established or known facts in your own words, for example 'The European Court of Justice (ECJ) consists of one judge for each member state,' you do not need to acknowledge the source of the information. However, if you refer to the provisions of a specific Act or Treaty, you must give information about the act or treaty. Thus, when you refer to the provisions of the Treaty on the Functioning of the European Union (TFEU), you acknowledge it as 'TFEU, art 289', for instance.

Needless to say, if you copy from a friend, your work will be dealt with as being plagiarised.

Good practice tip

Do not copy anything without acknowledging the source properly. Plagiarism is a serious academic offence.

SUMMARY

- It is necessary to distinguish between everyday English and academic English.
- Standard and formal vocabulary is used in academic and legal writing.
- In addition to a law dictionary, you need an English dictionary and a thesaurus to boost your vocabulary.
- One of the main features of academic writing is that each sentence must be grammatically correct.
- Each sentence must contain a subject and a verb.
- Another feature is the use of a wide range of sentences: short, long, simple, compound and complex.
- Two simple sentences can be joined together by a comma or a word, e.g. 'and', 'but', 'so', to form a compound sentence.
- A complex sentence has two parts: a main clause and a subordinate clause.
- The two clauses can be joined together by a linking word, such as 'although', 'despite', 'nevertheless', or a linking phrase, such as 'in case of', 'on condition that', 'in spite of'.
- When you use a linking word pay attention to the structure of the sentence, e.g. 'although' is followed by a subject and verb, but 'despite' is followed by a noun.
- Another way of forming a complex sentence is by using relative pronouns: to join two simple sentences, you can replace the subject of one sentence with a relative pronoun, such as 'which', 'who', 'whose'.
- In writing, the comma is used more often than any other punctuation mark.
- Paragraph writing: there is no rule regarding the length of a paragraph, but each paragraph must convey one point in the discussion.
- Make sure that one sentence follows another in such a clear, logical way that the reader or the examiner does not have to read a sentence twice.
- You need to follow the convention in writing an academic essay or article: start with an introductory paragraph, follow it with the main discussions, then finish with a concluding paragraph and include a list of your references.
- You should ask your tutor about the referencing system used in the department.
- Plagiarism: *do not* copy from a friend and *do not* copy any expression of an idea, interpretation or analysis without acknowledging the source.
- You must refer to the sources in the proper way.

Visit **www.mylawchamber.co.uk/mckay** to access further resources for practising legal language skills including additional exercises, listening activities and live weblinks for online research.

Chapter 2

Reading law at university

Learning objectives

This chapter will help you to:

- manage the demand for reading textbooks, statutes and cases;
- understand the language of law texts;
- develop your skills in making notes;
- understand law questions;
- develop your skills in case law and examination techniques.

INTRODUCTION

When you start studying for your law degree, you are expected to meet the demanding need for a substantial amount of reading. In order to be able to cope with such demands, you have to acquire various reading skills and adopt strategies which will help you get the most out of your reading and succeed in your studies. This chapter will explore reading techniques and note making to help you develop your own strategies. In addition, we shall examine the language of textbooks and cases. This will in turn help you improve your academic vocabulary for studying law and rephrasing. This chapter will also provide a guide for legal sources and research.

READING TECHNIQUES

Scanning

When you pick up the newspaper and your main interest lies in football, you quickly turn the pages over until you get to the sports section and, then, your eyes move quickly to locate the results or the story about the football match. This rapid reading to locate specific information is known as scanning.

This approach is used in academic reading to locate a specific topic in a textbook, for example you are studying homicide in criminal law and you are looking at provocation in cases of diminished responsibility. Suppose you are using Wilson's *Criminal Law*, 3rd edition, published by Pearson. You can look at 'Contents in detail' and find Homicide in chapter 12, then 12.6 Diminished responsibility, D 'Overlap with provocation,' page 365. Thus, you can locate a specific topic through the **contents** pages.

However, in some cases, it might be easier and quicker to locate the issue you are studying through the **index** pages at the end of the book. Now, we are going to look for 'alcoholism and diminished responsibility'. In the table of contents the word 'alcoholism' does not appear under 'Diminished Responsibility', but if we look at the index we find alcoholism under diminished responsibility, pages 363–4.

We follow the same approach when we look for a specific case or statute.

Skim reading

Once we have located the chapter or part of the chapter we need, we want to make sure that it deals with the specific aspects of the problem or research. In order to achieve this, we skim over the text without necessarily understanding every word to find out whether that text is useful for our studies or research. This way of speed reading for gist, i.e. to get the general idea of what the text is about, saves time.

In academic reading, skim reading is used to identify the key sentence in or the main idea of each paragraph. As an example, read the following paragraph quickly in order to decide what the paragraph is about and the main point raised:

> The protection of human rights, which is primarily a matter for the state in whose territory the rights may be enjoyed, cannot today be confined within national boundaries. The European Convention on Human Rights was signed in Rome in 1950, was ratified by the United Kingdom in 1951 and came into force among those states which had ratified it in 1953. The Convention is a treaty under international law and its authority derives solely from the consent of those who have become parties to it. It was a direct result of the movement of cooperation in Western Europe which in 1949 created the Council of Europe. Inspiration for the Convention came from the wide principles declared in the United Nations Universal Declaration of Human Rights in 1948. The Convention declares certain human rights which are or should be protected by law in each state. It also provides political and judicial procedures by which alleged infringements of these rights may be examined at an international level. In particular, the acts of public authorities may be challenged even though they are in accordance with national law. The Convention thus provides a constraint on the legislative authority of national parliaments, including that at Westminster.

By skim reading the above paragraph, you will find that:

(a) the paragraph is about the European Convention on Human Rights, and

(b) it explains how the Convention came into existence.

Exercise 2.1

Read the following paragraph quickly and decide on a heading for it:

In theory, the *actus reus* and *mens rea* elements of criminal offences are doing different jobs. The external (*actus reus*) elements of the offence approximately reproduce the substance of a society's 'rules of conduct' – the rules which tell all of us what we can and cannot do. If life was a game of golf, the *actus reus* of criminal offences would be like the golfer's rule-book. Golf rules, it should be noted, contain no mental element. A golfer who innocently hits the wrong ball or signs for the wrong score breaks

→

a rule regardless of his honest intention, and suffers penalty therefor. On this theory the mental element in crime (*mens rea*) is something quite distinct from the relevant rule of conduct. It operates to filter those deserving punishment for their wrong from those who do not and to grade liability according to their degree of fault. Theory does not tell the full story, however. A mental element may on occasions serve to define the wrong itself. A person commits no wrong by entering a shop. If he enters with the intention of stealing from it, however, he commits the crime of burglary. It is a burglar's state of mind which makes him a burglar, converting what might otherwise be a lawful act into a criminal wrong.

Skim reading is very useful in identifying the key point or sentence in a paragraph.

The key point is usually given in the first or second sentence as in the following example from a text on contract law:

Social arrangements are also presumed not to give rise to legal relations. In *Lens* v. *Devonshire social club*, *The Times*, 4 December 1914, it was held that the winner of a competition held by a golf club could not sue for his prize because no one involved in the competition intended that legal consequences should flow from entry into the competition. Competitions can, however, give rise to legal relations between the organiser of the competition and the participants, an example being the competitions that are now a regular feature of national newspapers.

Key point: **In cases of social agreements, the presumption is that the parties did not intend to create legal relations.**

However, the key point is sometimes given in the middle of or at the end of a paragraph.

Exercise 2.2

Skim read the following paragraph about manslaughter and then write down the key point:

Most unlawful homicides which are not classified as murder are manslaughter. There are two kinds of manslaughter: voluntary and involuntary. The basic difference between these two types of manslaughter is that for voluntary manslaughter the *mens rea* for murder exists, whereas for involuntary manslaughter it does not.

Deducing the meaning of a word from the text

While skim reading a text, we occasionally come across some unfamiliar words but, as we are reading quickly to get the main idea or point, we do not wish to slow the process of reading by stopping and looking the word up in a dictionary. So, we adopt some approaches to help us to think and find out the meaning of a word logically.

Now, let us look at the following paragraph and see how we can work out the meaning of the highlighted words:

> Theft, **befittingly**, lies at the heart of the Theft Act 1968. Not only is it in its own right, it also forms a key ingredient in a number of other crimes, for example burglary, robbery and handling. A knowledge of theft, then, is a necessary **prerequisite** to understanding the scope of coverage of these offences.
>
> (Wilson, 2008)

- 'Befittingly' is a formal word and you may not have seen it before. One way of understanding the meaning of this word is to look for its root or the smallest known part of it, which is 'fit'. You already know that 'fit' means right or suitable. You also know that you can form a verb by adding the prefix 'be' to the word, for example to 'befriend' is formed from 'friend'. So, 'to befit' means to be suitable, and now you understand the meaning: 'theft which rightly lies at the heart of the Theft Act 1968'.
- Another approach is to deduce the meaning of the word from the meaning of other words surrounding it in the sentence. The sentence in which the word 'prerequisite' appears means: 'if you want to understand the scope of these offences, you must have a knowledge of theft'. You already know that 'if' is used to express conditional statements, and you also know that the prefix 'pre' means 'before'. So, the word 'prerequisite' is a formal word and the meaning here is 'you must have the knowledge before understanding'

In a textbook, you will occasionally find that the meaning of a word is given in the same sentence, as in the following text about the law of contract:

> The general rule is that an offer may be **revoked**, i.e. withdrawn, at any time before acceptance. If there is an option attached to the offer as where the offeror agrees to give seven days for acceptance, the offeror needs not keep the offer open for seven days but can revoke it without incurring legal liability unless the offeree has given some consideration for the option.

The meaning is sometimes given in the next sentence, as in the following example of a text on appeals from the magistrates to the High Court:

> An appeal to the High Court may be made by either the accused or the prosecution by means of ***case stated***. This means that the magistrates must set out in writing their findings of fact together with the arguments put forward by the parties and their decision and the reasons for it.

Reading for detail

Having made a decision as to which part of the chapter or which case you need to study, you will read the text carefully, paying attention to details. This careful reading is much slower than reading the newspaper, a novel or any book which has an element of entertainment.

Good practice tips

- If you identify the subject and verb in each sentence, you will find it easier to understand the text (refer to sentence structure in Chapter 1).
- Noticing where the commas are placed will help you understand long sentences (refer to punctuation in Chapter 1).
- Use a law dictionary to find out the meaning of legal terminology.
- Try to deduce the meaning of an unknown word from the context in which it is placed, then use a general dictionary to ensure that you have understood the meaning of the word in that context.
- Make notes to use later for revision.

Now let us examine the following text on the procedure of government bills, adapted from a textbook on constitutional law (asterisks have been added to point out particular vocabulary):

In the case of government Bills, the sponsoring minister presents the Bill to the Commons; it receives a formal first reading and is then printed and published. There follows the second reading of the Bill, when the House may debate the general proposals contained in the Bill. If the second reading is opposed, a division may take place on an opposition amendment to postpone the second reading for three or six months or, more usually, on a reasoned amendment opposing the Bill. For a government Bill to be lost on second reading would be a serious political defeat. This setback has been avoided by most modern governments, but not by the government in 1986 when the Shops Bill, to reform the law on Sunday opening of shops, was defeated on second reading in the Commons by 296 votes to 282. Where a Bill involves new public expenditure or new taxation, the Commons must approve a financial resolution on the proposal of a minister before the clauses concerned may be considered in committee; the financial resolution is approved immediately after a Bill's second reading.

After second reading, a Bill is normally referred for detailed consideration to a standing committee, consisting of between 16 and 50 members nominated by the Committee of Selection. The Committee of Selection must have regard to the qualifications of the members and to the composition of the House, which means in practice that the parties are represented as nearly as possible in proportion to their representation in the House. It should be noted that a standing committee is constituted afresh for every Bill.

Whether a Bill is considered in standing committee or in committee of the whole House, the object of the committee stage is to consider the individual clauses of the Bill and to enable amendments to be made. While general approval has been given to the Bill on second reading, members opposed to the Bill may use the committee stage to propose amendments narrowing the scope of the Bill or in other ways rendering* it more acceptable to them. Members may be able to persuade the minister in charge of the Bill to reconsider a specific point, but the government expects to maintain its majority in committee and an amendment is not often made against the wishes of the government. After the amendments to a clause have been considered, there may take place a further debate on the motion that the clause, or the clause as amended, should stand part of the Bill.

When a Bill has completed its committee stage, it is reported as amended to the whole House. On the report stage, further amendments may be made to the Bill on the →

proposals of ministers, sometimes to give effect* to undertakings which they have given in committee, sometimes to remove amendments made in committee but not accepted by the government. The Opposition may use the report stage to urge further amendments upon the government although it is rare for these amendments to succeed and the Speaker has the discretion* to select the amendments which will be debated.

After a Bill has been considered on report, it receives its third reading; only verbal amendments may be made to a Bill at this stage. Such debates tend to be brief and formal. However, with a controversial Bill the Opposition may wish once more to vote against it.

Vocabulary

discretion: authority to decide, choose, determine or select

give effect: implement/put into practice/formalise

render: a formal word which means 'cause' or 'give'. Here in this sentence the meaning is: '. . . in other ways making more acceptable'

Use of similar words

The words 'defeat' and 'setback' are highlighted in this text to show you one way of using synonyms. Instead of repeating the word 'defeat', the word 'setback', which has a similar meaning, is used for linking the next sentence.

Use of the definite article 'the'

In general, the use of definite and indefinite articles is one of the most confusing areas in English usage. For this reason, you may put an article where it should not go or may miss one in spoken English. Inaccurate use of the articles in colloquial spoken English may be acceptable so long as you get your message across. However, in academic and legal writing you should use the articles correctly.

- Look at the beginning of the above text: 'In *the* case *of* government Bills'. When we have something that belongs to something else, 'the' is used.
- When you generalise you do not insert the definite article, e.g. 'Studying *law* requires developing many skills.' If you want to be specific and let the reader know which law you are referring to, the definite article is used, e.g. 'to reform *the law on* Sunday opening of shops.'
- In the sentence 'This setback has been avoided by *most* modern governments, . . .' the word 'most' means the majority of and no article is used. So, if you use the word 'most' in the sense of 'the majority of', do not use the definite article.
- If there is one thing of its own kind, we use the definite article 'the' when we refer to it, for example, 'by *the* government in 1986'. There is only one opposition in the House of Commons, so we refer to it as '*The* Opposition may use the report stage . . .'
- The same applies to anything which is unique, such as the moon or the sun.
- When we refer to people in a specific profession or a certain group, we use the definite article 'the' and the *singular form*. Rather than saying 'solicitors are . . .', we write '*The* solicitor is . . .', and, instead of 'young people', we refer to them as '*The* young'.

Use of indefinite articles 'a' and 'an'

Indefinite articles are used for countable nouns in the singular form. Use 'an' before a word starting with a vowel sound *NOT* a vowel letter and 'a' before a consonant sound, for example *'an* undertaking' and *'a* university'.

Good practice tips

- You must put an article ('a', 'an' or 'the') before a singular countable noun.
- Do not put an indefinite article before uncountable nouns or plural countable nouns.

(For more information on uncountable nouns, see Chapter 3.)

Exercise 2.3

Insert 'a', 'an', 'the' or nothing in the gaps in the following text:

In ______ 2007 British Crime Survey ______ crimes against property accounted for 78 per cent of all crime. Around ______ third of all crimes reported by victims involved theft of, or from, or damage to, ______ motor vehicles. The number of such crimes recorded is thought to be ______ small proportion of ______ level of offending. As with other forms of criminal activity ______ accuracy of ______ overall picture of ______ criminality is dependent upon ______ willingness of ______ victims to report and ______. Police to record ______ offence once reported. Many victims will not report ______ property crimes except to support ______ insurance claim. As a result ______ large proportion of minor thefts and burglaries go unreported. Those who are uninsured have ______ little incentive to report such offences unless they have evidence as to who ______ culprit was.

Much of ______ law relating to ______ punishment of ______ property offences is contained in ______ Theft Act 1968 and ______ Fraud Act 2006. It should be noted, however, that ______ social pattern of ______ offences of ______ dishonesty is not adequately represented by these Acts.

Exercise 2.4

Insert 'a', 'an', 'the' or nothing in the gaps in the following case:

***DPP* v *Majewski* [1976] WLR 723**

______ defendant was ______ drug addict who had consumed ______ large quantity of drugs before spending ______ evening drinking at ______ pub where ______ offences were committed. He appealed against ______ conviction of ______ assault of ______ police constable in ______ execution of his duty on ______ grounds that he was too intoxicated through ______ combination of drugs and alcohol to form ______ appropriate mens rea. ______ appeal was dismissed.

Rephrasing

Vocabulary

One way of rephrasing is to rewrite the sentence by replacing words. For example, in the text on p. 41 the phrase 'a standing committee is constituted afresh for every Bill' can be rephrased as follows: 'for every Bill a new standing committee is formed'.

Sentence structure

In compound and complex sentences, we can change the structure of one of the clauses into a phrase, i.e. we can replace the subject and verb by a phrase. For example, from the text on pp. 41–2:

- Look at the following complex sentence: 'Where a Bill involves new public expenditure or new taxation, the Commons must approve a financial resolution on the proposal of a minister before the clauses concerned may be considered in committee; the financial resolution is approved immediately after a Bill's second reading.'

  In the first clause the subject is 'a Bill' and the verb is 'involves', and we can change the clause into a phrase 'a Bill involving . . .' So, the sentence can be rephrased as: 'The Commons must approve a financial resolution on a Bill involving new public expenditure or new taxation proposed by a minister before the clauses concerned may be considered in committee . . .'
- In the sentence 'When a Bill has completed its committee stage, it is reported to the whole House,' the structure of the first clause can be changed. The sentence can be rephrased as: 'Upon completion of its committee stage, a Bill is reported as amended to the whole House.'
- The first part of the sentence 'After a Bill has been considered on report, it receives its third reading' can be rephrased as: 'Having been considered on report, a Bill received its third reading.'

NOTE MAKING

During your studies for a law degree – and later on in your professional career – you need the skills of note taking and note making in addition to the other skills covered in this book.

A distinction between **note taking** and **note making** should be made. When you attend a lecture, deliver a presentation, receive instruction from a client or sit while the police are interviewing the client, you jot down the important legal points, dates, names, incidents, etc. Imagine you are reading a book and while you are reading each paragraph you underline all the important words, statutes, dates, etc. The skill of jotting down and noting certain words is known as *note taking*, which will be dealt with in Chapter 7.

Note making is writing down in your own words what you have understood from the text. In other words, when you read a paragraph or a case, you stop, think, reflect on what you have read and then write the point(s) of law given in the text according to your understanding.

Making your own notes and keeping a record of them will be very useful later on. You will find such notes helpful for your written coursework and for examination revision.

Good practice tips

- When you start studying, get a notebook and divide it into sections: one section for each module, for example a section for criminal law, another for constitutional law, etc. and a section at the end for a glossary of legal terms, such as *obiter dictum*.
- Once you have finished reading and studying one specific point, make notes in your own words as follows:
  - your understanding of the principle of law and statutes related to the key point – you should also write the title of the Act and the year;
  - the name of the case and the year, together with brief notes as a reminder of the case;
  - reasons for a decision made by a judge;
  - in the glossary, record the definition of any term you have learnt.

It is also useful to use index cards. You can write on them and file them under relevant subject matters. They are then an invaluable revision source.

Studying cases

When you read a case, remember it is essential to make notes of the facts of the case, points of law, the decision made by the judge(s), the rationale behind their decision and any reference to binding precedent.

As already mentioned, you might find it useful to get some index cards and write down the important points of each case you are studying, such as the facts, legal issues and reasons for the decision. Then arrange the cards in a box, making your own index. The index cards will help you for examination revision.

Let us examine a case about the question of undue influence and inequality of bargaining power. (Highlighting of specific vocabulary to note has been added.)

Lloyds Bank Ltd* v *Bundy [1975] QB 326

The defendant, Mr Bundy, an elderly farmer, shared the same bank as his son and his son's company. The company's affairs deteriorated over a period of years, and the company ran into financial difficulties. So the defendant gave a guarantee in respect of* the company to the bank, the guarantee being secured by a charge over the farmhouse. The fortunes of the company failed to improve and the defendant was then approached by his son and the manager of the bank, who informed him that the bank was unwilling to continue to support the company without additional security. In response to this approach, and without seeking independent advice*, the defendant extended the guarantee and with it the charge over his property. Eventually, the company went into receivership* and the bank sought* to enforce its security against the house. The defendant pleaded undue influence based on the fact that there was a long-standing relationship between himself and the bank, and as such he had placed confidence in it in that he looked to the bank for financial advice. Clearly the bank in having a financial interest in the company could not present itself as being able to give independent financial advice. It was incumbent upon* the bank to advise the defendant to seek* such advice, which they failed to do, and as such could not rebut* the presumption of undue influence.

Vocabulary

in respect of: concerning; regarding. Note the use of prepositions, we can use 'in respect of' or 'with respect to'

incumbent upon: necessary as part of the bank's duties. Note the use of preposition, either 'incumbent upon' or 'incumbent on'

rebut: refute; disprove; argue that the claim is not true

seek/sought: to try to obtain; to ask for

to go into receivership: to be dealt with by a receiver to administer the property under litigation

Study notes

You will have noticed that the name of the case is followed by the year in square brackets, then the law report from which the case was obtained, i.e. Law Reports Queen's Bench Division, abbreviated as QB. Since cases are recorded in different law reports, you may find that this case is cited in another textbook from All England Reports and appears as *Lloyds Bank* v *Bundy* [1974] 3 All ER 757.

Confusing words

'advise' (v) and 'advice' (n)
You *advise* a client, but you give him *advice*.

Now read the following commentary and analysis of the case of *Lloyds Bank* v *Bundy*, paying attention to the principle of law in the court decision and the way in which it is described.

> While the majority of the Court of Appeal (Cairns LJ and Sir Eric Sachs) were content to decide the appeal on the conventional ground that a fiduciary relationship existed between the bank and its customer (which is to suggest that a new fiduciary relationship has come into being), Lord Denning took the opportunity to break new ground by deciding that, in addition to avoiding the contract on the grounds of fiduciary relationship, Mr Bundy could also have done so on the basis of 'inequality of bargaining power'. Lord Denning set out the following general principle:
>
> > English law gives relief to one who without independent advice enters into a contract upon terms which are very unfair or transfers property for a consideration which is grossly inadequate, when his bargaining power is grievously impaired by reason of his own needs and desires, or by his own ignorance or infirmity, coupled with undue influence or pressure brought to bear on him by or for the benefit of the other.

Law reports abbreviations

The following abbreviations are used for citing some of the main law reports and other sources:

AC	Law Reports, Appeal Cases (1891–current)
All ER	All England Law Reports (1936–current)
All ER (D)	All England Law Reports (Direct) (Online)
All ER (EC)	All England Law Reports (European Cases)
All ER (Comm)	All England Law Reports (Commercial Cases)
BCLC	Butterworths Company Law Cases (1983–current)

B & CR	Reports of Bankruptcy and Companies Winding-up Cases (1918–current)
BYIL	British Yearbook of International Law
Ch	Law Reports Chancery Division (1891–current)
CLY	Current Law Year Book (1947–current)
CMLR	Common Market Law Reports (1962–current)
EHRR	European Human Rights Reports
HC	House of Commons Paper
HC Deb	House of Lords Debates (Hansard)
HL	House of Lords Paper
HL Deb	House of Lords Debates (Hansard)
ICR	Industrial Court Reports 1972–74; Industrial Cases Reports (since 1974)
KB	Law Reports, King's Bench Division (1901–52)
LGR	Local Government reports (1902–current)
P & CR	Planning and Compensation Reports (1949–current)
PIQR	Personal Injuries and Quantum Reports
QB	Law Reports, Queen's Bench Division (1891–1901) and (1953–current)
WLR	Weekly Law Reports (1953–current)
YBEL	Yearbook of European Law

LEGAL SOURCES

For a detailed study of some points of law, and in order to provide logical analysis of the legal issues related to a problem question or an opinion, you need to understand and refer to legislation, case law and other materials about law. There are two main types of sources:

- **Primary sources:** Legislation and case law are very important sources of the legal rule: Acts of Parliament, statutory instruments, law reports and EU legislation.
- **Secondary sources:** These sources provide statements of the law, explanation and commentary for law students, articles of interest to legal practitioners, critical perspective on the law: textbooks, law journals, such as *Law Quarterly Review*, *Law Society's Gazette* and *Cambridge Law Journal*, and legal encyclopaedias.

Remember therefore that original sources of law, such as Acts of Parliament (statutes), international treaties, EU Directives and case reports, are sometimes referred to as 'primary' authorities. Other sources of law are sometimes referred to as 'secondary' or 'subsidiary' sources, i.e. those sources which are delegated legislation or relate the law 'secondhand' (in other words the law in its original form would exist even if the text didn't). Examples of secondary sources of law include statutory instruments and practitioner texts. It is also important to cite these authorities accurately, e.g. the 'Companies Act 2006' and not simply the 'Companies Act' (which would confuse it with the Companies Act 1985 and earlier Acts).

Further details of sources of law and legal research are provided in Appendix 1.

Reports on cases are regularly reported in national newspapers, such as in *The Times* in the UK on Thursdays.

To achieve higher grades for your law degree, you need to develop your skill in searching for and analysing information obtained from both primary and secondary sources. You will find useful information on these sources and websites in the appendix section at the end of this book.

SUMMARY

- Scanning: you scan the table of content or the index of a textbook or the 'home' page of a website to locate the chapter or section you need to read.
- Skim reading: you read a paragraph, section or page quickly to get the gist of it. This will help you to decide whether the text is important for your study or research. While skim reading you do not have to understand every word.
- Once you have found the text needed for your studies/research, read the text again for detail and make notes.
- You can understand the meaning of a new or unfamiliar word by finding the root of the word, i.e. by removing a prefix or a suffix from the word.
- In a textbook, most authors explain the meaning of a legal term either before or after the word.
- Definite article 'the': in English when you refer to something general, the definite article is not used. Use the definite article when you are specifying the noun or you refer to a noun you mentioned in a previous sentence, i.e. it is known to the reader.
- Indefinite articles 'a' and 'an': they are used for singular countable nouns; 'a' is used before a word starting with a consonant sound, and 'an' is used before a word starting with a vowel sound.
- When you write a singular countable noun, you must use a definite or indefinite article.
- You can rephrase a sentence by using other words of similar meaning.
- You can also rephrase a sentence by changing the sentence structure.
- Note making: after reading a text or a court judgment in detail, write down what you have understood in your own words.
- Making your own notes is a very useful skill as you will need these notes later at the time of examination revision.
- Studying cases: read the facts of the case and then examine the principle of law applied to the case. Look for the reasoning of the judgement and make a distinction between binding precedents and the views of a judge.
- Primary sources: all types of legislation: Acts of Parliament, case law, law reports, EU legislation.
- Secondary sources: textbooks, academic journals, books and journals for practitioners.

Visit **www.mylawchamber.co.uk/mckay** to access further resources for practising legal language skills including additional exercises, listening activities and live weblinks for online research.

Chapter 3

Writing letters, e-mails and internal documents

Learning objectives

This chapter will help you to:

- write professional legal correspondence including letters, e-mails and memoranda;
- learn vocabulary relevant to writing letters, memoranda and file notes;
- use language and grammar effectively for legal practice.

INTRODUCTION

This chapter concentrates on legal writing (correspondence) typically used in legal practice. In particular, it will cover writing letters, facsimiles (faxes), e-mails, file notes, attendance notes, and memoranda. Drafting of legal documents is considered in Chapters 4 and 5.

LETTER WRITING IN PRACTICE

The purpose of legal writing in practice is to provide information, suggestions and advice as well as to record information. The reader of your legal writing may rely on what you have written when making important, real-life decisions. What you write must therefore be clear and precise. In the following letter the main points to keep in mind when writing a letter in legal practice are shown in blue side notes.

STRINGWOOD & EVANS
Solicitors
18 Bond Street
London W1 1KR
Tel: +44 (0)20 7538 2892

Name and address of sender

Mr C. Horton
Flat 3
Mancunian Mansions
Mayfair
London, W1 2GB

Name and address of person receiving letter

Our Ref. A1245
Your Ref

Your firm's reference here. (If recipient of letter has provided a reference then also indicate that reference here.)

Insert date 23 June 2011

Dear Mr Horton

Start letter with salutation of 'Dear Mr/Ms/Mrs or Miss' + last name. If last name is not known, use 'Dear Sir/Madam'. Only use first name if on first name terms or invited to use it.

Ravenscourt Limited

Provide title to indicate subject of letter

Further to our meeting last week I am writing to confirm that I am happy to act for you in forming a private limited company in the UK in the name of Ravenscourt Limited ('Ravenscourt'). In accordance with your instructions I have now drafted the company documentation necessary to incorporate Ravenscourt. This documentation includes a memorandum, model articles of association and form IM01.

In further compliance with your instructions, you have been named on this documentation as the sole shareholder and director of Ravenscourt. You will recall that during our discussion it was pointed out to you that the Companies Act 2006 stipulates that a private company limited by shares no longer requires a company secretary. You nevertheless indicated that you wish Ravenscourt to have a company secretary, namely Jennifer Oranuba and I have therefore named this person on form IM01 as company secretary.

→

Further details of this new company, as requested, will be as follows. The registered office of the company is to be 19 Connaught Terrace, Holborn, London, EC1 2GB. In addition, the company is to be formed with an initial share capital of £100 sterling, consisting of 100 ordinary shares of £1 each. You will also be the shareholder of these shares.

Please now check the details on the enclosed forms to ensure that they meet with your requirements and return the forms to me duly signed and dated. I will then arrange for the paperwork to be forwarded to Companies House, along with the appropriate fee, in order to incorporate the company.

My hourly rate for all work undertaken in connection with forming Ravenscourt and advising you on the procedure and legal requirements in this connection will be £250 per hour plus VAT. I am a partner with this firm and if at any time you are dissatisfied with any aspect of my work then please contact me and I will endeavour to resolve the matter. If, however, you then remain dissatisfied you can contact Martin Mendoza, who is the partner who deals with our complaints procedures. I look forward to hearing from you.

Yours sincerely

Peter Arkhurst

Letter starts with recipient's last name, so ends with 'Yours sincerely'. If letter starts with person's first name then also use 'Yours sincerely' or 'Yours'. If recipient's name is unknown (and 'Sir' or 'Madam' has been used), then end with 'Yours faithfully'. Also note that 'sincerely' and 'faithfully' start with small letters, while 'Yours' starts with a capital letter.

2

Number all pages after page 1

Points to note on letter content

If you are writing on behalf of a firm, use the first person plural, we, and use it consistently throughout the correspondence. Avoid overly emotional expressions or over-emphasis (e.g. using !!!). Acknowledge the last communication. For instance, Thank you for your letter dated...

Summarise what both you and the person you are writing to (whether a client, colleague, etc.) are to do next.

Use of the active and passive voices

The active voice is used when writing legal correspondence, being more personal and direct. You should write as if you were speaking directly to the person to whom you are writing. Compare for instance:

> Ms Susan Fitzsimmons is writing an important letter to the court (active voice)
>
> An important letter to the court is being written by Ms Susan Fitzsimmons (passive voice).

The passive voice is more appropriate when a more detached impression is needed, such as in court documents. Drafting of such documents is considered in Chapter 4.

Use of multi-word (or phrasal) verbs

When a verb is used with one or two particles (i.e. a preposition or an adverb) and they *together* have one meaning, it is called a **multi-word verb** (also a **phrasal verb**). For example, to 'put off' is a multi-word verb which means the same as 'to postpone'. Multi-word verbs are commonly used in legal English.

Exercise 3.1

The following such verbs are commonly used in legal correspondence:

call for the witness	take down a statement	draw up a court order
take over	make progress	was found in

Complete the following sentences by inserting the appropriate expressions from the list above into each of the blank spaces below.

1. We expect the judge to ______ shortly.
2. My lawyer has told me he is now going to ______ for approval by the court.
3. We are now starting to ____________ in negotiating a settlement agreement.
4. My client ____________ possession of a firearm.
5. I have arranged for my secretary to ______ from the independent witness.
6. My corporate client will ______ the target company by the end of this week.

Exercise 3.2

Complete the following statements by selecting the correct expression to place in the blank spaces from the list below.

extremely generous	**severely injured**	**deliberately mislead**
solemnly declare	**strongly suggest**	**successfully defended**
dismissed without notice	**totally objective**	**settle out of court**
substantially increase	**refrain from**	**extremely fruitful**

1. I ____________ you accept the present offer.
2. Our offer is an ______________ one.
3. I do __________ that the contents of my statement are true.
4. The defendant __________ the claim against her.
5. The negotiation was ________.
6. You will need to _____ your present offer if settlement is to be achieved.
7. The claimant was ______ in the course of his work.
8. A judge must be _______ in the course of arriving at his decision.
9. An advocate must never ________ the court.
10. The court ordered the defendant to _______ working for a competitor.
11. The employee was _________.
12. My client is hoping to ________.

Exercise 3.3

Charles Scoville, a client of your firm (Stringwood & Evans, solicitors), has recently confirmed that he would accept the sum of £25,000 in settlement of his case. The following letter is addressed to Roderick Krugman, the lawyer acting for Bannerman and Law (the solicitors for the other party). It sets out proposals for settlement of the dispute. Complete this letter by inserting the correct words from the box below into the corresponding spaces in the letter.

prospects of success	**damages**	**award**
employment tribunal	**unfairly dismissed**	**mitigate**
settlement	**applicant**	**instructions**
misconduct	**disciplinary hearing**	**dismissal**
contract of employment	**legal grounds**	**notice period**

→

STRINGWOOD & EVANS
18 Bond Street
London W1 1KR
Tel: +44 (0)20 7538 2892

To: Weir & Co.
45 Richmond Hill
Richmond
Surrey, KT8 9BU

WITHOUT PREJUDICE

21 December 2010

Dear Mr Krugman

Charles E. Scoville v *Bannerman and Law*

We act on behalf of the **(1)** ______ in the above **(2)** ____________ proceedings. It appears clear from our **(3)** ______ that our client has been **(4)** ____________ ____________.

In particular, there does not appear to have been any valid or acceptable reason for his **(5)** ____________. The dismissal was also procedurally unfair. For instance Mr Scoville was not provided with the opportunity to explain, there having been no **(6)** ____________. Similarly, he was denied his legal right to have a representative present when confronted with the allegation of **(7)** ______________. He was not provided with the opportunity of working the three months **(8)** ____________ ____________ provided for in his **(9)** ____________ ___ ____________. There were no **(10)** ____________ ______________ for his summary dismissal. We are confident therefore that our client's **(11)** __________ ___ ___________ are high.

Mr Scoville has not obtained further employment despite having made efforts to **(12)** ________ his loss. We are confident therefore that the Employment Tribunal would **(13)** ______ significant **(14)** ______.

Entirely without prejudice, however, we would propose **(15)** _______ of this matter on the basis that your client pays the sum of £25,000 within twenty-one days. If this matter has not been satisfactorily resolved within twenty-one days then legal proceedings will be commenced. We are confident that the tribunal will award damages. We look forward to hearing from you.

Yours sincerely

STRINGWOOD & EVANS
Specialist Court and Company Lawyers

Prefixes

In the above letter there are examples of prefixes (letters placed at the beginning of a word). Prefixes are often used in English to create an opposite or negative meaning to what the word means without the prefix. For instance, 'un' has been added to the adjective 'fair' and 'mis' to the noun 'conduct'. Further examples of prefixes include: 'dis', 'il', 'im', 'in', 'ir', 'mis', 're', 'un'.

Here's another example: 'quantum is an *in*exact science' – 'in' is used as a prefix to modify 'exact'.

Exercise 3.4

Put the following adjectives and verbs under the correct prefix column in the table below to create an opposite or negative meaning.

legal
reliable
obedient
honour
fair
literate
legible
mature
valid
accurate
relevant
responsible
direct
certain
comfort
represent
able
possible
ease
logical
avoidable

ir	un	dis	im	in	il	mis

Suffixes

A suffix is added to the end of a word to change its part of speech, e.g. to change a verb into a noun or to change an adjective into an adverb. The following suffixes can be added to the end of words to create new words:

able ably al ance ate ion ful ist ive ous some less

For example, we can change the word 'accept' (verb) by adding suffixes as shown here:

accept<u>able</u> (adjective)

accept<u>ably</u> (adverb)

accept<u>ance</u> (noun)

Exercise 3.5

Put the following nouns and verbs under the correct suffix column in the table below to create a new word. (Note: there may be more than one appropriate choice for some words.)

person | hope | rest
worth | use | awe
law | suggest |

able	al	ate	ion	ful

ive	ous	some	less	ist

Exercise 3.6

Now write the following words into the correct prefix column in the table below in order to create the opposite meaning. You may not require all of the headings.

comfort | represent | able
satisfaction | legal | possible
logical | responsible | avoidable

ir	im	il	dis	re	un	mis

Conditional sentences

Note the use of the conditional sentence in the letter in Exercise 3.3: 'If this matter has not been satisfactorily resolved within twenty-one days then legal proceedings will be commenced.' Such conditional sentences are regularly used when acting for a client. (Conditional sentences are considered in further detail in Chapter 7.)

Exercise 3.7

Insert the correct tense form of each word in brackets in the blank spaces to complete the following sentences.

1. If you offer £25,000, my client ______________ (accept) it.
2. If no reply ______________ (receive) within fourteen days, I ______________ (commence) legal proceedings.

Exercise 3.8

Here is another example of a letter addressed to the lawyers for the other party in a breach of contract dispute. The letter sets out details of a claim being made on behalf of Travelgraph Limited. The letter is to inform Matrix Printers Limited that Travelgraph Limited will issue legal proceedings in court for breach of contract unless Matrix Printers pays compensation for loss of profit.

Complete the letter on behalf of Travelgraph Limited by filling in the blank spaces, using the selection of words and phrases from the list below.

our instructions	**contract**
breach of contract	**express term**
legal proceedings	**proposals to compensate**
satisfactory proposals	**act on behalf of**

STRINGWOOD & EVANS
18 Bond Street,
London W1 1KR
Tel: +44 (0)20 7538 2893

The Directors
Matrix Printers Limited
18 Tottenham Court Road
London, W1 1LB

5 August 2011

Dear Sir or Madam

We ________________ **(1)** Travelgraph Limited of 44 Princess Diana Walk, South Kensington, London, W2 3SL, in relation to a ____________ **(2)** between our clients and yourselves. This written contract, entered into on 7 May 2011, stipulated that two 'Ultra-Print 123 Series' printing machines would be supplied by yourselves to our client, which would each be capable of printing one hundred A4 pages per minute. It is clear from ____________ **(3)**, however, that despite this _________ **(4)** each machine is in fact only capable of printing at a maximum rate of fifty pages per minute. You are therefore liable to our client for ________________ **(5)**, as a direct result of which our client has lost anticipated profit to date in the sum of £100,000.

Please provide us with your ___________________ **(6)** our client accordingly within fourteen days of receipt of this letter. If no ______________ **(7)** are received within this time then ______________ **(8)** will be commenced without further reference to yourselves.

Yours faithfully

STRINGWOOD & EVANS
Specialist Court and Company Lawyers

STRUCTURE AND STYLE

The style of language used in actual legal practice differs from academic writing (considered in Chapters 1 and 2). The general rule of prioritising and addressing issues in a logical order nevertheless applies to writing in practice just as it does to essay writing.

Sentence structure

Logical sentence structure will make your writing more effective and persuasive.

Example 1

> An unfair dismissal claim must, within three months of the date of dismissal by the employer, be filed with the employment tribunal.

This can be written with a more logical and clear sentence structure as:

> An unfair dismissal claim must be filed with the employment tribunal within three months of the date of dismissal.

Example 2

> A defence must, within twenty-one days after service of the claim form has been effected, be filed with the court.

This can be better structured as:

> A defence must be filed with the court within twenty-one days following service of the claim form.

Note that in both examples the subject and verb have been brought closer together by placing the formerly intervening words at the end of the sentence.

Keep sentences relatively short, the meaning clear and the grammar accurate. Deal with one idea per sentence. Remember the general rule that each paragraph should address one particular topic. Similarly, each sentence in that paragraph should deal with one particular aspect of the topic. The following complex sentence contains a number of subordinate clauses (highlighted) and makes a range of points:

> Mrs Matthews, who remains in hospital as a result of the recent accident she sustained at work, is unable to visit the office to provide a statement, although I have informed her that you are willing to visit her in hospital out of office hours she does not want that but instead wants to meet with you in her home once she is discharged from hospital, provided you are happy with that.

The information contained in this sentence can be expressed more clearly by separating the various points being made into shorter sentences. The sequence of events being explained is as follows:

1. Mrs Matthews has had an accident and remains in hospital.
2. She is unable to visit the office.

3. She has been informed you are willing to visit her in hospital out of office hours but she doesn't want that.
4. Provided you are agreeable, she would like to meet with you in her home once she is released from hospital.

Exercise 3.9

Finish the following two sentences from the above:

1. Mrs Matthews who ____________________
2. Instead of visiting her ____________________

Sub-clauses can also be used to provide a range of information in one sentence. This involves using a main sentence followed by sub-clauses. Consider for instance the following lengthy sentence:

> To be eligible to undertake the vocational Legal Practice Course required to become a solicitor, every applicant must be registered as a student member of the Law Society and have successfully completed a qualifying law degree or a postgraduate diploma in law.

This can be rewritten more concisely with a main sentence followed by tabulated sub-clauses:

> An applicant will only be eligible to undertake the Legal Practice Course required to qualify as a solicitor by having:
>
> (i) become a registered student member of the Law Society; and
>
> (ii) either successfully completed a qualifying law degree or a postgraduate diploma in law.

Exercise 3.10

Now rewrite the following by using sub-clauses:

The Occupiers Liability Act 1957 provides that the occupier of premises owes a common law duty of care to visitors, regardless of whether a specific contract has been entered into between the occupier and visitor, this tortuous duty of care therefore being independent of any contractual duty of care which may also exist.

Precision

Clear and precise writing requires accurate spelling, punctuation and grammar. Errors can obviously have serious consequences as well as reflecting badly on your professional reputation.

Consider for instance how the lack of use of a comma (,) affects the meaning of what is being said in the following sentences:

The accused said the judge is a professional criminal!

The accused, said the judge, is a professional criminal!

Exercise 3.11

Sentence writing

Complete the following sentences by entering the appropriate words into each blank space from the list below.

contract for	**negotiate with**	**act for**
appeal against	**decide against**	**enter into**

1. The Defendant has decided to ________ ________ the judgment.
2. My client has agreed to enter into the ________ ______ the purchase of two printers.
3. We are confident that the judge will ________ ________ our opponent.
4. He wants to ________ ________ discussions with a view to becoming a director of the company.
5. He intends to ________ ________ the company to purchase some shares.
6. I ______ ______ the claimant in the case of *Travelgraph Limited* v *Matrix Printers Limited*.

List of words/expressions

The following is a further list of examples of vocabulary used in legal English correspondence.

act for	appeal against	charge with
contract for	decide for/against	enter into
file for	find against	legislate for/against
negotiate with/for	prohibit from	rule against
settle for	swear in	withdraw from

You will also write more concisely by avoiding repetition and use of redundant words. Redundant phrases or compound expressions can often be written in simpler language.

Exercise 3.12

Replace the following compound constructions with simpler language. The first one is done for you by way of example:

Compound	Simple form
hereinafter	*below*
aforementioned	
save as aforesaid	

Exercise 3.13

Replace the words underlined with simpler vocabulary (for instance, a suitable alternative to the first word underlined would be 'begin').

We intend to **commence** (1) legal proceedings tomorrow against Hendragin Limited. **Subsequent to** (2) that, we will await a defence to the court action being filed at court by the defendant. Hopefully the directors of Hendragin Limited will then take a rational and commercial approach to the litigation, however, and negotiate a settlement of the dispute. That would **terminate** (3) the court proceedings **prior to** (4) the court listing the case for trial. **In the event that** (5) the case does not settle, it will be necessary to prepare witness statements **in regard to** (6) the evidence which remains in dispute.

1. ______________________ **4.** ______________________

2. ______________________ **5.** ______________________

3. ______________________ **6.** ______________________

Other examples of complex words and expressions along with their plain English alternatives shown in brackets include:

forthcoming (next) in light of the fact that (since)
in the event that (if) provide a response (reply)

Keep in mind who will be reading and relying on what you write when choosing your vocabulary. For instance, using technical language or terms would not normally be appropriate when writing to a lay client (i.e. a client not trained as a lawyer). Such technical language may, however, be appropriate when writing to another lawyer.

As with other professions, the law has its own 'jargon' of English vocabulary. Some jargon nouns and verbs are specific to legal English. Through convention and practice, some are still generally used because they have a very specific legal meaning. Even where such language is appropriate, however, always consider whether it will be readily understood by the reader. Your writing will usually be more effective if you use plain English wherever possible. Keep in mind that as a practising lawyer your work will not only be read by other lawyers. So, as you write, keep in mind the question: will the reader have a clear understanding of the words I have chosen? Choose language you would use when speaking in a formal situation to the person you are writing to.

Exercise 3.14

Writing concisely

Always consider whether a particular word could be used in place of a group of compounded words. Select a word from the following list which has the same meaning and could be used as an alternative to each of the phrases in the 'Compound construction' column in the table below. Write each corresponding word in the 'Simple form' column. The first entry has been completed for you by way of illustration.

if	associated	like
until	below	near
then	later	otherwise
before	set out above	
due to/since/because	because	

→

Compound construction	Simple form
in the event that	If
at a later date	
as a consequence of/for the reason that	
until such time as	
similar to	
at that particular time	
prior to	
in close proximity to	

Exercise 3.15

Now rewrite the following sentence more concisely.

American courts award damages in personal injury cases which are higher than English courts award when determining damages in the course of making judgments in personal injury cases.

Exercise 3.16

Letter writing

Complete the following letter to Addison, Rais and Partners on behalf of a client named Nicholas Tiessen by filling in the blank spaces, selecting the relevant phrases from the list below.

referred to	award damages	independent witness
obtain a statement	full and final settlement	are instructed

STRINGWOOD & EVANS
18 Bond Street
London W1 1KR
Tel: + 44 (0)20 7538 2892

To: Addison, Rais & Partners
18 Aldgate Crescent
London

WITHOUT PREJUDICE

10 February 2012

→

Dear Sir or Madam

N Tiessen v M Gluck and Londinium Delivery Co. Ltd

Accident 20 October 2011

We note that you act on behalf of the defendants in the above matter. It appears clear from the facts of the case that the First Defendant caused the accident ____________ **(1)** above. We have managed to ____________ **(2)** from an ____________ **(3)** which appears to indicate clearly that liability will be established for negligence. If the case proceeds to trial we are confident that the court will ____________ **(4)** to our client. To avoid further unnecessary legal costs therefore we ____________ **(5)** to propose settlement, entirely without prejudice, in terms whereby:

1. Your clients pay damages in the sum of £25,000 to our client within twenty-eight days in ____________ ____________ **(6)** of this matter.
2. In addition, your clients pay our client's reasonable legal costs.

We look forward to hearing from you in the earnest hope that this matter may now be resolved amicably in the above terms.

Yours sincerely

Signature

Recording agreed settlement terms by correspondence

The following letter from Addison, Rais and Partners is in reply to the above letter from Nicholas Tiessen's solicitors dated 10 February 2012. Read the letter on page 64 then answer the questions which follow in Exercise 3.17.

Exercise 3.17

Comprehension

1. What did Addison, Rais and Partners do before writing this letter?
2. What are they agreeing to on behalf of their client?
3. How soon are they going to provide the agreed settlement amount?
4. What further information are they asking for?

ADDISON, RAIS & PARTNERS
18 Aldgate Crescent
London

Stringwood & Evans
18 Bond Street
London, W1 1KR

24 February 2012

WITHOUT PREJUDICE

Dear Sir/Madam

Nicholas Tiessen* v *Matthew Gluck & Londinium Delivery Company Limited
Accident 20 October 2011

We refer to your letter dated 10 February 2012 setting out without prejudice proposals in regard to the above matter. Having taken our clients' instructions we confirm that our clients agree to the terms of settlement proposed in full and final settlement. We will forward a cheque for the agreed damages amount of £25,000 to your office within twenty-eight days. In the meantime please provide us with details of your client's legal costs and date of birth.

Yours sincerely

A. Lawyer

Good practice tips

- Keep sentences short (especially when writing to a client).
- Be concise and use the 'active' voice.
- Use language appropriate to the reader (this will be different depending on whether the reader is a client or a fellow solicitor, for instance) and write in the same way that you might speak to the person to whom you are writing.

WRITING INTERNAL DOCUMENTS

Memorandum (or 'memo')

An internal memorandum (also known as an inter-office or 'in-house' memo) is a document for communicating with colleagues in your firm or company. Some legal jargon can therefore be used. A memo typically sets out written details of a client's instructions and concerns. It should concentrate on the specific issue, question or problem it is intended to address. Memos are often relied upon when making important decisions on the future conduct of a client's file.

Exercise 3.18

Some firms have their own 'house styles' of format or layout. All memos should, however, provide the information indicated in the blue side notes in the following memorandum. The memorandum is addressed to you from the Head of the Business Law Department. It sets out the steps now required to complete your client's instructions. Eight words or phrases have been omitted. Fill in these missing prepositions and phrases in the numbered blank spaces from the list below (you may need to use some words more than once).

of to in good time in terms of by within

STRINGWOOD & EVANS

MEMORANDUM

Heading

From: Jacqueline Hanratty (Head of Business Law Dept.)
To: [ ]
Client: Travelgraph Limited
File Ref: T4536G
Date: 20 October 2011

Who from

Who to (the recipient)

Name of client/date/ file reference

TRAVELGRAPH LIMITED

Brief heading of subject matter

Thank you for doing such a good job ______ **(1)** preparing the necessary company documentation for this client company. The company also now wishes ______ **(2)** confirm the appointment ______ **(3)** another director, namely Kadir Salleh.

Relevant background details, for reader to understand what the matter is about

It is now necessary ______ **(4)** update the company's Register of Directors and notify the Registrar of Companies of Kadir Salleh's appointment to the board ______ **(5)** completing a Form AP01 and forwarding it to the Registrar of Companies ______ **(6)** 14 days.

Brief statement of facts/issues/matters for consideration or 'actioning'

We must ensure we do this ______________ **(7)** therefore. ______________ **(8)** fees this is a valuable client. I'd be very grateful therefore if you could please attend to these matters for me while I am at a meeting with other clients in Paris. I will then check your work when I return to the office on Thursday.

Regards

Jacqueline Hanratty

Sometimes memos are addressed to outside parties. They are known as 'external memos' and are usually intended to persuade a party to accept another party's point of view in a legal dispute. External memos are less common than internal memos (although sometimes used in the USA in particular).

E-mails

E-mails are increasingly used for legal correspondence and are usually laid out in similar fashion to more traditional correspondence such as letters. Language should remain appropriately formal.

Read the following e-mail from your secretary at Stringwood & Evans, then answer the questions which follow.

From: Tracey Hongzhi <tracey.hongzhi@unilaw.univ>
Date: 7 July 2011
To: Alex Reader <a.reader@legal.unilaw.univ>
Subject: Appointment tomorrow with Cadmium Aerospace

Dear Alex

The Sales Director of Cadmium Aerospace Limited, Frederick Johannsen, telephoned this afternoon. I have made an appointment for him to see you in your office tomorrow at 11.00 a.m. He wants to discuss an agency agreement with you that his company is considering entering into with another company called MacFadyen Aviation Limited. In particular, he wants you to advise him concerning:

- Whether Cadmium Aerospace can appoint other agents within Europe and North America during the course of the agency agreement.
- Whether the principal can sell directly to customers within Europe and North America as well as through MacFadyen Aviation Ltd while the agreement remains in force.
- Details of how the principal is required under the agreement to assist the agent to achieve sales.
- An explanation of how the agent's commission is to be calculated in accordance with the agreement and what minimum sales the agent is required to achieve under the agreement.

Kind regards

Tracey

Exercise 3.19

Comprehension

1. Why is Frederick Johannsen coming into your office tomorrow?
2. Which other company is involved in the proposed agency agreement?
3. What in particular does Frederick Johannsen want advice on concerning Europe and North America?
4. What in particular does he want to know about the agent's rights and obligations under the proposed agency agreement?

Attendance notes

An attendance note records what was said, agreed and decided while talking to a client, a witness or indeed another lawyer (whether in person or by telephone). They are therefore largely composed of reported speech.

Reported speech indicates what was said but not in exactly the same words. Verbs commonly used in reported speech include 'said', 'told, 'explained', 'suggested', 'asked', 'wondered' and 'advised'. For instance, 'He told me that the meeting had taken place.' Be careful to use the correct verb tense.

Imagine the following discussion between a lawyer and her client:

Lawyer: 'How did the accident happen?'
Client: 'I tripped over a pot of paint.'

This would be written in reported speech (in the first person) as:

I asked her (or 'the client') how the accident happened. She told me that she had tripped over a pot of paint.

Or, more concisely:

She (or 'the client') told me she had tripped over a pot of paint.

Good practice tip

- Direct speech is placed in speech marks (inverted commas).
- Pronouns and tenses alter in indirect speech.

Exercise 3.20

Rewrite the following in reported speech using 'I asked' or 'I said that'.

1. 'What is your job Mr Anderson?'
2. 'We'll meet again next week Mrs Kennedy.'
3. 'An employer will usually agree to provide a reference.'

Attendance notes are kept in a client's file and should contain the following details:

- date and time of attendance;
- names of everyone present at the meeting, event or discussion being recorded by the file note;
- duration of attendance (with starting and finishing times);
- what was discussed – including all relevant facts;
- what advice, decisions and conclusions were reached;
- what further action was agreed (what are the next steps for the client and lawyer to take).

Attendance notes can later be useful for checking and proving:

- what a client's specific concerns or instructions were;
- details of what was said and agreed with other parties (including, for instance, details of a telephone conversation with a lawyer acting for another party);
- exactly what a client informed you of or asked you to do when a dispute arises!

Now read the following attendance note, noting how reported speech is used.

Exercise 3.21

As you read the attendance note, try to spot the two sentences containing irrelevant information!

Lambros & Co.
Solicitors

ATTENDANCE NOTE

Date: 21 July 2011
File Ref: H3547

Attended on Mrs Catherine Hawkins, a new client. She set out what happened to her on Thursday 30 June 2011. She tripped over a tin of paint on the ground floor of an office building at 32 Chancery Lane, London, while heading towards a client's office. She sustained a broken finger on her right hand as well as a fractured right arm. This client turned up twenty minutes late for our meeting. Mrs Hawkins works for an advertising agency and she is concerned that these injuries may affect her ability to do her job, which involves a good deal of written work. The accident happened at approximately 10 a.m. Mrs Hawkins clearly remembers that the tin of paint had been left on the floor of the corridor by decorators who had not fenced off the area in which they were working. There were also no warning signs to indicate that decorating work was being carried

→

out. She did admit, however, that, off the record, she was not fully paying attention to where she was going because she was in a hurry.

She wishes to pursue a civil claim for damages for the injury and loss sustained on the grounds of the decorators' negligence. She also told me that one of the decorators was wearing a dirty old shirt. We agreed that I would write a letter to the company which owns the building. I advised that she is likely to be successful with her claim.

Time engaged on attendance on client: 30 minutes

Uncountable nouns

There are some nouns in English which are uncountable, i.e. they have no plural form (such as having an 's' on the end). In the above file note, for instance, 'negligence' is uncountable. The following words are also uncountable and regularly used in legal correspondence and documents.

malice	information	advice	evidence
research	employment	discrimination	legislation

File notes

File notes are regularly used in legal practice to create an accurate record of work and legal research undertaken on a particular client's file.

File note checklist

File notes should contain:

- date, time and any file reference number;
- duration (time taken for both the work undertaken which the file note is recording and for writing the file note);
- all relevant facts, findings, conclusions and details of work undertaken (whether letter writing, drafting documents or legal research, etc.).

File notes can then be subsequently referred to when reviewing the client's file. The file may, for instance, have to be reviewed for the purpose of:

- preparing for trial
- becoming familiar with a client's file when taking over conduct of it from a colleague.

Time spent on tasks such as writing correspondence, drafting documents and legal research is recorded in file notes. So file notes are also useful when calculating the fees to charge your client! Read the following file note, noting how reported speech is used.

STRINGWOOD & EVANS
Solicitors

FILE NOTE

7 July 2011

Fee Earner's Reference: WRM
File Number: L8453

Client: Michelle Lohan

Conducted legal research into share holding required by one share holder to compel a company incorporated in the United Kingdom to hold a general meeting of the shareholders. Ascertained that this now requires 5 per cent shareholding (reference – website of UK Department of Business, Innovations and Skills).

Drafted necessary notice to company on behalf of client to call a general meeting and covering letter.

Time engaged: 1 hour

SUMMARY

- Use headings and separate paragraphs for separate issues.
- Proofread carefully for correct grammar, punctuation and spelling.
- When describing events or occurrences, it can be helpful to structure the content of your correspondence in date order (i.e. chronologically).
- Check you have included all key facts and information.
- Use appropriate headings to 'signpost' issues and topics and set out content in a logical order.

Visit **www.mylawchamber.co.uk/mckay** to access further resources for practising legal language skills including additional exercises, listening activities and live weblinks for online research.

Chapter 4

Drafting legal documents for business

Learning objectives

This chapter will help you to:

- become familiar with company documentation and procedure;
- understand the language of legal agreements and business documents;
- consider the sentence structure and grammar of commercial legal documents;
- practise drafting and amending business documentation.

INTRODUCTION

Legal drafting is the process of preparing legal documents. Typical examples of such documents include:

- company documents, such as articles of association of a company, company resolutions and minutes of company meetings;
- commercial agreements, including partnership agreements, agency and distribution agreements, merger and acquisition agreements and intellectual property agreements;
- statements of case (formal court documents used in court proceedings).

This chapter will address the first two of these types of documents, i.e. company legal documents and commercial agreements. The next chapter will look at drafting court documents for court proceedings, i.e. documents for litigation, generally known as statements of case.

The purpose of drafting business and commercial documentation is principally to create documents which accurately set out agreements reached between individuals and/or companies – generally referred to as the parties. It is essential to use the appropriate vocabulary and write grammatically correct sentences to ensure that the documents you produce convey precisely the intended meaning. Otherwise a dispute may subsequently arise as to the meaning of a term in the drafted agreement, particularly when the language used can be interpreted as having alternative and different meanings which would lead to ambiguity. In that case a court will interpret (construe) the term as having the meaning least beneficial to the party which drafted the ambiguous term. This is known as the ***contra proferentem*** doctrine. However, if the document is well drafted, being clear and concise, then any misunderstanding or dispute can be determined by reference to the document, avoiding a dispute in court. So precision of meaning is crucial.

When drafting documents, it is common practice to use precedents (existing, previously used documents). Precedents provide a range of standard words and phrases for you to use but they must be selected carefully. Many precedents deliberately retain some traditional vocabulary or dated words (i.e. not in everyday current use), where such words have been tried and tested, sometimes in court, as to their specific meaning. If you replace such words with your own choice of words, you should ensure that they retain the specific meaning intended.

In this chapter you will have the opportunity to examine the language and grammar used in some sample precedents.

DRAFTING COMPANY DOCUMENTS

Incorporating a company

Assume that you are a solicitor at Stringwood & Evans, a law firm in London. You have been instructed by a new client, Thomas Shapiro, to incorporate a company for him. Mr Shapiro wishes to establish a private company limited by shares, to be named 'Maplink Limited'. Here are the details of the proposed new company.

Registered Office:	44 Princess Diana Walk, South Kensington London W2 3SL Telephone: (020) 7429 8137	
Directors:	(1) Mr Thomas Shapiro 23 Essex Street, Hampton Court, Surrey KT8 1NQ (2) Professor Dimitris Yavaprapas 'The Manor', 2 Queen Elizabeth Street, London SE1 5NP	
Company Secretary:	Ms Gisela Wirth 15 Robin Hood Way, Mansfield, Nottingham NG2 7CX	
Authorised Share Capital:	£10,000.00 divided into 10,000 ordinary shares of £1.00 each	
Members and shareholdings:	Thomas Shapiro	4,500
	Dimitris Yavaprapas	3,000
	Gisela Wirth	2,500

Articles of association

The articles of association set out regulations (rules) for conducting the business of a company and its internal management. The Companies Act 2006 provides newly incorporated (established) companies with 'model articles'. These are a simple set of articles and provide basic rules for a company.

Maplink Limited has model articles of association ('articles'). Excerpts from the company's articles are set out below for the purpose of exploring how English is used and to help you to develop your language skills in understanding a legal text. Now read these articles carefully, paying particular attention to the way language is used.

> **PART 2**
> **DIRECTORS**
> **DIRECTORS' POWERS AND RESPONSIBILITIES**
>
> **Directors' general authority**
>
> **3.** Subject to the articles, the directors are responsible for the management of the company's business, for which purpose they may exercise all the powers of the company.
>
> **Shareholders' reserve power**
>
> **4.**—(1) The shareholders may, by special resolution, direct the directors to take, or refrain from taking, specified action.
>
> (2) No such special resolution invalidates anything which the directors have done before the passing of the resolution.

These model articles are deliberately drafted in plain English for clarity of meaning. Many legal documents nevertheless continue to use old-fashioned phrases. Consider, for instance, the following:

hereinafter: in a later part of this document

hereby: as a result of this document

save: except

Use of adverbs for legal English

The words 'hereinafter' and 'hereby' are adverbs. Other similar adverbs are commonly used in legal documents and official statements. For example:

> In testimony whereof I have hereunto* set my hand and affixed my seal of office in the City of London, this sixth day of June two thousand and eleven.

Vocabulary
hereunto: to this document

Exercise 4.1

Match the adverbs (1–9) with their corresponding meaning (from *a* to *i*):

1. hereby	(*a*) below, later in this document
2. herein	(*b*) in a preceding part of this document, earlier in this document
3. hereinafter/hereafter	(*c*) together with this document
4. hereinbefore/heretofore	(*d*) as a result of this statement, by this means
5. hereof	(*e*) in consequence of this, at this point
6. hereto/hereunto	(*f*) in this document, in this matter
7. hereunder	(*g*) in a later part of this document, starting from this time
8. hereupon	(*h*) to this matter or document
9. herewith	(*i*) of this document

When reviewing the articles of association of companies incorporated (created) before October 2009, you will find more extensive use of such dated language. Consider for instance the following further articles of a company established prior to October 2009 (when the more modern 'model articles' shown above were introduced). Also note how each clause is structured:

SHARES

3. Subject to the provisions of the next following Regulation the Directors are authorised* for the purposes of Section 80 of the Act to exercise the power of the Company to allot* shares to the amount of the authorised but unissued share capital of the Company for the time being and the Directors may allot grant options over or otherwise dispose of such shares to such persons on such terms and in such manner as they think fit provided always that:–

(i) Save as provided in sub-paragraph (ii) of this Regulation the authority given in this Regulation to the Directors to exercise the power of the Company to allot shares shall expire five years after the date of incorporation* of the Company.

(ii) The Members in General Meeting* may by Ordinary Resolution*:

(a) renew the said authority (whether or not it has been previously renewed) for a period not exceeding five years; but such resolution must state (or restate) the amount of shares which may be allotted under such authority or renewed authority or as the case may be, the amount remaining to be allotted thereunder, and must specify the date on which the authority or renewed authority will expire;

(b) revoke or vary any such authority (or renewed authority).

4. The proviso to Regulation 12 of Table A shall not apply to the Company.

LIEN

5. The lien* conferred by Regulation 8 of Table A shall attach to all shares whether fully paid or not and to all shares registered in the name of any person indebted or

→

under liability to the Company whether he be the sole holder thereof or one of two or more joint holders. The Company shall have a first and paramount lien on every share (not being fully paid) for all moneys (whether presently payable or not) called or payable at a fixed time in respect of that share and the Company shall also have a first and paramount lien on all shares (including fully paid shares) registered in the name of any person indebted or under liability to the Company whether he be the sole holder thereof or one of two or more joint holders for all moneys presently payable by him or his estate to the Company: but the Directors may at any time declare any shares to be wholly or in part exempt from the provisions of this Regulation. The Company's lien, if any, on a share shall extend to all dividends payable thereupon*.

6. The liability of any Member in default in respect of a call shall be increased by the addition at the end of the first sentence of Regulation 18 in Table A of the words "and all expenses that may have been incurred by the Company by reason of such non-payment".

Vocabulary

Note the terminology used and the corresponding meaning:

allot (shares): to issue or distribute shares to raise capital for the company
authorised: permitted (typically used to refer to directors being permitted by company law or the articles to do something, such as issue shares
general meeting: a meeting of the shareholders
incorporation of the company: formation or creation of the company
lien: right(s) or security which the company retains over shares it has issued
ordinary resolution: a proposal (such as to remove a director of the company) which requires more than half of the votes cast to be in favour of the resolution for it to be 'passed'
resolution: proposal/decision (usually of shareholders)
thereupon: consequently; accordingly

Use of the passive

We use two forms of the verbs: the active (e.g. exclude, shall offer), and the passive (e.g. am/is/are excluded, shall be offered). Look at the following expressions typically found in documents such as these and notice how the verb is formed in each sentence:

... they *are excluded*

No shares ... *shall be offered*

... the Directors *are authorised*

... it *has been* previously *renewed*

The liability ... *shall be increased*

The **passive** is widely used in academic writing and legal English since it conveys a more formal and objective impression.

Good practice tip

When forming the passive, put the verb 'to be' in the tense of the original verb + the *past participle* of the verb, and start the sentence with the object of the original one.

Verb 'to be'

Present simple	Present continuous	Present perfect simple
am is are	am being is being are being	has been have been
Past simple	**Past continuous**	**Past perfect simple**
was were	was being were being	had been
Future simple		**Future perfect simple**
will be shall be		will have been shall have been

Note: Verb 'to be' is not used in the following tenses:

- present perfect continuous – past perfect continuous
- future continuous – future perfect continuous

The passive is used to draw the attention of the reader to the importance of the process, for instance:

The liability of any Member in default *shall be increased* ...

- When there is a general rule that applies to all parties:

  Consideration *must be given* to support a contractual promise, unless made by deed.

- when the subject of the original sentence is assumed and does not need identification, e.g: '... the authority, police or shareholders ...'

  Special measures *were taken* to allow the victim to give evidence by pre-recorded DVD and TV link.

  It *has been agreed* to postpone the meeting due to unforeseen circumstances.

Note: The verbs 'base' and 'entitle' are usually used in the passive form.

Changing a sentence into the passive form

1. ***Active***: They *may excuse a director* if he or she took every step that a reasonably diligent person would have taken to minimise loss to creditors.

   Passive: *A director may be excused* if he or she took every step that a reasonably diligent person would have taken to minimise loss to creditors.

2. ***Active***: People *see the breaking of criminal law* as different from the breaking of other kinds of law.

   Passive: *The breaking of criminal law is seen* as different from the breaking of other kinds of law.

3. ***Active***: *They agreed* to appoint an auditor.

   Passive: *It was agreed* to appoint an auditor.

Exercise 4.2

Change the following sentences into their passive equivalent:

1. The committee will have published the report by the end of next month.
2. Their lawyer is currently drafting the terms and conditions of the agreement.
3. They have listed your case for hearing next Wednesday.
4. The firm of solicitors has submitted all the necessary documents to court.
5. They will appoint a new director as soon as possible.
6. Last week the company's legal adviser explained the reasons for amending some clauses in the draft contract.
7. They may disqualify a director for breach of health and safety law.
8. A compromise agreement must contain the terms of the settlement.
9. Employment Tribunals calculate the compensatory award on the basis of net pay.
10. They have decided to hold a conference to discuss the impact of the new regulations.

Drafting point

Arrange clauses and sub-clauses in logical order and according to their degree of importance.

Analysing the grammar of long, complex sentences

Many companies were established before October 2009. You are therefore likely to encounter 'old style' articles of companies when advising corporate clients. Lengthy and complex sentences are often encountered in such articles.

The following article (article 17), which provides protection for directors from personal financial liability for business-related costs, is a typical example. You will note that sub-clause (a) consists of two sentences; the first sentence is very long and complex while the second one is much shorter.

INDEMNITY

17. (a) Every Director or other officer of the Company shall be indemnified out of the assets of the Company against all losses or liabilities which he may sustain or incur in or about the execution of the duties of his office or otherwise in relation thereto, including any liability incurred by him in defending any proceedings, whether civil or criminal, in which judgment is given in his favour or in which he is acquitted or in connection with any application under Section 144 or Section 727 of the Act in which relief is granted to him by the Court, and no Director or other officer shall be liable for any loss, damage or misfortune which may happen to or be incurred by the Company in the execution of the duties of his office or in relation thereto. But this Article shall only have effect in so far as its provisions are not avoided by Section 310 of the Act.

The first sentence in article 17 (a) is very long and complex. Your understanding of such provisions can, however, be developed by examining how English is used.

The basic sentence here is:

[1] Every Director shall be indemnified against all losses or liabilities.

First, we wish to add two points:

(a) the rule applies to any other officer of the company as well as the directors;

(b) the indemnity shall be paid out of the assets of the company.

So, the first part becomes:

Every Director or other officer of the Company shall be indemnified out of the assets of the Company against all losses and liabilities.

The next part specifies and identifies such losses and liabilities:

[2] He (the director or the officer of the company) may sustain or incur such losses and liabilities in or about the execution of the duties of his office – or otherwise in relation to the execution of his duties.

The two parts refer to *all losses and liabilities*, so we can link them using the relative pronoun 'which' (refer to Complex Sentences in Chapter 1). Thus, the new sentence becomes:

[3] Every Director or other officer of the Company shall be indemnified out of the assets of the Company against all losses or liabilities which he may sustain or incur in or about the execution of the duties of his office or otherwise in relation thereto.

This clause deals with indemnity against losses or liabilities, and we can add another sentence to include other liabilities. The next sentence would read:

Such liabilities include any liability incurred by him (a director or any other officer of the company) in defending any proceedings or in connection with any application under Section 144 or Section 272 of the Act.

Rather than starting a new sentence, this part can be added to sentence [3] by replacing the subject (such liabilities) and the verb (include) with the word 'including'. So, our main sentence now reads as follows:

[4] Every Director or other officer of the Company shall be indemnified out of the assets of the Company against all losses or liabilities which he may sustain or incur in or about the execution of the duties of his office or otherwise in relation thereto, including any liability incurred by him in defending any proceedings or in connection with any application under Section 144 or Section 727 of the Act.

The reader might think that these proceedings relate to civil cases only, in fact they relate to both civil and criminal cases. So, we need to insert 'whether civil or criminal' after the word 'proceedings':

[5] Every Director or other officer of the Company shall be indemnified out of the assets of the Company against all losses or liabilities which he may sustain or incur

> in or about the execution of the duties of his office or otherwise in relation thereto, including any liability incurred by him in defending any proceedings, whether civil or criminal, or in connection with any application under Section 144 or Section 727 of the Act.

Notice the *use of the comma* for a list: loss – damage – misfortune.

> The loss, damage or misfortune may happen to or be incurred by the Company in the execution of the duties of his office or in relation hereto.

- Instead of writing 'any director ... shall not be ...', the sentence starts with 'No' to replace 'not'. So, it becomes: 'No Director or other officer shall be liable ...'
- The word 'which' is used to replace 'the loss, damage or misfortune'.

The additional sentence reads as follows:

> No Director or other officer shall be liable for any loss, damage or misfortune which may happen to or be incurred by the Company in the execution of the duties of his office or in relation thereto.

To join the above sentence to further relevant information, we simply add a comma and the word 'and'. For instance:

> Every Director or other officer of the Company shall be indemnified out of the assets of the Company against all losses or liabilities which he may sustain or incur in or about the execution of the duties of his office or otherwise in relation thereto, including any liability incurred by him in defending any proceedings, whether civil or criminal, in which judgment is given in his favour or in which he is acquitted or in connection with any application under Section 144 or Section 727 of the Act in which relief is granted to him by the Court, and no Director or other officer shall be liable for any loss, damage or misfortune which may happen to or be incurred by the Company in the execution of the duties of his office or in relation thereto.

Commas are also used in legal drafting to indicate exactly which items within the same sentence or list are included in a particular category. Consider, for instance, the following excerpt from an insurance contract which sets out what items or activities are covered by insurance:

> This insurance policy provides insurance cover to the insured party for damage to and arising from *newspaper, deliveries and publishing.*

Since the comma has been placed between 'newspaper' and 'deliveries', this conveys the meaning that the insured will be insured if loss results from 'newspaper' regardless of whether the loss results from 'newspaper delivery'. If the comma had not been used in this way the insurance policy would be likely to be construed as meaning that there would only be insurance cover for loss caused by newspapers *being delivered.* (Further guidance on these aspects of language can be found in the accompanying website materials for this chapter.)

Exercise 4.3

Further language practice

Match the following adverbs (1–12) with their corresponding meaning (*a*–*l*):

1. thereafter	(*a*) to that; in addition
2. thereby	(*b*) in that document; in that respect
3. therefor	(*c*) with that; soon after that
4. therein	(*d*) from that point in time
5. thereinafter	(*e*) in accordance with that stated below in the document
6. thereinbefore	(*f*) as a result of that; by that mean
7. thereof	(*g*) in consequence of that; immediately after that
8. thereto/thereunto	(*h*) later in this document
9. theretofore	(*i*) of that
10. thereunder	(*j*) before that time
11. thereupon	(*k*) earlier in this document
12. therewith	(*l*) for that purpose

COMPANY MEETINGS AND RESOLUTIONS

Company law dictates that certain business decisions concerning a company need shareholders approval. Shareholders' meetings are particularly needed when major changes to the company are being proposed. Proposals for such changes are put to a shareholders' meeting in the form of resolutions.

Board meeting

Having been incorporated, Maplink Limited has held its first board meeting. The following document is the minutes of that first board meeting (i.e. directors' meeting) of the company. The minutes record what was discussed and agreed at the meeting.

Exercise 4.4

Complete the minutes by selecting the most appropriate word from those given in brackets below.

Maplink Limited

Minutes of the first meeting of the board of directors of Maplink Limited ('the company') held at 44 Princess Diana Walk, South Kensington, London, W2 3SL on 16 May 2011 at 10.00 a.m.

Present: Thomas Shapiro
Dimitris Yavaprapas
In Attendance: Gisela Wirth

→

1. Thomas Shapiro and Dimitris Yavaprapas accepted office as directors of the company. It was resolved that Thomas Shapiro be appointed Chairperson of the board.
2. It was ________ (**restitution/resolution/resolved/determined**) that [insert your name here] be appointed solicitor to the company.
3. It was resolved that Gisela Wirth be ________ (**employed/appointed/selected/commissioned**) secretary of the company.
4. It was resolved that the ________ (**classified/head/official/registered**) office be at 44 Princess Diana Walk, South Kensington, London, W2 3SL.
5. It was resolved that the quorum necessary for the transaction of the business of the directors should be two directors personally present.
6. A draft notice of an extraordinary general meeting of the company was ________ (**disclosed/indicated/presented/represented**) to the meeting and approved. It was further resolved that such meeting be ________ (**collated/convened/assembled/ accumulated**) and that notice of this be ________ (**given/provided/catered/supplied**) forthwith to the shareholders.
7. The meeting thereupon adjourned. Upon resumption it was reported that the ________ (**intentions/proposals/resolve/resolutions**) set out in the notice of the extraordinary general meeting had been passed respectively as ordinary and special resolutions of the company.
8. Upon there being no further competent business the meeting was then ________ (**declared/proclaimed/affirmed/publicised**) closed by the Chairperson.

Drafting point

Those attending the board meeting who are entitled to vote at the meeting, i.e. the directors, are indicated as being '**Present**'. Anyone else who is attending but is not entitled to vote (the company secretary in this meeting since she is not also a director) is indicated as being '**In Attendance**'.

Exercise 4.5

Convening a board meeting

Answer the following questions on the minutes you have just finalised for Maplink's first board meeting.

1. What is meant by convening a meeting?

2. Why do you think multi-national companies sometimes conduct board meetings by audio-visual conferencing?

→

3. Suggest one reason why a director may wish to call a board meeting.
4. Paragraph 5 of the minutes indicates that the quorum for board meetings is two. What is a quorum?

NOTICE OF GENERAL MEETING

The following document is a notice of the first shareholders' meeting of Maplink Limited. A shareholders' meeting is usually called a 'general meeting'. This meeting is being held to:

1. appoint a third director, namely Kadir Salleh, of 4 Kensington Palace Gardens, London, W2 4AJ (date of birth 4 April 1969); and
2. change the name of the company from Maplink Limited to Travelgraph Limited.

Read the notice carefully and look at how it is phrased.

COMPANY NUMBER 3467609

NOTICE OF GENERAL MEETING

COMPANIES ACTS 1985 AND 2006
COMPANY LIMITED BY SHARES
MAPLINK LIMITED
('The Company')

Notice is hereby given that an extraordinary general meeting of the Company will be held at 44 Princess Diana Walk, South Kensington, London W2 3SL, on 16 May 2011 at 11.00 a.m. for the purpose of considering and if thought fit passing the following resolutions respectively* as ordinary and special resolutions of the Company.

ORDINARY RESOLUTION

That Kadir Salleh be appointed a director of the Company.

SPECIAL RESOLUTION

That the name of the Company be changed to Travelgraph Limited

By order of the board

____

Gisela Wirth

Secretary

Date: 14 May 2011

Registered office: 44 Princess Diana Walk, South Kensington, London W2 3SL.

Note: A shareholder who is entitled to attend and vote at the meeting convened by the notice set out above is entitled to appoint a proxy to attend and vote in his place. A proxy need not be a member of the Company.

Vocabulary

attorney: a person appointed to act for or represent another for certain purposes. The formal instrument by which a person gives the authority to another to act for him is called **power of attorney**.

proxy: a person authorised to represent another at a meeting or to vote for him/her.

respectively: for each resolution separately and in the same order as mentioned.

Exercise 4.6

Minutes of general meeting

Here are notes of the general meeting held on 16 May 2011 as per the above notice. Study the notes and draft the minutes of the meeting.

Attended: Thomas Shapiro, Dimitri Yavaprapas & Gisela Wirth

1. notice – given quorum – present
2. chairperson: proposed → ordinary resolution → Kadir Salleh, a director
   show of hands
   declared: resolution passed unanimously
3. chairperson: proposed → special resolution → change of company name
   show of hands
   declared: resolution passed unanimously

Close of meeting

Minutes of the General Meeting

Exercise 4.7

Comprehension

Answer the following questions relating to shareholders' (general) meetings.

1. What is meant by a 'unanimous agreement'?
2. Name another term meaning the same as 'shareholder'.
3. What is a 'casting vote'?
4. What does it mean to 'requisition' a meeting?
5. At the foot of the notice calling the general meeting there is a clause stating that a shareholder is entitled to appoint a proxy. What do you think is meant by a proxy?

Use of prepositions to refer to place and time

We can see from this chapter that prepositions are used in relation to company meetings to refer to place and time:

Place:

The shareholders' meeting was held *at* the company's registered office.

The annual general meeting will be *in* the main hall.

Time:

The general meeting took place *at* 11.00 a.m.

The next board meeting will be sometime *during* February.

The next meeting must be convened *before* September.

Geographical variation

Note that there is some degree of variation internationally in the manner in which prepositions are used, particularly in spoken English. For instance, whereas in England it would be common to state 'you have *until* Wednesday to lodge the document at court', in the US the word 'through' is often used in place of 'until'. Hence in the US you would be more likely to hear 'you have *through* Wednesday to lodge the document at court'. It is also common in 'American' English to omit the preposition which would otherwise be placed in a clause immediately before reference to a day in the week. Thus in the US you might hear 'we'll reconvene this meeting first thing Monday', whereas in England this would be stated as 'we'll reconvene this meeting first thing *on* Monday'.

DRAFTING LEGAL AGREEMENTS

The following document is an agreement typically entered into between a company and one of its directors. This particular document relates to the terms agreed between the newly appointed director, Kadir Salleh, and Travelgraph Limited (the company formerly named Maplink Limited). It sets out the terms of his employment with the company (such as salary, other benefits and his duties as an employee as well as a director of the company).

General principles for drafting a legal agreement

Heading

Note that the agreement below is headed with the name of the document.

Commencement

The nature and purpose of the document is then indicated. This is known as the 'commencement' and begins 'This agreement is made on...' Note that the date of the agreement is also indicated here. (In the US the practice is to put the month first, e.g. June 10, 2011.)

Names

The names of the parties are then set out (in capital letters) and are usually referred to by their position in the agreement (e.g. buyer, seller, agent, principal).

Recitals

More detailed documents also set out some background details and information as to what the agreement is about and this is known as the 'Recitals' section.

Definitions

Definitions used in legal documents are then commonly placed in a definitions clause (e.g. 'the Board'). Definitions can also consist of initials, e.g. KL for Klondyke Limited (do not use initials to define the names of persons). Definitions can be convenient. They avoid having to repeat the same key terms or descriptions when referring to them throughout a document. By defining particular words you can also specify clearly the precise intended meaning of the word(s) in the context of the agreement. Definitions are placed in alphabetical order. Once you have used a definition, be careful to use the definition throughout the rest of the document when referring to the word(s) you have defined. Start each definition with a capital letter (e.g. 'Intellectual property' below).

Operative part

The main provisions of the agreement (price, delivery and payment details, etc.) are contained in what is termed the *operative* part of the agreement. Each clause within the document should address one specific matter. Clauses are commonly divided into sub-clauses (2.1, 2.2, etc.). Notice how headings are used for different aspects of the agreement (such as the Sales Director's duties and holiday entitlement in the example below). Also note that headings are underlined.

Execution

When the agreement is signed and dated this is referred to as *executing* the document. This final part, setting out the names of the parties, their signatures and the date of the agreement, is termed the 'execution' part.

The following document is Kadir Salleh's service contract with Travelgraph Limited. Read it carefully, noting its content and structure.

DIRECTOR'S SERVICE AGREEMENT

THIS AGREEMENT IS MADE ON 10 JUNE 2011 BETWEEN:

(1) TRAVELGRAPH LIMITED ('the Company'), whose registered office is at 44 Princess Diana Walk, South Kensington, London W2 3SL

AND

(2) KADIR SALLEH ('the Sales Director') of 4 Kensington Palace Gardens, London W2 4AJ.

IT IS HEREBY AGREED that the aforesaid Kadir Salleh will serve as Sales Director of Travelgraph Limited on the following terms and conditions.

1. DEFINITIONS

In the agreement the following expressions shall have the meanings set out below:

1.1 'the Board'	the board of directors of the Company
1.2 'Intellectual property'	trade marks, copyrights, inventions and confidential information

2. TERMS OF ENGAGEMENT

2.1 The Sales Director shall be employed by the Company for an initial fixed-term period of three years commencing from 10 June 2011. This agreement may be terminated thereafter by either party providing to the other not less than six months' notice in writing.

3. DUTIES

3.1 The Sales Director shall during his employment with the Company:

3.1.1. endeavour to promote and develop business on behalf of the Company.

4. REMUNERATION

4.1 The Sales Director shall be paid an annual salary of £75,000, payable monthly in arrears on the 28th of each month by direct credit transfer.

5. COMPANY VEHICLE

5.1 The Company shall provide the Sales Director with a Mercedes 300E motorcar and will pay all running costs of said vehicle, including insurance and maintenance.

6. PENSION SCHEME

6.1 The Sales Director will throughout his employment with the Company be eligible to become and remain a member of the Company's pension scheme. The Company will pay into the Company's pension scheme on behalf of the Sales

→

Director an amount equal to 4% of his annual salary during his employment with the Company.

7. HOLIDAY ENTITLEMENT

7.1 The Sales Director shall be entitled to 25 working days' holiday in each calendar year. This is in addition to normal public holidays.

8. CONFIDENTIALITY

8.1 In order to protect the confidentiality of the Company's affairs, business and/or Intellectual property rights, the Sales Director hereby agrees not to disclose to any other party during the course of his employment or thereafter any confidential information relating to the Company nor to use any such information in any way for any purpose following termination of employment with the Company. This restriction is to remain valid for a period of 12 months from termination of the Sales Director's employment with the Company.

9. RESTRAINT OF TRADE

9.1 The Sales Director hereby covenants with the Company that he shall not for a period of 12 months following termination of employment with the Company either directly or indirectly engage in or be involved in any activity or business in competition with the Company.

10. LEGAL JURISDICTION

10.1 This agreement shall be governed by English law and the parties hereby submit to the exclusive jurisdiction of the English courts.

SIGNED BY THOMAS SHAPIRO

For and on behalf of Travelgraph Limited

SIGNED BY KADIR SALLEH

Of 4 Kensington Palace Gardens, London, W2 4AJ

Dated this 10th day of June 2011.

Vocabulary

aforesaid: mentioned earlier
covenants with: agrees with
endeavour to promote: try hard to promote

Confusing words

eligible and illegible

'Eligible' (a person): to fulfil the required conditions; to be entitled to.

'Illegible' (of handwriting): not clear enough to be read.

Further typical vocabulary for such documents includes:

emoluments (earnings) **expeditiously** (quickly) **seized of** (own).

Use the simpler form (shown here in brackets) whenever possible.

Exercise 4.8

Answer the following:

1. What is Kadir Salleh's yearly (annual) salary?
2. What is his job title?
3. How many days annual holiday is he entitled to?
4. In the event of a dispute arising concerning Kadir's service agreement, which country's law governs the agreement?
5. For what period of time is Kadir to be employed by the company according to the agreement?
6. Can Kadir terminate his employment with the company prior to then and if so how much notice is he required to provide to do so?

Expressing obligation

In legal documents the word 'shall' means 'must', as in the following examples:

> The Sales Director *shall endeavour to promote and develop* business on behalf of the Company. [Clause 3]
>
> This agreement *shall be governed* by English law. [Clause 10]

Another way of expressing obligation in legal and formal English is the use of the verb to be plus the infinitive, as in the following example:

> This restriction *is to remain* valid for a period of 12 months. [Clause 8]

So, obligation can be expressed in different ways:

1. The supplier *shall* deliver the printers by the end of May. (legal English)
2. The supplier *is to* deliver the printers by the end of May. (legal/formal English)
3. The supplier *must* deliver the printers by the end of May. (standard English)
4. The supplier *needs to* deliver the printers by the end of May. (standard English/semi-formal English)
5. The supplier *has to* deliver the printers by the end of May. (standard English/semi-formal English)
6. The supplier's *got to* deliver the printers by the end of May. (spoken/informal English)

Note that 'need to' and 'have to' are used for *both* standard and semi-formal English. 'Have got to' is used in spoken and informal English; the verb 'to have' is normally used in the contracted form, e.g. 'I've got to', 'She's got to'.

Exercise 4.9

The following sentence is written in standard English, rewrite it to show different degrees of formality:

He must attend the meeting.

____

Sales agreement

The following sales agreement concerns two parties which are contracting for the sale and purchase of printing machines. Read the agreement carefully then complete the exercise which follows.

SALES AGREEMENT

DATE : 1 August 2011

PARTIES : (1) MATRIX PRINTERS LIMITED, a company registered in England and Wales with its registered office at 18 Tottenham Court Road, London W1 1LB ('the Seller'); and

(2) TRAVELGRAPH LIMITED, a company registered in England and Wales with its registered office at 44 Princess Diana Walk, South Kensington, London W2 3SL ('the Buyer').

1. DETAILS OF SALE

1.1 The Seller is a manufacturer of printing machines and the Buyer is a publisher of maps and tourist guides. The Seller agrees to sell and the Buyer agrees to purchase two printing machines ('the Machines') as specified in Schedule 1 of this Agreement.

1.2 The price for each of the Machines is £45,000 and is payable by the Buyer to the Seller immediately upon delivery of the Machines to the Buyer.

2. DELIVERY

The Seller hereby agrees to deliver the Machines to the Buyer's factory in London on 15 August 2011.

3. LEGAL TITLE

Title in the Machines shall remain vested in the Seller until all monies specified in clause 1.2 have been received by the Seller.

4. RISK AND INSURANCE

It is hereby agreed that all risk of loss and damage shall pass to the Buyer upon delivery of the Machines.

→

5. WARRANTIES

The Seller warrants to the Buyer that the Machines are of satisfactory quality.

6. GOVERNING LAW

This Agreement shall be governed by and construed in accordance with English law. In addition, this Agreement constitutes all terms of agreement between the parties with respect to the subject matter of this Agreement. In the event of any dispute arising, it is hereby irrevocably agreed that the English courts will have exclusive jurisdiction.

SCHEDULE 1

(Details of the Machines)

2 Ultra-Print '123 Series' printing machines

SIGNED by ______________________________

(an authorised representative of Matrix Printers Limited)

SIGNED by ______________________________

(an authorised representative of Travelgraph Limited)

Vocabulary

irrevocably (adverb): cannot be changed

Exercise 4.10

Comprehension

1. How many printing machines is Travelgraph purchasing?
2. How much will Travelgraph pay in total for its purchase in accordance with the agreement?
3. Will Matrix Printers be in breach of contract if the machines are delivered on 8 September 2011? Explain your answer.
4. When does legal title in the printing machines pass to Travelgraph in accordance with the agreement? Explain your answer.
5. Why should Travelgraph arrange for insurance to be in force as soon as the machines are delivered? Explain your answer.

Vocabulary

The word 'satisfactory' in clause 5 headed 'Warranties' of the above sales agreement is formed from the verb 'to satisfy':

satisfy (v.) satisfactory (adj.) satisfactorily (adv.) satisfaction (n.)

We can add the prefix 'un' to have the negative forms of both the adjective and adverb: unsatisfactory; unsatisfactorily.

Satisfy is a regular verb, so the simple past is 'satisfied' and past participle is 'satisfied'. The past participle of most verbs can be used as an adjective; for example, we can use 'satisfied' to describe a person.

Note that for the negative form of 'satisfied' and 'satisfaction', we can add the prefix 'un' or 'dis':

unsatisfied = dissatisfied

Sponsorship agreement

'Heads of agreement' is a term used to refer to a list of basic terms which two parties (typically two companies) have agreed between themselves. Corporate clients then typically ask their lawyers to draft a legal document which incorporates those proposed terms. The following heads of agreement relate to terms which a city law firm intends to enter into with a promising young tennis player named Antonio Perez. The agreement provides that the law firm (Bannerman and Law) is to sponsor Antonio Perez in return for the tennis player agreeing to promote the law firm.

Exercise 4.11

Draft the sponsorship agreement based on the heads of agreement set out below. (Keep in mind the above guidance on drafting, including appropriate use of abbreviations.)

Heads of Agreement

1. Date: 17 October 2011
2. Parties: Antonio Perez (the player) and Bannerman and Law, of 11 The Strand, London (the sponsor)
3. Bannerman and Law will sponsor Antonio Perez to play tennis internationally
4. Further duties: social and business events, including a minimum of 4 days of exhibition tennis matches per year
5. Player to wear a sports shirt showing 'Bannerman and Law – Worldclass Lawyers'
6. Remuneration: £90,000 per annum and use of a Jaguar XKR motor vehicle
7. Duration of agreement: 2 years
8. Conditions for earlier cancellation: bankruptcy; adverse publicity
9. Agreement governed by English law

The phrase 'on or before' can be used to indicate that the clause is intended to *include* the date stated, e.g. 'Delivery is to be made on or before 21 March 2012'. 'Before' can be used to indicate that the clause is intended to *exclude* the date stated, e.g. 'Delivery is to be made before 21 March 2012'.

The following terms, used carefully and appropriately, can also help to prevent future dispute as to the exact meaning conveyed:

on before from but excluding from and including

commencing on [date] exclusive of and/or

It is fairly common in legal English for adverbs to be used at the beginning of a sentence to connect the sentence to the rest of the text. Such sentence adverbs and adverbials which can assist you to write clear legal English include:

accordingly	alternatively	conversely	on the contrary
in any event	finally	furthermore	however
in addition	in particular	similarly	therefore

Agency agreement

Exercise 4.12

The following agreement relates to the appointment of an agent by an aircraft manufacturer called Cadmium Aerospace Limited. Complete this agency agreement on behalf of Cadmium Aerospace Limited by selecting the appropriate word to enter in each blank space from the alternatives in brackets.

AGENCY AGREEMENT

THIS AGREEMENT is made on the 19th day of July 2011

BETWEEN:

CADMIUM AEROSPACE LIMITED, whose registered office is at 168 Hanover Square, London, W1 ('the Principal')

AND

MACFADYEN AVIATION LIMITED, whose registered office is at 115 Duxford Road, Cambridge, CM3 ('the Agent').

1. APPOINTMENT

The Principal **(1)** ________ [hereby / thus / thereafter] appoints the Agent and the Agent agrees to act as the Agent of the Principal for the purpose of promoting and selling the Principal's aircraft throughout Europe and North America ('the Territory'). It is **(2)** ________[nevertheless / whereby / further] agreed that this agreement shall be valid for a period of two years. **(3)** ________[Hereunder / Moreover / Whereby] the Principal agrees not to appoint any other agent in the

→

territory and **(4)** _______ [hereof / conversely / furthermore] agrees not to seek nor enter into sales itself within the Territory during the period of the Agreement.

2. <u>AGENT'S OBLIGATIONS</u>

2.1 The Agent **(5)** _______ [hereunder / hereof / hereby] undertakes to use its best endeavours to market and achieve sales of the Principal's aircraft in the Territory. The Agent is also **(6)** _______ [henceforth / subsequently / hereinafter] authorised to enter into contracts for the sale of the Principal's aircraft for and on behalf of the Principal.

2.2 **(7)** _______ [Herein / Alternatively / In addition], the Agent undertakes to provide the Principal with market reports on monthly sales and competitors' activities.

2.3 The Agent shall make appropriate credit checks on potential customers in order to ensure their creditworthiness.

3. <u>PRINCIPAL'S OBLIGATIONS</u>

3.1 The Principal hereby agrees that **(8)** _______ [hereto / during / meanwhile] the continuance of the Agreement it will:

3.1.1 provide the Agent with training on the Principal's aircraft;
3.1.2 provide customers with technical and servicing report;
3.1.3 provide the Agent with marketing and publicity material to assist the Agent with marketing the Principal's aircraft **(9)** _______ [within / nevertheless / hereafter] the Territory.

4. <u>REMUNERATION</u>

4.1 The Agent shall receive from the Principal in consideration of its services hereunder commission as follows:

4.1.1 at a rate of 5% of the Net Selling Price for each single-engined 'Strato-Line' aircraft sold;
4.1.2 at a rate of 7% of the Net Selling Price for each twin-engined 'Skymaster' aircraft sold.

<u>EXECUTED BY</u> _____________ (Sales Director)

For and on behalf of CADMIUM AEROSPACE LIMITED

<u>EXECUTED BY</u> _____________ (Chief Executive Officer)

For and on behalf of MACFADYEN AVIATION LIMITED

Exercise 4.13

Sentence structure

Cadmium Aerospace has now notified you that it wishes to include a further clause in the agreement providing either party with the right to terminate the agreement at any time with three months' notice. Rearrange the following clauses in the correct order to produce an appropriate sentence which fulfils this purpose:

This agreement shall continue in force / three calendar months notice in writing / be terminated by either party providing to the other / for a period of two years save and except that it may.

Exercise 4.14

It has now been agreed between the two parties to the agreement that Cadmium Aerospace may terminate the agreement at the end of the first year in the event that MacFadyen Aviation Limited does not achieve sales of at least £750,000 by that time. Rearrange the following clauses in the correct order to produce an appropriate sentence which fulfils this purpose:

£750,000 within / the Principal shall be entitled / by notifying the Agent in writing accordingly / In the event that / to terminate this Agreement / the Agent fails to achieve a minimum total sales amount of / twelve months of the commencement of this Agreement.

As with legal writing generally, remember to avoid making your sentences too long and complicated. This can result in double-negatives, which can make sentences confusing and misleading. Consider for instance:

> The court staff will not let the administration office not to be opened to the general public by 10.30 a.m. on each and every week day.

Do you think this sentence conveys the meaning intended? It actually fails to state accurately that the administration office must be open to the public by 10 a.m. Redraft the sentence to remove the double-negative.

Exercise 4.15

Drafting

The parties to the agreement have further agreed that the Agent is to receive a bonus in addition to the commission already agreed if the Agent achieves sales exceeding £1,250,000 by the end of the first year of the agency agreement. This bonus will be 1% of total net sales made by the agent within this first year of the agreement.

1. Draft a suitable clause which complies with these further instructions.
2. Which paragraph number would be a suitable place to locate this additional clause within the agreement?

(Further drafting practice exercises can be found in the corresponding website materials for this chapter.)

Exercise 4.16

Matching pairs

Match the correct pairs from the words listed below.

draft	meeting
business	a resolution
convene	interests
written	a document
propose	interests
bankruptcy	a meeting
board	agreement
pension	property
intellectual	meeting
sponsorship	order

Exercise 4.17

Drafting concisely

There is an increasing trend towards the use of simple language in legal documentation. By using simple or plain language rather than repetitive or redundant words your drafting will be more concise. Match up the following compound constructions with their simple form equivalents.

Compound construction	Simple form
for the reason that	now
hereinafter	due to/since/because
aforementioned	while
save as aforesaid	like
in the nature of	set out above
at this point in time	by
by means of	below
in the event that	if
in order to	monthly
on a monthly basis	otherwise
until such time as	to
during the time that	until

Some jurisdictions (particularly states within the USA, including California) have passed laws requiring rules and regulations to be written in plain language. Law firms are also increasingly requiring the use of plain language, so avoid unnecessary additional words. Consider for instance the following excerpt from an agency agreement:

> The agent **hereby further** agrees to make **said** best endeavours to maximise sales of the product in the **said** territory from the date of this agreement **herefrom.** The agent will **accordingly** receive the **hereby** agreed commission as **and when** the **same** commission shall become payable under the **herein** terms of this agreement. If **and in the event that**

→

> the agent fails to make **said** best endeavours, this agreement shall **henceforth cease and** terminate, in which **said** event the principal **hereby** reserves the right to **forthwith** recover all stock still in **and persisting in** the agent's possession.

Notice how all words in bold can be removed without affecting the meaning and indeed making the meaning clearer.

Developing competence in drafting

When drafting legal documents you should aim to:

- comply with your client's requirements and instructions;
- generally use the active voice;
- write in the present tense rather than the future tense;
- ensure clarity of meaning and careful selection of appropriate vocabulary;
- ensure correct use of grammar and punctuation.

If a court is required to determine the disputed meaning of any ambiguous part of a legal document it will generally find against the party seeking to rely on the ambiguous word or term. Clarity of meaning in what you write is therefore crucial.

There are several legal principles which a court can apply when deliberating on the meaning of words or phrases in a document.

The 'ejusdem generis' *rule*

There are many 'general' words in the English language which have potentially wide meaning. Take for instance the word 'property'. This can mean a wide range of things. The *ejusdem generis* rule assists in interpreting the intended meaning within a particular document by restricting the meaning of general words to include in the meaning only items within a similar category to those words which *precede* the general word. Consider, for instance, the following section from a settlement agreement reached between Travelgraph Ltd and Kadir Salleh concerning their legal dispute in Chapter 6.

> **It is hereby agreed that the Respondent will deliver to the Applicant within 7 days: computer discs, sales ledgers, customer records and any other property.**

Consider what is meant by the term at the end of the agreement, 'any other property'. A literal interpretation of this could include any property of any description in Kadir Salleh's possession. The *ejusdem generis* rule, however, restricts the meaning of 'any other property' in this context to items of a similar nature to those preceding the general word 'property' (i.e. items like computer discs, sales ledgers and customer records).

Exercise 4.18

Consider each of the items in the list below and decide which of these items would come within the intended meaning of the general word 'property' contained in the above terms of settlement. Write these words in column A of the table below. Then write in column B the remaining words which you think would not come within the intended meaning.

Travelgraph's customer lists
Kadir's CD collection
Travelgraph's stock records
Travelgraph's accounting records
Kadir's driving licence
Copies of letters written by Kadir applying for employment
Kadir's desktop computer
Travelgraph's sales records
Kadir's academic diplomas
Travelgraph's expansion plans
The motorcar in the garage belonging to Kadir's wife
Kadir's CV (resumé)
The computer desk in Kadir's study
Travelgraph's purchasing policies
Computer access codes to Travelgraph's computer records
Travelgraph's software programmes

Column A (items within same category)	Column B (items not within same category)

'Noscitur a sociis' rule

The meaning of general words can also be interpreted by the courts as being limited to the subject matter or the context within which the general word is being used. Viscount Simonds described this principle in the case of *Attorney-General* v. *Prince Ernest Augustus of Hanover* [1957] as follows:

> **'. . . general words, cannot be read in isolation: their colour and content are derived from their context.'**

Further points of drafting practice and procedure

When a draft document is being exchanged between the parties involved, with changes (amendments) being made, the document is sometimes referred to as a 'travelling draft'. Amended drafts are traditionally coloured consecutively: red, green, violet, yellow. It is common drafting practice to indicate reinsertment of deleted wording by writing 'stet' alongside the wording to be reinserted into the draft.

When referring to male and female ('his' and 'her', etc.) consider using gender neutral language such as 'they' and 'their'. A gender neutral clause can also be used, such as for example:

> Words used to refer to the male gender include the female gender and vice versa.
>
> or
>
> Words denoting any gender are to be construed as including all genders.

Vocabulary

Inter alia: among other things
Null and void: legally unenforceable
Prima facie: appears on the face of it

Good practice tips

- Start with a checklist of matters which must be included in the document you are drafting.
- Use precedents critically, being careful to amend them to suit your specific requirements.
- As with legal writing, keep sentences short and language simple whenever possible.
- To emphasise the relative importance of the main provisions of the agreement, set them out in order of importance (most important first and so on).
- Use double spacing in your early drafts (this provides space for changes and additions).
- Date your drafts and number them '1st draft', '2nd draft', etc. (you will then be sure which is the most recent!).
- Proofread carefully, checking spelling, punctuation and concise use of language.
- Also check grammar carefully – remember that grammatical errors can also fundamentally alter the meaning of a contract.
- A good dictionary is useful for referring to standard dictionary definitions (such as *The Longman Dictionary of Law*).

Exercise 4.19

Latin expressions

Legal English contains some words that originate from other languages, including many expressions from Latin. For instance, the expression '*pari passu*' is a Latin expression meaning 'in equal measure/with equal speed' and is a term commonly used in business and commercial agreements. Column A below contains a list of further Latin expressions used in legal documents (note that common expressions are not italicised). Match each of these expressions with its corresponding meaning from the list of meanings in column B.

Column A	Column B
1. ad hoc	(*a*) genuine
2. bona fide	(*b*) without notice
3. *ex gratia*	(*c*) reason
4. *ex parte*	(*d*) beyond the powers
5. *ratio*	(*e*) the Queen
6. Regina	(*f*) the existing state of affairs
7. status quo	(*g*) not permanent
8. ultra vires	(*h*) as a favour/for free

SUMMARY

- Remember to use precedents critically when drafting.
- Headings in a document are in bold and underlined.
- Adverbs such as 'hereinafter' and 'hereby' are in common use in legal documents and official statements.
- The passive is formed by adding the verb 'to be' in the appropriate tense to the 'past participle' of the verb.
- The passive form of the verb is used widely in academic and legal English. It is used to show the importance of the process, when there is a general rule and when the subject is assumed.
- The verbs 'base' and 'entitle' are usually used in the passive form.
- When drafting a document, arrange the clauses and sub-clauses in accordance with their degree of importance.
- In order to fully understand a long, complex sentence, your best approach is to notice where the commas are and divide the sentence into smaller units. This will help you understand how additional parts are inserted and linked to the main part.
- Another group of adverbs, such as 'thereafter' and 'thereby', are in common use in legal documents and official statements.
- For board meetings, use the term 'present' for those who are entitled to vote and the term 'in attendance' for those who are not entitled to vote.
- In drafting legal agreements, use the name of the agreement as the heading. Then write the nature and purpose of the document, followed by the names of the parties. Definitions

should be given and must be used throughout the rest of the agreement. The final part contains names of the parties, their signatures and the date of the agreement.

- Obligation can be expressed in legal English by the use of 'shall' and 'am/is/are to'. In other forms of English 'must', 'need to', 'has/have to' and 'has/have got to' are used to express obligation.

Visit **www.mylawchamber.co.uk/mckay** to access further resources for practising legal language skills including additional exercises, listening activities and live weblinks for online research.

Chapter 5

Drafting for court

Learning objectives

This chapter will help you to:

- draft clear and accurate court documents;
- develop skills in writing concisely and persuasively for court;
- master the relevant grammar for drafting.

DRAFTING DOCUMENTS FOR COURT

Many court documents are referred to in England and Wales as 'statements of case' (previously known as 'pleadings'). Statements of case set out the facts and allegations concerning a court case.

Exercise 5.1

Drafting

The document on pages 102–3 is an example of a typical claim form (a statement of case used when commencing a claim in court). This claim form has been partially completed. Complete the claim form by entering the correct words from the list below in each of the numbered areas of the claim form.

claimant	**claims**	**contract**
Matrix Printers Limited	**recover**	**damages**

For many types of legal documents (particularly court documents), many well-established and recognised forms (known as precedents) have been published and are generally available (including electronically). A precedent is a document which was prepared for a previous and similar type of legal claim (or action) which is suitable as a 'template' for the document currently required.

Precedents can provide standard phrases and be useful guides for describing a particular type of claim clearly and precisely. Always remember, however, that a precedent will have to be amended to suit the particular circumstances of the case you are working on. Be careful therefore to use them selectively.

A statement of case known as 'particulars of claim' is regularly used when legal proceedings are commenced in court. The sample 'particulars of claim' on pp. 104–5 concerns the same breach of contract claim as in the claim form on pp. 102–3. It provides more detailed information about the claim. Both a claim form and particulars of claim are commonly lodged (i.e. filed) at court. Read the particulars of claim, noting the guidance on correct content and format provided in the blue text.

Claim Form

In the High Court of Justice
Queen's Bench Division

	for court use only
Claim No.	
Issue date	

Claimant(s)
Travelgraph Limited,
44 Princess Diana Walk, South Kensington, London, W2 3SL.

SEAL

Defendant(s)
Matrix Printers Limited

Name and address of Defendant receiving this claim form

Matrix Printers Limited
18 Tottenham Court Road
London
W1 1LB

Amount claimed	to be assessed
Court fee	
Solicitor's costs	to be assessed
Total amount	

The court office at the Admiralty and Commercial Registry, Royal Courts of Justice, Strand, London WC2A 2LL is open between 10 am and 4.30 pm Monday to Friday. When corresponding with the court, please address forms or letters to the Court Manager and quote the claim number.

N1(CC) Claim form (CPR Part 7) (03.02)

Claim No.

Brief details of claim

The claim is for ________________ [1] for breach of a written ___________ [2] dated 7 May 2011 made between the ___________ [3] and the Defendant for the manufacture and delivery of 2 Ultra-Print 123 Series printing machines. The Claimant also ___________ [4] interest pursuant to section 35A of the Supreme Court Act 1981.

The Claimant expects to ___________ [5] more than £15,000.

Particulars of claim (*attached)

Statement of Truth

*~~(I believe)~~(The Claimant believes) that the facts stated in this claim form *(~~and the particulars of the claim attached to this claim form~~) are true.

* I am duly authorised by the claimant to sign this statement

Full name Thomas Shapiro

Name of *(claimant)(~~'s solicitor's firm~~) Travelgraph Limited

signed Thomas Shapiro position or office held Managing Director

*(Claimant)(~~'s solicitor~~) (if signing on behalf of firm, company or corporation)

delete as appropriate

Stringwood & Evans, Solicitors,
18 Bond Street, London.

Claimant's or solicitor's address to which documents or payments should be sent if different from overleaf including (if appropriate) details of DX, fax or e-mail.

Heading and title

IN THE HIGH COURT OF JUSTICE
QUEEN'S BENCH DIVISION **CLAIM No. 2011 HC 1829**

BETWEEN:

Claimant	**TRAVELGRAPH LIMITED**
	AND
Defendant	**MATRIX PRINTERS LIMITED**

PARTICULARS OF CLAIM

Facts and allegations relating to the claim are set out in numbered paragraphs

1. The Claimant is and was at all material times a company carrying on business as publishers of maps and tourist guides. The Defendant at all material times carried on business as a manufacturer and seller of printing machines.

2. By a written contract ('the Contract') entered into between the Claimant and the Defendant and signed by both parties on 1 August 2011, the Defendant in the course of its business agreed to manufacture and sell to the Claimant and the Claimant agreed to buy from the Defendant 2 Ultra-Print 123 Series printing machines at a price of £45,000 each.

The third person is used and parties are referred to as 'Claimant' and 'Defendant' throughout

3. The Contract included an express term that the machines would each be capable of printing at a rate of 100 pages per minute using A4 size paper. The Defendant is in breach of that term.

4. The Contract included an implied term that the machines would be of satisfactory quality.

5. Pursuant to the contract, on 1 August 2011 the Defendant delivered to the Claimant two printing machines ('the delivered machines') which the Claimant installed at its registered office.

6. In breach of the aforesaid express and/or implied term, neither of the delivered machines were capable of printing at a rate exceeding 50 pages per minute.

7. As a result of the matters set out above, the Claimant has suffered loss and damage.

→

PARTICULARS OF LOSS

Loss of profit

(a) From 1 August 2011 until 8 February 2012:

(i) estimated receipts from warranted output	£200,000
(ii) actual receipts	£100,000
	£100,000

(b) Continuing from 9 February 2012 at the following annual rate:

(i) estimated receipts from warranted output	£400,000
(ii) estimated actual receipts	£200,000
	£200,000

8. Further the Claimant claims interest pursuant to section 35A of the Supreme Court Act 1981 on the amount found to be due to the Claimant at such rate and for such period as the Court thinks fit.

AND the Claimant claims:

This summary of the claim is known as the 'prayer'

(1) Damages

(2) Interest pursuant to section 35A of the Supreme Court Act 1981 to be assessed.

STATEMENT OF TRUTH

The Claimant believes that the facts stated in these Particulars of Claim are true.

Dated this 8th day of February 2012.

The form is signed to confirm its contents are entirely truthful and dated

[Signature]

Stringwood & Evans, Solicitors, of 18 Bond Street, London.

Solicitors for and on behalf of the Claimant.

Use of prepositions

Many nouns, verbs and adjectives are used with particular prepositions. The following expressions are used in the particulars of claim for instance:

enter into	agree to	capable of
pursuant to	in breach of	on behalf of

The following examples show how the verb 'agree' is followed by different prepositions, depending on what follows after the preposition:

agree *to* a proposal or suggestion	agree *on* a matter for decision
agree *with* someone	agree *about* something

Exercise 5.2

Complete the following sentences by inserting the appropriate preposition from the following list in each of the blank spaces. You may have to choose some words more than once.

of between into in on to

1. A lawyer has to be capable ______ summarising key legal principles.
2. Their deposit showed their intent to enter ______ an agreement.
3. The sales director cannot sell to customers directly while the agreement remains ______ force.
4. He claims interest pursuant ______ section 69 of the County Courts Act 1984.
5. The lawyer is trying to comply ______ her client's instructions.
6. The client claims interest ______ this amount.
7. It was held that the position of a controlling shareholder in a company was not incompatible ______ being an employee for the purposes of an unfair dismissal claim.
8. There is a distinction ______ dishonesty at work in relation to an employer and dishonesty outside work.

The defence

This document sets out the position and response of the party the claim is being made against (termed the 'defendant'). For example:

IN THE HIGH COURT OF JUSTICE
CASE NO. 2011 HC 1829
QUEEN'S BENCH DIVISION
BETWEEN:

Heading and title

TRAVELGRAPH LIMITED **Claimant**
AND
MATRIX PRINTERS LIMITED **Defendant**

Text in third person, referring to the parties as 'Claimant' and 'Defendant'

DEFENCE

When an allegation is denied, the reason for the denial should be given. Notice the use of the passive tense. This is more objective and generally used in this legal context.

1. Paragraphs 1 to 5 of the Particulars of Claim are admitted.
2. The allegation in paragraph 6 of the Particulars of Claim is denied. The delivered machines were capable of printing 100 pages per minute.

Each and every allegation in the Particulars of Claim (see above) must be either: 'admitted', 'denied' or 'required to be proved' (if defendant is unable to admit or deny).

→

3. The Defendant has no knowledge of the alleged losses claimed by the Claimant and the Claimant is required to prove the losses alleged in paragraph 7 of the Particulars of Claim.

SIMON NAGANO

If the document is drafted by a barrister (counsel), counsel's name is indicated here

Statement of Truth

The Defendant believes that the facts stated in this defence are true.

Signed:

Alfredo Schaefer

Managing Director of Matrix Printers Limited

Dated this 20th day of February 2012

More complex wording for statements of case

If you need to admit part of an allegation but deny another aspect of the same allegation, the sentence can be commenced with 'Except that'. For example:

Except that it is denied that the Defendant is in breach of the term, paragraph 3 of the Particulars of Claim is admitted.

Exercise 5.3

Statements of case also include the documents in column A below. Fill in column B by indicating which party (claimant or defendant) prepares each of these statements of case. The first one is done for you by way of illustration.

A	B
Claim form	*Claimant*
Particulars of claim	
Defence	
Defence and counterclaim	

Vocabulary and prepositions

The following phrases, associated with criminal law, are also used in witness statements and other court documents.

prosecuted *for* charged *with* convicted *of* sentenced *to* acquitted *of*

Exercise 5.4

Complete the following statement by inserting the most appropriate phrase from the list above in each blank space.

Eric Jones was arrested at home and __________ **(1)** fraud. At court he was ____________ **(2)** fraud and _____________ **(3)** two years in prison.

Exercise 5.5

Now identify which one of the above phrases can be used to rewrite the following sentences.

1. He was put on trial for burglary. = He was __________ burglary.
2. The bank manager was found guilty of fraud. = The bank manager was __________ fraud.

Using plain English

There is an increasing trend towards the use of plain English when drafting. So use readily understood vocabulary whenever possible rather than old-fashioned legal jargon. Statements of case have traditionally contained a certain amount of old-fashioned language.

There have, however, been recent reforms encouraging greater use of plain English by lawyers. For instance, a procedural code, known as the 'Civil Procedure Rules', has introduced some new terminology.

A range of words in legal English sound rather old-fashioned. Some of these words are still used, however, having become standard and recognised phrases, because they have proved through time to be particularly apt and descriptive. For much of this old-fashioned vocabulary, however, there is a plain English alternative.

The following table provides some examples. The first column lists words and phrases which have traditionally been used in statements of case over many years. The second column of the table provides a suitable modern English equivalent for the old-style words and phrases in the first column.

Old fashioned/dated language	Equivalent modern language
action	claim
Anton Piller order	search order
discovery	disclosure
ex parte	without notice (to other parties)
inter-partes hearing	hearing with notice (to other party)
interlocutory hearing	interim (as opposed to final) hearing
interrogatory	request for further information
leave	permission
mandamus order	mandatory order
mareva order (or injunction)	freezing injunction
prohibition order	prohibiting order
request for further and better particulars	request for further information
setting down for trial	listing (scheduling) for trial
specific discovery	specific disclosure
subpoena	witness summons
summons (to commence proceedings)	claim form
summons for directions	case management conference
thereafter/thereinafter	subsequently/then
therein	contained within

Exercise 5.6

Vocabulary

In the list below, the first column provides some further examples of dated or old-fashioned language which you are still likely to see today in court documents. The second column provides a selection of suitable alternative modern English words and phrases. Match each expression in the first column with its equivalent in the second column. For instance, the first one is done for you – 'in camera' should be matched with 'in private'.

Old fashioned/dated language	Equivalent modern language
aforesaid	in private
aver/plead	in public
in camera	claim form
in open court	stated previously
save that/save insofar	noted below
plaintiff	claimant
pleading	contend/allege
prescribed by	provided by/indicated by
undernoted	statement of case
writ	except that

The following is a precedent for an injunction order (a court order preventing or prohibiting someone from doing something). This particular order is to prevent Kadir Salleh from joining a company named Worldlink Limited. (See Chapter 4 for details of Kadir's service agreement with another company called Travelgraph Limited.)

Exercise 5.7

Complete the drafting of the injunction by:

1. deleting clauses in square brackets within the draft as appropriate;
2. completing the blank spaces using relevant information from the text above as well as by selecting appropriate entries from the following list.

Phrases for inserting in draft injunction order

contempt of Court	Solicitor
Order	to the Court
Respondent	set aside this Order
sent to prison	Respondent shall pay the Applicant
confidential information relating to Travelgraph Limited	Applicant's

DRAFT INJUNCTION ORDER

IN THE HIGH COURT OF JUSTICE **Claim No. 2011 HC 4045**

QUEEN'S BENCH DIVISION

MR JUSTICE JACKSON

Date ________

BETWEEN:

Travelgraph Limited	Applicant
and	
Kadir Salleh	Respondent

DRAFT INJUNCTION ORDER

IMPORTANT
NOTICE TO THE RESPONDENT

→

[1] This Order **[prohibits you from doing] [obliges you to do] (1)** the acts set out in this Order. You should read it carefully. You are advised to consult a _________ **(2)** as soon as possible. You have a right to ask the court to vary or _________ **(3)**.

[2] If you disobey this Order you may be found guilty of _________ **(4)** and may be _________ **(5)** or fined or your assets may be seized.

Upon hearing Counsel for the Applicant and Counsel for the Respondent,

IT IS ORDERED that:

THE INJUNCTION

1. For a period of 12 months commencing from 20 October 2011 the _________ **(6)** must not: (i) Enter into or continue in the employment of Worldlink Limited; (ii) Divulge to Worldlink Limited, their officers, employees and/or agents or to any other person or entity any computer files(s) or ___________________________ **(7)**.

COSTS OF THE APPLICATION

2. The ____ **(8)** the costs of this Application.

VARIATION OR SETTING ASIDE OF THIS ORDER

The Respondent may apply __________ **(9)** at any time to vary or set aside this __________ **(10)** but if he wishes to do so he must first inform the __________ **(11)** solicitors in writing at least 48 hours beforehand.

NAME AND ADDRESS OF APPLICANT'S SOLICITORS

The Applicant's solicitors are:

Name: _________________________ **(12)**

Address: _______________________

Telephone number: ______________

All communications to the Court about this Order should be sent to Room E15 Royal Courts of Justice, Strand, London, WC2A 2LL quoting the case number. The office is open between 10 am and 4.30 pm Monday to Friday. The telephone number is 020 7936 6148 or 6336.

Exercise 5.8

Verbs

The words in column A of the following list appear in the injunction order. Match each of these verbs with their corresponding meaning in column B.

Column A	Column B
1. may	(*a*) it is compulsory
2. must	(*b*) will
3. shall	(*c*) it is possible

Vocabulary

Note the following terms and expressions from the injunction order above.

contempt of court: disregard of and disobedience to the authority of the court
divulge: reveal, disclose or make files or confidential information known
entity: an individual or body that has its own independent existence
set aside: to annul or revoke
to vary: to amend or alter

Word formation

One way of building your vocabulary is by developing your skills in forming new words by adding suffixes. For instance: 'ment', '-tion'. Similarly, prefixes such as 'im-' and 'un-' can be added. Prefixes can be used in this way to form the negative of the word. For example:

apply (v) application (n) applicant (n) applied (adj) applicable (adj) inapplicable (adj negative)

Exercise 5.9

The following verbs are typically used in court orders such as the 'Injunction Order' above. Complete the remaining sections of the grid below by writing the appropriate word in each column, based on the verb in the left column (X = not possible).

Verb	Noun	Adjective	Negative
advise	advice	advisable	inadvisable
consult			X
continue			
obey			
employ			
pay			
prohibit			X
respond			
vary			

Use of the past tense

Consider the following sentences:

I *tried* to explain to Mr Moore that I *had done* nothing wrong.

All I *knew* was that I *was being dismissed*.

Form	Use
Past simple	This is used to refer to anything that happened in the past, whether the time is stated in the same sentence or in a previous sentence, e.g. On the following day Charles *received* a letter confirming his dismissal. 'Time words' used with the past tense include, 'last night', 'yesterday', 'in June', 'on Monday', etc.
Past perfect simple **'had' + past participle**	When we refer to two incidents in the past in a sentence, the verb used for the earlier incident is in the past perfect tense, e.g. When I spoke to the manager, he *had* already *dismissed* Mr Scoville.
Past continuous **'was/were' + ...ing**	This is usually used to show that something was taking a longer time when it was interrupted by another action, e.g. When the police officer arrived, Charles *was sitting* at reception. Or two long incidents happened at the same time, e.g. While the police officer *was interviewing* Charles, Mr Moore *was writing* a letter.
Past perfect continuous **'had been' + ...ing**	This is mainly used to show a longer action was happening before another action, e.g. When Charles applied for the job, he *had been working* for another law firm for eight years.

It is also worth noting the present perfect tense which 'has/have + past participle'. This tense is not a true past tense, but it indicates that the 'action' is not yet complete and is still being connected with the present. It is often used with words such as 'since', 'yet', 'never', 'ever', 'just' and 'ready', e.g. 'I *have longed* to own a Ferrari since childhood.'

Exercise 5.10

Look at the following sentences and explain the meanings for each, noting how they differ:

1. When I arrived, they discussed the case.
2. When I arrived, they were discussing the case.
3. When I arrived, they had discussed the case.
4. When I arrived, they had been discussing the case.

Exercise 5.11

Put the verbs between brackets in the correct past tense and in the appropriate active or passive form.

1. She (tell) us last Thursday that she already (offer) a new job.
2. A meeting (hold) after we (receive) new instructions.
3. The witness was very nervous when he first (talk) because he (not appear) in court before.
4. When I (see) the motorist, he (hold) a mobile telephone.
5. They waited until everyone (be) ready and then they (start) the meeting.
6. He (travel) at a speed of over 70 mph when the accident (take place).
7. When Phil (come) to my office, I (write) a report for three hours.
8. Lucy (tell) us the rationale behind her decision after we (ask) her twice.
9. While he (interview) the witness, Lisa (prepare) the documents.
10. We (thank) Christine for all what she (do) for us.

Exercise 5.12

Using correct verb tenses

The following document is a witness statement of a dentist named Jason Garfinkle, who witnessed an accident on 20 October 2011. Read the witness statement and correct it by putting the verbs in brackets into the correct form in the spaces provided.

WITNESS STATEMENT OF JASON GARFINKLE

1. I **(1)** ________ (*be*) a forty-seven-year-old dentist and live at 15 Gray's Inn Road, London. I make this statement concerning a road traffic accident I **(2)** ________ (*witness*) at the junction between Regent Street and Oxford Street, London, on Thursday 20 October 2011. At approximately 4.00 p.m. that day I **(3)** ________ (*drive*) along Oxford Street towards Oxford Circus. It **(4)** ________ (*be*) a lovely afternoon and the sun was shining. I **(5)** ________ (*come*) back from a dental conference at Earls Court Exhibition Centre and was **(6)** ________ (*head*) into the West End of town to buy a birthday present for my wife. I **(7)** ________ (*drive*) behind a blue Honda Accord motor car which **(8)** ________ (*travel*) at approximately 30 miles per hour.

2. As I **(9)** ________ (*approach*) Oxford Circus I **(10)** ________ (*can*) see that the traffic lights **(11)** ________ (*show*) green. The aforesaid Honda motor car **(12)** ________ (*proceed*) through the traffic lights and I **(13)** ________ (*begin*) to follow. I then suddenly **(14)** ________ (*catch*) sight of another vehicle off to my right, a silver Ford Galaxy. It **(15)** ________ (*head*) at high speed along Regent Street towards the Honda in front of me. I **(16)** ________ (*can*) see that the driver of the silver Ford **(17)** ________ (*hold*) a mobile telephone. He

→

also **(18)** ________ (*appear*) to be having an argument with the woman sitting in the front passenger seat of the vehicle. He was clearly not paying attention to his driving or the traffic lights, which were showing red from his direction. The Ford **(19)** ________ (*come*) straight through the traffic lights into the junction between Oxford Street and Regent Street.

3. The driver of the Ford then **(20)** ________ (*brake*) hard but his vehicle skidded straight into the driver's door of the blue Honda. I was able to stop just in time to avoid also being involved in the collision. I have no doubt that the driver of the silver Ford was entirely to blame for the accident.

I believe that the facts stated in this witness statement are true.
Signed
Dated

One of the drivers involved in the accident on 20 October 2011 referred to above, Nicholas Tiessen, has decided to issue legal proceedings in court. (Correspondence concerning this case can be found in Chapter 3.) Now read the particulars of the claim below and complete the sentences which follow.

IN THE CENTRAL LONDON COUNTY COURT **CASE NO. KR 65739**

BETWEEN:

NICHOLAS TIESSEN	**CLAIMANT**
and	
MATTHEW GLUCK	**FIRST DEFENDANT**
and	
LONDINIUM DELIVERY COMPANY LIMITED	**SECOND DEFENDANT**

PARTICULARS OF CLAIM

1. At about 4.00 p.m. on Thursday 20 October 2011 the Claimant was driving his Honda Accord registration number HL16 GNT along Oxford Street, London, in an easterly direction. At all material times the Second Defendant was the owner of a Ford Galaxy motor car registration number FT23 FLK, which was being driven by the First Defendant as servant or agent for the Second Defendant.

→

2. A collision occurred when the said Ford motor car, travelling in a northerly direction along Regent Street, drove into the Claimant's vehicle at the junction between Oxford Street and Regent Street. The said junction is a crossroads controlled by traffic lights which were showing green in favour of the Claimant.

3. The collision was caused by the negligence of the First Defendant, acting in the course of his employment.

PARTICULARS OF NEGLIGENCE

The First Defendant was negligent in that he:

(a) failed to keep any or any adequate lookout;

(b) failed to observe or heed the presence and progress of the Honda Accord motor car;

(c) drove too fast;

(d) drove into collision with the Honda Accord motor car when, by the exercise of reasonable driving skill and care, such collision could have been avoided.

(e) failed to stop, steer, manage or control his motor vehicle in such a way as to avoid a collision;

(f) failed to sufficiently apply the brakes of his said vehicle in time or at all. The Second Defendant is negligent by virtue of vicarious liability, being the employer of the First Defendant and owner of the aforesaid Ford Galaxy motor car registration number FT23 FLK.

4. By reason of the matters aforesaid the Claimant has suffered pain and injury, loss and damage.

PARTICULARS OF INJURY

The Claimant, who was born on 18 March 1980, sustained the following injuries.

The Claimant, who was wearing a seatbelt, sustained injury to his neck. Hospital treatment was required, the Claimant having been taken by ambulance to Chelsea and Westminster Hospital, Fulham Road, London. The Claimant was retained in hospital for four days. Following medical examination a whiplash injury was diagnosed. The Claimant was unable to return to work as a computer programmer for five weeks due to continuing symptoms of neck pain, radiating to the right shoulder. This has necessitated physiotherapy treatment, which has now alleviated the symptoms. Full particulars are set out in the medical report of Mr Paulo Jarvis, consultant orthopaedic surgeon, dated 1 December 2011.

→

PARTICULARS OF SPECIAL DAMAGE

5.	(1) Value of Honda Accord motor car damaged beyond repair	£ 7,500
	(2) Loss of earnings: 4 weeks at £1,000 per week	£ 4,000
	(3) Cost of ruined clothing as a result of accident (shirt and jacket)	£ 200
	(4) Cost of 12 sessions of physiotherapy at £25 per session	£ 300
		£ 12,000

AND THE CLAIMANT CLAIMS:

1. Damages not exceeding £50,000;
2. Interest pursuant to section 69 of the County Courts Act 1984.

STATEMENT OF TRUTH

The Claimant believes that the facts stated in these Particulars of Claim are true.

____

Dated this 2nd day of December 2011.

Stringwood & Evans, Solicitors, 18 Bond Street, London.
Solicitors for the Claimant
Tel. No. +44 (0)20 7126 8983

Exercise 5.13

Relative pronouns

Note the sentence in the particulars of claim above that says: 'The Claimant, who was born on 18 March 1980, sustained the following injuries'. In this clause 'who' is a relative pronoun relating to the Claimant. Complete the following sentences by inserting the correct relative pronoun in each blank space from the list below (note that some words may be applicable more than once while others may not be applicable at all).

which **that** **who** **whom**

1. The remedy __________ the court may grant for breach of contract is damages.
2. The lawyer wrote a letter to the company _______ manufactured the machines.
3. The individual against _____________ a claim is commenced is known as the Defendant.
4. Thomas Shapiro, _____________ is the Managing Director of Travelgraph Limited, was disappointed with the printing machines.

Exercise 5.14

1. Which of the following sentences suggests that he has more than one brother?
   (a) My brother, who is a lawyer, is working in New York.
   (b) My brother who is a lawyer is working in New York.
2. Which of the following sentences suggests that there were some claimants who did not receive any money
   (a) The Claimants, whose cases were below £2000, all lost.
   (b) The Claimants whose cases were below £2000 all lost.

IDIOMATIC USE OF LEGAL ENGLISH

Note the following phrases in the above particulars of claim:

'at all material times' (i.e. always and continuously throughout the incident being referred to)

'by virtue of vicarious liability' (i.e. as a result of being legally liable for the fault or wrong of another – such as an employer being liable for the negligence of an employee acting in the course of his employment)

Exercise 5.15

Comprehension

Write out answers to the following questions concerning the above particulars of claim.

1. Who are the defendants?
2. What make of car was Nicholas Tiessen driving?
3. On what date did the accident occur?
4. Where did the accident occur?
5. Where was Nicholas Tiessen taken immediately after the accident?
6. What is Nicholas Tiessen's occupation?
7. How much income did Nicholas Tiessen lose as a result of the accident?
8. Why do you think Nicholas Tiessen has named the Londinium Delivery Company Limited as a second defendant?

Exercise 5.16

Language practice

The following statements are typical of those likely to be made by Nicholas Tiessen's lawyer in the course of preparing for trial. Complete the statements by selecting the most appropriate expression to place in each of the blank spaces from the panel below.

witness statements	negligence	was at fault
medical evidence	the claimant's bundle of documents	on the balance of probabilities
be calling	will have to rule on	the claimant

→

1. I act for ______________ and understand that you act for the defendant.
2. I intend to send ______________ to the court tomorrow.
3. Please confirm that you will send me your ______________ by post this evening.
4. This is a ______________ claim for damages.
5. This case involves considering firstly whether the defendant ______________ and thereby caused this accident.
6. There is ______________ which confirms my client's injuries.
7. The claimant has to establish ______________ that the defendant drove negligently.
8. Those are the issues the court ______________.
9. I will ______________ three witnesses.

Counsel's opinion

Assume that you are now acting as counsel (i.e. as a barrister) for Nicholas Tiessen, the claimant, in the case of *Nicholas Tiessen* v *Matthew Gluck and Londinium Delivery Company Limited*. You have now been instructed to advise your client on quantum regarding his claim. When representing a client with a monetary claim it is important to ascertain clearly the likely amount or 'quantum' of the claim. The term 'quantum' in a legal context means the monetary amount or value of the claim. If the claim is settled between the parties or an award is made by a court then the monetary amount of compensation agreed or awarded is known as 'damages'.

The advice you are being asked to provide (known as 'counsel's advice') is urgently required. A meeting between the parties has been scheduled for early next week for the purpose of seeking to negotiate a settlement of the case. A medical report has been obtained which details your client's injuries and prognosis. This medical report is set out below. Read the medical report then write a short summary of Mr Tiessen's injuries (in no more than 50 words).

MEDICAL REPORT

On: Nicholas Tiessen

Prepared by: Mr P. Jarvis BSc FRCS (Orth)
Consultant Orthopaedic Surgeon

Prepared at the request of: Stringwood & Evans, solicitors,
18 Bond Street, London

BACKGROUND DETAILS

Mr Nicholas Tiessen is a thirty-six-year-old computer programmer. This medical report has been prepared in relation to injuries sustained by Mr Tiessen in a

→

road traffic accident on Thursday 20th October 2011. Mr Tiessen was driving his Honda motorcar through the junction between Oxford Street and Regent Street in central London that afternoon when another vehicle, a Ford Galaxy, came through a red traffic light from Regent Street and collided with his vehicle.

He recalls being thrown forward when the collision occurred. He was wearing a seatbelt and his car was equipped with head-rests. He did not lose consciousness but recalls feeling pain and stiffness in his neck. An ambulance was called and he was taken to Chelsea and Westminster Hospital in London. I have seen the hospital notes, which confirm that Mr Tiessen was diagnosed as having a moderate hypertension sprain of the cervical spine (commonly known as a 'whiplash' injury) on arrival. By the next morning his neck felt stiffer and the pain from the neck injury had increased. He was retained in hospital for four days.

CURRENT SITUATION

Mr Tiessen told me that he thinks his symptoms have now improved but that he still experiences occasional neck discomfort along with occasional headaches. The neck discomfort occurs approximately once a week, particularly when he is playing tennis. He has now returned to work, having been off work for five weeks as a result of his injuries.

MEDICAL OPINION AND PROGNOSIS

I examined Mr Tiessen on 1st December 2011. His description of his injuries appeared to me to be genuine and devoid of exaggeration. He demonstrated a good range of neck movement but displayed slight discomfort on full extension. He also displayed full and pain-free movement in the right shoulder, in which he endured a moderate degree of discomfort for several weeks following the accident. I have reviewed the medical records provided to me by his general practitioner and can confirm that he has no prior medical history of neck injury.

Mr Tiessen has made a good recovery. The whiplash injury limited his lifestyle for about three months post accident due to residual pain and discomfort around the neck and right shoulder along with occasional headaches. In particular, he was off work for five weeks and unable to play tennis for around three months. In the last month or so the symptoms have, however, settled, save for intermittent neck discomfort and headaches approximately once per week. I do not expect any deterioration of his condition in the future as a result

→

of this accident. I would further anticipate that his remaining residual symptoms will dissipate within six to nine months of the date of the accident and that he will therefore make a full recovery within this time period.

DUTY TO THE COURT

I understand that my duty in writing this report is to assist the Court in the matters within my expertise. I further understand that this duty overrides any obligation to the party by whom I am instructed and by whom I am being paid. I further confirm that in so far as the facts stated in my report are within my own knowledge I have made clear which they are and I believe them to be true and that the opinions I have expressed represent my true and complete professional opinion.

____

Mr Paulo Jarvis BSc FRCS (Orth)
Consultant Orthopaedic Surgeon
Date: 1st December 2011

Language practice: choosing the correct part of speech

As we have seen, adjectives, nouns, verbs, prepositions and so on are known as parts of speech, or grammatical classes. Each has a different function in the structure of an English sentence. For example:

The oil company employed (verb) Alan Johnson as Chief Executive.

Alan Johnson was an employee (noun) of the oil company.

As a result of his injuries in the accident, Alan Johnson is no longer considered employable (adjective).

Exercise 5.17

Put *noun, verb, adjective* or *adverb* against each of the following words as appropriate (the first entry is done for you).

quantum	Noun	compensation		requisite	
quantify		compensate		advise	
quantifiable		compensatory		advice	
claim		require		advisable	
claimant		requirement		inadvisably	

Exercise 5.18

Now choose the appropriate words from the table to complete the sentences below. You need to think about the meaning and the part of speech required in each case (there are only 10 sentences, so you will not need to use all the words given above). The first sentence has been completed as an example.

1. It is important to ascertain the likely amount, or quantum, of the damages in each case.
2. Counsel will ________________ the client on the appropriate quantum.
3. It is ______________________ to take account of precedent when assessing damages.
4. A medical report is a ____________________ when claiming damages for physical injury.
5. The ___________________ is the person who states that he/she is entitled to damages.
6. The other driver very ______________________ went through a red light, and collided with Mr Tiessen's vehicle.
7. The driver drove with undue care and attention, that is he did not take the ______________ care.
8. He claimed _______________________ for no longer being able to play the drums.
9. The amount of compensation which should be paid in this case is not exactly _____________________, but an approximate estimate can be made.
10. The client should listen to the _______________ of his/her counsel when deciding whether to go ahead with the case.

Exercise 5.19

Having considered the medical report detailing your client's injuries it is now necessary to draft counsel's advice on quantum in accordance with your instructions. Complete the following counsel's advice therefore by selecting the appropriate phrases and words from the list below and writing them in the appropriate spaces in the opinion.

full recovery
symptoms
injuries sustained
consultant orthopaedic surgeon
whiplash injury
advise Mr Tiessen on quantum

assessing
road traffic accident on 20th October 2011
report
an award
opinion
as a computer programmer

claim
medical report
from his injuries
FT23 FLK
these instructions
date of the accident

→

IN THE CENTRAL LONDON COUNTY COURT **CASE NO. KR 65739**

BETWEEN:

NICHOLAS TIESSEN	**Claimant**
and	
MATTHEW GLUCK	**1st Defendant**
and	
LONDINIUM DELIVERY COMPANY LTD	**2nd Defendant**

COUNSEL'S ADVICE ON QUANTUM

Background Details

1. I am asked to **(1)** ________________________ in regard to **(2)** ____________________ in a **(3)** ____________________. The accident occurred when another vehicle collided with the claimant's vehicle. This other vehicle, a Ford Galaxy registration number **(4)** __________, drove through a red traffic light, entering the junction between Oxford Street and Regent Street in London from Regent Street.

2. Instructing solicitors have kindly enclosed with **(5)** ________________ the **(6)** ________________ of Mr Paulo Jarvis, **(7)** ________________, dated 1st December 2011. This report indicates that Mr Tiessen incurred a moderate hyperextension sprain of the cervical spine, commonly referred to as a 'whiplash' injury. This injury incapacitated him for 5 weeks, during which time he was unable to work. Following a course of physiotherapy, however, Mr Tiessen has now returned to work **(8)** ________________________. He now considers that he has almost completely recovered, save for continuing to suffer occasional **(9)** ______________ of stiffness in the neck and intermittent headaches. According to Mr Jarvis such symptoms are likely to continue for several months and Mr Tiessen is expected to make a complete recovery **(10)** __________________ within 6 months from the date of the accident.

Damages

3. Mr Tiessen sustained a relatively minor **(11)** ________________ resulting in moderate symptoms. There are some continuing symptoms although Mr Jarvis's report has provided an encouraging prognosis in his **(12)** ________, indicating that he expects Mr Tiessen to make a full recovery within 6 to 9 months of the **(13)** ______________________. Mr Tiessen was off work for several weeks but has not had his career prospects adversely affected by the accident.

4. The Guidelines for the Assessment of General Damages provided by the Judicial Studies Board (JSB) indicate that the level of appropriate damages for a whiplash injury of this nature is within the range of £750 to £2,500. The following

→

cases further assist in **(14)** ______________ the level of damages a court would be likely to award.

(a) *Evans* v *Morton* 3rd March 1998 (Oxford County Court)
The award for pain, suffering and loss of amenity (PSLA) was £1,675. The facts of this case are fairly similar to those in Mr Tiessen's case. The claimant was involved in a road traffic accident and sustained a whiplash injury. The claimant experienced immediate neck pain and was taken to hospital. He was unable to work for several days as a toolmaker. There were continuous symptoms of neck pain and shoulder pain from which the claimant made a **(15)** ______________ in approximately 7 months. The extent of injury was broadly of the same degree of severity as sustained by Mr Tiessen. Taking account of inflation the award of £1,675 represents an award at today's value of approximately £1,950.

(b) *Sangster* v *Kensington Building Services* 4th April 1997 (Birkenhead County Court)
The claimant sustained a whiplash injury in a road traffic accident and suffered continuing pain and stiffness in the neck as well as headaches, making a full recovery in approximately 6 months. The claimant was off work for 2 days and was unable to play football as a pastime for 2 months. The total award for PSLA was £1,500. Uplifted for inflation this represents **(16)** __________ today of approximately £1,800.

5. Taking account of these cases and the JSB Guidelines I am of the **(17)** ___________ that an award of £2,000 represents the likely value of Mr Tiessen's **(18)** ________ for pain, suffering and loss of amenity.

A. LAWYER

Justice Chambers

9th December 2011

RECORDING TERMS OF SETTLEMENT

Following negotiation between the lawyers acting for the parties in the 'Tiessen' case, the dispute has now been resolved (settled). (The process of negotiation is considered further in Chapter 8.) The terms of settlement are as follows.

TERMS OF SETTLEMENT
The two defendants have agreed to jointly pay the claimant £14,250 damages, payable by 6th January 2012. This is to be in full and final settlement of the claim, including:

- damages for personal injury
- special damages (agreed as per the figures in the particulars of claim)

The defendants will also pay the claimant's legal costs.

Exercise 5.20

It is now necessary to draft a consent order (i.e. a court order setting out the agreed terms). Complete the following consent order by writing the correct details in the blank spaces, taking account of the settlement terms above.

IN THE CENTRAL LONDON COUNTY COURT **Case no. KR 65739**

BETWEEN:

NICHOLAS TIESSEN **Claimant**

and

MATTHEW GLUCK **1st Defendant**

and

LONDINIUM DELIVERY COMPANY LIMITED **2nd Defendant**

CONSENT ORDER

Upon the parties having agreed terms of settlement of this claim, IT IS HEREBY ORDERED BY CONSENT THAT:

1. The First and Seconds Defendants shall by **(1)** ________________ pay to the **(2)** ____________ the sum of **(3)** £________.

2. The Defendants shall jointly pay the **(4)** ____________________ of this action, to be taxed on the standard basis in default of agreement.

3. These terms are in **(5)** _____________________________ of this claim and that upon payment of the above mentioned damages and costs the **(6)** ____________ be discharged from any further liability to the Claimant in respect of this action.

District Judge Hemmings

Dated this 16th day of December 2011

Employment tribunal case

Imagine you have been consulted by a new client named Charles Edward Scoville. Charles has recently been dismissed by his employer, a firm of solicitors named Bannerman and Law. You have agreed to issue legal proceedings on his behalf for unfair dismissal. Read the following statement of your client. Your secretary has just completed typing it for you in readiness for issuing proceedings in the employment tribunal (assume that today's date is Thursday, 5 May 2011).

IN THE EMPLOYMENT TRIBUNAL

BETWEEN:

CHARLES E. SCOVILLE **Claimant**

and

BANNERMAN AND LAW (a firm) **Respondent**

STATEMENT OF THE APPLICANT

I, Charles Edward Scoville, of 18 Lower Richmond Road, Putney, London, SW15, hereby states as follows.

1. I am the claimant in these Employment Tribunal proceedings. I commenced employment with the Respondent on 4 April 2007. I was based at the firm's Head Office at 11 The Strand, London, WC2, where I worked until 26 April 2011 as one of a team of four legal cashiers.

   On Tuesday, 26 April 2011 I arrived at the office at approximately 8.50 a.m., to start work as usual at 9.00 a.m. I had just parked in the firm's car park and was entering the building when I noticed Mr Henry Moore, the firm's Managing Partner, running towards me. He appeared very angry. I was then very taken aback as he grabbed my arm while stating to me, 'You're dismissed as of now, Scoville. I want your office keys. Don't think you're going anywhere, the police are on their way!'

2. I tried to explain to Mr Moore that I had done nothing wrong and didn't understand what all this was about. I was given no details at this stage of what I was being accused of. All I knew was that I was being summarily dismissed.

3. It was only when the police arrived that I began to get an explanation. Detective Constable Clouseau told me that I was being accused by Mr Moore of stealing several million pounds of client monies. I was astounded by this. I stated in reply that I would never dream of doing such a thing. I have worked as a legal cashier for a number of prestigious legal and accountancy firms in the city and have an unblemished record for my professionalism and honesty.

4. DC Clouseau then asked me, 'How do you account for the new Ferrari sports car sitting out there in the car park then?' I explained that I had been

→

the very fortunate winner of a large sum of money on the National Lottery several days previously. At that time the only purchase I'd made from my winnings was the Ferrari, a vehicle I have longed to own since childhood. Ironically I was intending to continue with my job at Bannerman and Law since I love my work. I also explained this to DC Clouseau and his colleague, Police Constable Capriati.

5. The following day I received a letter in the post from Bannerman and Law confirming my dismissal with immediate effect along with a cheque for my salary up to and including Monday, 26 April 2011. The letter was signed by Henry Moore. That day I visited the offices of Chameleon, who run the National Lottery. There I provided Mandy Renwick, Chameleon's Chief Executive, with authority to disclose information to the police confirming my win. When I went to the police station the next day I was relieved to be informed by the police that they had concluded their inquiries and were now satisfied that there were no criminal charges for me to answer. They had received a written statement from Mandy Renwick confirming that I had indeed recently won the lottery.

6. I have subsequently written a letter to Bannerman and Law asking for an appeal hearing against my dismissal. I want the opportunity to be heard and to explain to the firm that I am entirely blameless. I have not, however, received any response to my letter to date. I have many friends there and miss their companionship very much. Nevertheless, I no longer want to work for Bannerman and Law after the way I have been treated.

7. The contents of this statement are true to the best of my knowledge and belief.

Signed ____________________

CHARLES E. SCOVILLE

Date ____________________

Vocabulary

Note the following language as used in the above statement:

summarily dismissed: dismissed without notice
taken aback: to be taken aback (phrasal verb) = to be surprised (Other words of similar meaning: to be flabbergasted (informal), amazed, astonished)
unblemished record: a very good, faultless record

Confusing words

'subsequently' and 'consequently'

'Subsequent to': happened following another event
'Consequently': as a result

For instance: '*Subsequent to* leaving Bannerman and Law, the claimant has not been able to find another job. *Consequently*, he cannot afford to go on holiday.'

Exercise 5.21

Comprehension

Answer the following questions:

1. Why did the policeman think that Charles had stolen money from the firm?
2. What explanation has Charles provided for the allegation made against him?
3. What proof has Charles obtained in support of his explanation?
4. State in a few sentences why Charles has been unfairly dismissed.

Direct speech

There are examples of direct speech in the above statement. For instance, 'You're dismissed as of now, Scoville.' Remember that direct speech is placed between speech marks and conveys exactly what was actually said.

Indirect (reported) speech

Indirect speech is used to report or describe what was said without quoting the actual words that were said. It is regularly used in written court and tribunal decisions as well as in witness statements. (Note, for instance, the use of reported speech in the employment tribunal decision and witness statements in this chapter.) Verbs commonly used in reported speech include 'said', 'told', 'asked' and 'explained'. For example:

Direct speech: 'You are being accused of stealing client money.'

Indirect (reported) speech: DC Clouseau told me that I was being accused of stealing client money.

In this example the present continuous 'are being accused' has been changed into the past continuous 'was being accused'. Note the following example:

Direct speech: 'You're dismissed as of now, Scoville.'

Indirect (reported) speech: Henry Moore told Charles Scoville that he was dismissed.

Other changes that commonly occur when converting direct speech into indirect or reported speech are:

- Pronouns usually convert from: 'I' to 'he'/'she'; 'my' to 'his'/'her';
- 'Tomorrow' becomes 'the following day'/'yesterday' becomes 'the previous day'.
- Modal verbs change so that you often find for instance that: 'can' becomes 'could'; 'will' becomes 'would'; 'may' becomes 'might'.

Exercise 5.22

Rephrase the following statements by Henry Moore to change them from direct speech into reported speech:

1. 'I've got him, the Ferrari-driving swindler!'
2. 'You're dismissed as of now, Scoville!'

Exercise 5.23

Drafting

The following document is an application form used for submitting a claim for unfair dismissal to an Employment Tribunal (ET). To complete the application it is necessary to set out details of your client's unfair dismissal claim. Complete the drafting of the application on behalf of your client, Charles E. Scoville, by selecting the most appropriate form of each verb from the verbs in italics. Draw a line through the other forms.

CHARLES E. SCOVILLE *v* BANNERMAN and LAW

1. I *to begin / beginning / began* **(1)** employment with Bannerman and Law ('the Respondent') on 4 April 2007. I *employing / was employed / to employ* **(2)** as a legal cashier, *worked / to work / working* **(3)** in a team of four within the Respondent's accounts department. My work principally involved double-entry book-keeping of the firm's client account and client ledgers. The Respondent is an international law firm, *have / having / to have* **(4)** several overseas offices.
2. At my annual appraisal meeting in March 2011 I was *telling / to tell / told* **(5)** by my manager that management were very pleased with my work. I was *to give / given / give* **(6)** a pay rise to reflect this. I have never received any disciplinary warnings.
3. However on Tuesday 26 April 2011 I *arriving / to arrive / arrived* **(7)** at work as usual at about 8.50 a.m. I am in the habit of *driving / drove / to drive* **(8)** to work since there is a staff car park. I had just parked and was *to enter / entering / enter* **(9)** the building when I was suddenly confronted by Mr Henry Moore, the Respondent's Managing Partner. He started *shouting / shout / to shout* **(10)** at me. I was shocked and confused. Then he suddenly *to tell / told / tell* **(11)** me I was sacked. I tried to reason with him but he was too angry to listen.
4. Shortly after that the police *arrived / arrive / to arrive* **(12)**. They *inform / to inform / informed* **(13)** me that I was being accused of stealing a large amount of money from the Respondent. I told Detective Constable Clouseau that was absurd. I *explaining / explained / to explain* **(14)** that I had done nothing wrong. The police subsequently accepted this and discontinued their inquiries.

→

5. I was nevertheless summarily *dismiss / to dismiss / dismissed* **(15)** on Tuesday 26 April 2011 for alleged gross misconduct. I therefore respectfully *contend / contending / to contend* **(16)** that I have been unfairly dismissed. There was no valid nor acceptable reason for my dismissal.
6. My dismissal was also procedurally unfair. In particular I was not granted a disciplinary hearing. I was therefore *to deny / deny / denied* **(17)** the opportunity *providing / to provide / provide* **(18)** an explanation. In addition I have been denied an appeal hearing.

Charles Scoville's case has now been heard and the employment tribunal has issued a written decision:

THE EMPLOYMENT TRIBUNAL

Case no. 128942/02

BETWEEN

Claimant		**Respondent**
Charles E. Scoville	**AND**	**Bannerman and Law (a firm)**

DECISION OF THE EMPLOYMENT TRIBUNAL

HELD AT: London (Central) ON: 26 AUGUST 2011

CHAIRMAN: Mr Claude Rumbelow MEMBERS: Thomas Stringfellow
Carol Kendall

Appearances

For Applicant: Richard Vaughan, Counsel and
Nancy Watkins, Solicitor

For Respondent: Jonathan Stevenson, Counsel and
Samantha Ponsonby, Solicitor

DECISION

The unanimous decision of the Tribunal is that: the Applicant was unfairly dismissed.

THE DECISION OF THE EMPLOYMENT TRIBUNAL

The tribunal has reached a unanimous decision in this matter. Firstly, it is accepted that there was a dismissal. What was in dispute, however, was

→

whether the dismissal was fair or unfair. The Respondent contended the former and the Applicant the latter. The Respondent is a city firm of solicitors, being a partnership with its head office in London. It also has four overseas offices. The Claimant was employed as a legal cashier for approximately 4 years prior to being dismissed by the Respondent on 26 April 2011. The Respondent contends the dismissal was justified by reason of gross misconduct. We are satisfied that the reason for dismissal was the employee's conduct relating to the alleged theft of £2 million. This is a potentially fair reason for dismissal as provided by section 98 of the Employment Rights Act 1996 (ERA). We then considered whether the dismissal was fair in all the circumstances, as further required by section 98(4) ERA. A relevant issue here was whether the employer had adopted a fair procedure in the course of dismissal. The Advisory, Conciliation and Arbitration Service (ACAS) Code of Practice on Disciplinary Procedure provides a helpful set of guidelines. It states that the following matters should be taken into account by an employer in the course of taking disciplinary action against an employee in order to ensure procedural fairness. The employee should be provided with detailed information concerning the allegations in advance of the disciplinary hearing (preferably in writing). The employee should also have the opportunity to make representations in his or her own defence. The employee is also entitled to be accompanied by a representative at a properly convened disciplinary hearing.

We also took into account the instrumental finding in *British Home Stores* v *Burchell* [1980], as recently confirmed by *Boys and Girls Society* v *MacDonald*. This was in relation to considering the reasonableness of the employer's actions in dismissing the employee in the particular circumstances.

These cases held that in order for the dismissal to be fair in a case of alleged misconduct, the employer must satisfy three criteria. Firstly, that the employer genuinely believed the employee had done wrong. Secondly, that there were reasonable grounds for that belief. Thirdly, that the employer reached that conclusion of misconduct after having carried out a reasonable investigation into the matter.

In the tribunal's view it was clear from the evidence we heard that this dismissal was procedurally unfair. Virtually none of the above requirements for a fair dismissal were adhered to by the employer. The Claimant was 'ambushed' by Mr Moore, the Respondent's Managing Partner. In other words the Claimant was dismissed without being provided with any advance notice of the allegation being made against him. Nor was he provided with the opportunity

→

to reply to the allegation. Similarly, details of the allegation were not even made clear to the Claimant at the time of dismissal. Neither was there any proper disciplinary hearing. Quite simply Mr Moore had already made up his mind that the Claimant had stolen this money without even listening to what he had to say in response.

By Mr Moore's own admission he summarily dismissed the Claimant in front of colleagues. He also divulged details of Mr Scoville's dismissal to a number of clients in reception. It further appears from the evidence that there was no reasonable or proper investigation carried out. Mr Moore simply leapt to the conclusion that the Claimant was the culprit. This procedural unfairness was then compounded by denying the Claimant an appeal hearing.

In further deliberating on the fairness of the dismissal in all the circumstances we took account of the decision in *Iceland Frozen Foods* v *Jones* [1983] ICR 17. This case continues to be recognised in law as providing the traditionally recognised test referred to as the 'band of reasonable responses'. In other words, did dismissal in the circumstances fall within the band of reasonable responses which a reasonable employer might invoke? This is an objective test as opposed to subjective. Therefore we would be erring in law if we decided this case on the basis of whether we as individuals on this panel would or would not have dismissed Mr Scoville in the circumstances. It is rather a question of what a reasonably minded person would think.

Taking account, however, of the evidence, this tribunal is unanimous in deciding that dismissal in the circumstances of this case was not a reasonable response to be expected of a reasonable employer. We were particularly swayed here by the evidence of Mrs Mandy Renwick, Chief Executive of Chameleon Gaming Systems, who we regarded as a credible and helpful witness. Mrs Renwick's evidence appears to clearly confirm the Claimant's version of events. We were also assisted by DC Clouseau's evidence which has satisfied us that there was in fact no wrongdoing on the part of Mr Scoville. Indeed DC Clouseau's evidence further indicates that the actual perpetrator was one of the Respondent's own partners.

This tribunal therefore finds that the Claimant was dismissed unfairly. I thereby declare that this was an unfair dismissal. The Claimant was on a gross salary of £25,000 per annum, i.e. £1,500 per month net. His immediate loss of earnings from date of dismissal until the date of this hearing therefore amount to £6,000. The Claimant remains unemployed despite having made efforts to

→

> find similar work. The tribunal hereby awards future loss of earnings for a period of a further eight months. In addition we award a sum of £2,000 as a basic award to represent compensation for his length of service with the Respondent. The Respondent is therefore ordered to make a total payment accordingly to the Claimant in the sum of £20,000 within 14 days.
>
> <u>Claude Rumbelow</u>
>
> CHAIRMAN

Vocabulary

adhered to: maintained; followed
compounded by: made worse by; combined with
culprit: guilty person
erring: doing wrong
gross misconduct: unacceptable behaviour justifying immediate (i.e. summary) dismissal
invoke: apply; resort to
leapt to the conclusion: quickly reached a conclusion; *jump to an opinion*
perpetrator: person who has done something wrong
swayed: influenced

Confusing words

adopt (v) and adapt (v)

'To adopt': to choose to follow a course of action

'To adapt': to adjust in order to suit different uses

The following words are contained in the judgment. Note how they are pronounced:

de-$\overline{\text{ci}}$-sion	(decision)
pro-$\overline{\text{ce}}$-dure	(procedure)
re-pre-$\overline{\text{sen}}$-ta-tive	(representative)
al-le-$\overline{\text{ga}}$-tion	(allegation)

Exercise 5.24

Now practise pronouncing the following further words from the judgment. Read out loud each word from the list, taking care to use correct stress patterns.

The correct stress patterns for each word can be checked in the answer key at the back of the book.

→

decision	dismissal	conduct	considered
procedure	fairness	information	hearing
representative	misconduct	investigation	evidence
allegation	admission	employer	wrongdoing
misappropriation	tribunal	declare	respondent

Exercise 5.25

Summarise the main conclusions of the above judgment of the employment tribunal in less than 100 words by restating in different words (i.e. paraphrasing) the important points and findings of the tribunal. (You will also look at paraphrasing and summarising in Chapter 7 in relation to interviewing and advising.)

Subject–verb inversion

Examine the following sentences in the above employment tribunal document and pay attention to the position of the subject and verb:

'Nor was he provided with the opportunity to reply to the allegation.'

He was not provided with the opportunity to reply to the allegation, either.

'Neither was there any proper disciplinary hearing.'

There was not any proper disciplinary hearing either.

Note how the verb comes before the subject, i.e. 'was he' and 'was there'. The subject–verb inversion happens in questions, but if the sentence starts with a negative adverbial, such as 'nor', 'neither', 'little' or 'not only', then you must put the verb before the subject.

Here are some further examples of subject–verb inversion:

Never had the police encountered such a mysterious case.

Little did Charles Scoville imagine that the firm's Managing Partner would accuse him of dishonesty.

Not only did the employment tribunal decide that the applicant was unfairly dismissed, but it also awarded him a compensation for loss of earnings

Note that the verb must come before the subject if the sentence is introduced by any of the following: 'nor', 'neither', 'never', 'not only', 'hardly', 'rarely', 'seldom', 'little', 'under no circumstances', 'at no time', 'no sooner than'.

Exercise 5.26

Rephrase the following sentences using the words in brackets:

1. They are not to be disturbed while holding a meeting. (under no circumstances)
2. The solicitor will not submit the documents until she has finished preparing the case. (only)
3. As soon as he started the car engine, the police asked him to produce his driving licence. (no sooner)
4. The defendant never showed remorse for his crime. (at no time)

Exercise 5.27

Pronunciation practice

The endings of regular past tenses in English ending in 'ed' are usually pronounced either as 'd', 'id', or 't' (not as 'ed'). Put the following words from the Employment Appeal decision under the column for the correct pronunciation.

Reached accepted contended employed dismissed provided considered entitled believed carried decided

't'	'd'	'id'

Exercise 5.28

Comprehension

Read the following application to the court (known as an 'application notice') and answer the following:

1. Who is making the application?
2. In which court?
3. What do you think is meant by 'real prospects of success'?
4. What order is being asked for?
5. What is summary judgment?
6. Write out a brief explanation of what the main case is about.

IN THE CENTRAL LONDON COUNTY COURT **CASE No. SL4 56473**

BETWEEN:

DARYL COSIMO **Claimant/Applicant**

and

ANTONIO AHMAN **Defendant/Respondent**

APPLICATION NOTICE

We, Stringwood & Evans, solicitors, on behalf of the Claimant intend to apply for an order for summary judgment on the grounds that the Defendant remains indebted to the Claimant in the sum of £20,000 for building work done and materials supplied at the Defendant's work premises. The Claimant contends that on the basis of the evidence the Defendant has no real prospect of successfully defending the claim and knows of no other reason as to why the disposal of this claim should await trial.

→

If the Defendant wishes to rely on written evidence at the hearing he must file that evidence and serve copies on every party to the application at least 7 days before the summary judgment hearing.

____

Stringwood & Evans
Claimant's solicitors

Address to which documents about this claim should be sent:
Stringwood & Evans, 18 Bond Street, London, W1 1KR

Good practice tips

- Analyse and research your case before starting to draft (see further guidance in Appendix: Legal study and research guide).
- Consider the facts and relevant law.
- Use plain English as much as possible.
- As a general rule, set out only one idea, argument or concept per paragraph.

SUMMARY

- Set out the facts accurately and in a logical order, with suitable headings.
- Be careful when using precedents – use them critically by amending them as necessary to suit your particular case.
- Use definitions to define terms which you repeatedly refer to in your draft (and be careful to then use those defined terms consistently).
- Comply with any applicable practice or court rules.
- Proofread carefully, checking that all grammar and punctuation is correct and language appropriate.
- Be completely honest! Professional codes of conduct in the legal profession require lawyers to ensure they do not provide misleading information or in any other way deceive the court.

Visit **www.mylawchamber.co.uk/mckay** to access further resources for practising legal language skills including additional exercises, listening activities and live weblinks for online research.

Part 2

Oral communication skills

Chapter 6

Oral presentation skills

Learning objectives

This chapter will help you to:

- be well prepared for effective oral presentations including debates, moots, interviews and other public speaking events;
- deliver a presentation clearly and persuasively, using appropriate language;
- develop your skills for presentation at university;
- improve your pronunciation;
- reflect on your own presentation and develop your analytical skills;
- understand the English courts of law system;
- develop your skills for winning a moot.

INTRODUCTION

The purpose of making virtually any presentation is to persuade whoever you are addressing. You must therefore communicate accurately and clearly. Presentations are usually made in public and often on behalf of someone else (such as when made in the course of making an application in court on behalf of a client). Such public speaking imposes a duty of care on you to deliver the required message effectively. Many people are nervous when they start to speak in public but this natural nervousness can be eased with practice and by keeping in mind some basic techniques.

These public speaking skills will also be of use to you in legal practice (such as when you appear in court on behalf of a client). Competency in advocacy stems from the skills addressed in this chapter. (Advocacy will be considered in Chapter 9.)

Skilful presenters and advocates vary their pace of speech, increasing it, for instance, to emphasise an important point and increase the persuasiveness of what they are saying. Altering the pace and volume of your voice can also help to maintain the listener's attention.

You can obtain valuable experience in public speaking by getting involved in debates and moots. A moot is a mock trial. Debates and moots are commonly organised by universities and colleges. Involvement in these is a good way of starting to develop the skills you will need as an advocate in court.

ORAL PRESENTATION AT UNIVERSITY

In order to develop these skills, you need to go through three stages:

- preparation;
- delivery;
- feedback and reflection.

Stage one: preparation

Gathering information

Make sure that you have carried out your research thoroughly and collected all the information you need for the presentation. In Chapter 2 there is a guide for sources of legal information and legal research to help you gather the information you need for your presentation.

Plan your talk in a logical order

Once you have obtained all the information you need, start planning your talk in a logical order so that the audience can follow you easily. Focus on one point at a time.

Make your own notes

Since we have to retain a substantial amount of information, we are bound to forget some names, dates or other details, particularly when a presentation has to be delivered within a limited time.

To avoid such awkward situations, prepare notes on a small card – preferably A5 size. These cards should contain the main points along with any details that you may have difficulty remembering at the time of delivery. It is important to number the cards because you might be nervous immediately before your turn comes for speaking and shuffle the cards. Putting numbers on the cards will help you put them in the right order quickly.

It is also important to remember that you will put the cards on the desk, table or next to the computer keyboard. So, your written notes should be made in such a way that you can read them without lifting them off the desk.

Prepare visual aids

Visual aids, such as boards, flip charts, computers and laptops, are commonly used in oral presentations. An experienced presenter uses at least two of the visual aids in a presentation.

When you prepare, for example, 'PowerPoint' slides, write only the main points so that the audience are reminded of each area of discussion you are addressing. *Do not* write a text in full. However, it is useful to write a quotation in full. Acknowledging the source is essential, so you must write the source clearly.

Be prepared for questions from the audience

Once you have finished writing your notes and PowerPoint slides, review all the points you are going to raise in your discussion. At the end of each point *stop* and *think*; someone from the audience might ask a question directly related to the point or might raise a counter-argument. So, you need to prepare additional notes to reply to any question you expect at the end of the talk.

Stage two: delivery

Appropriate language

Your choice of language should take account of your intended audience. If you use vocabulary with which the listener is not familiar then the listener may fail to understand you correctly. You also then risk alienating the listener. So vernacular or 'slang' words should be avoided. You should use shared vocabulary, i.e. vocabulary with which both you and the listener are familiar. Legal 'jargon' should therefore generally be avoided (unless you are presenting an application on a point of law solely in front of a legally qualified judge). Plain English will be better understood by non-lawyers (i.e. lay persons).

Terminology

When starting to speak in a moot, address the judge or person you are addressing with words such as,

> 'My Lord [etc.], I am [name] and I represent [the "claimant", etc.]. My learned friend Ms [name] represents [the "defendant" etc.].'

When referring to a case, use a phrase such as,

> 'I would refer you ['Your Lordship', etc., if addressing a judge] to the case of...'

End your submission with for instance,

> 'My Lord [etc.], that completes my submissions for [the 'appellant', etc.]'

Good practice tip

Cases are usually written as '*Hadley* v *Baxendale* (1854)', etc. If it is a civil case the 'v' is pronounced 'and'. If it is a criminal case, however, the 'v' is expressed orally as 'against'. Do not say 'versus' or 'vee'!

Appearance

Although formal wear is not required at university, most lecturers expect you to wear smart, casual clothes. There are no specific rules as to your appearance. There are, however, certain things you should not do.

Good practice tips

Do not do any of the following in an oral presentation:

- appear scruffy;
- use inappropriate greetings, such as 'Hi, guys';
- put your hands in your pockets;
- chew gum;
- lean against a desk or a chair.

Confidence

The feeling of nervousness and fear of making mistakes is quite normal and understandable if you are addressing an audience in public for the first time.

To overcome such feeling, always remind yourself that:

- you have carried out all the preparation;
- you are now well prepared;
- you have in-depth knowledge of certain areas that the others have not prepared.

Voice quality

The speed and volume of your speech, pronunciation, the tone of your voice and intonation are important factors which affect the quality of your voice. In order to improve the quality of your voice, read the following guidelines carefully and follow the instructions.

When you deliver a presentation, make sure that you speak at the right pace and your voice is audible and clear.

Do not speak very fast or very slowly

Nervous speakers typically speak too fast (often to get the ordeal of speaking in public over with as quickly as possible!). Nervous, inexperienced speakers often combine this with speaking continually without pausing. This results in 'ums' and 'ers', etc., known as 'fillers'. Try to replace such fillers with pauses.

Pauses are useful tools and can be used to:

- indicate a change or transition from one topic or point to another;
- emphasise the point you are making (try this by stopping what you are saying and watch how your listeners suddenly look up from their notes to see why you have stopped);
- give the audience time to think, understand and take note of what you are saying (by continuously speaking rapidly, the listener is likely to miss something which might be of importance);
- allow you to take a breath.

Do not speak very loudly or very softly

Make sure you speak at a volume appropriate to the surroundings. Be careful not to keep your head down when addressing the audience. When you stare down at your notes, your voice is then projected downwards rather than towards the audience, which may result in an inaudible, unclear voice.

Pronunciation

By now you have realised the importance of speaking at the right speed so that the audience can hear you clearly. Another factor of producing a clear voice is the way you pronounce words.

Some people may wrongly believe that they will not give a good performance in a presentation because of their accent. Your accent will *not affect* your performance. Remember that, if you speak at a slower pace when you deliver a presentation, your speech becomes much clearer and you performance will be much better. So, *do not* speak very fast.

Vowel sounds

When people speak very fast, some vowel sounds become unclear, though their friends and those who are familiar with their voice will have no problems in understanding them.

You already know that there are five vowels in English; they are the vowel letters only. But, when we speak, there are in fact twenty vowel sounds in English. To help the reader pronounce a word correctly, dictionaries provide the pronunciation of each word using the International Phonetic Alphabet (IPA). IPA is a system of symbols, each symbol represents a sound. There is a list of the IPA symbols, for consonants and vowels, in most dictionaries. Some dictionaries show the British, American and Australian pronunciation, when it is applicable.

Word stress

In many languages the stress is distributed equally on all the syllables of the word, but in English the main stress in a word lies on one syllable only. So, when you give a presentation it is important to stress the correct syllable.

There are many rules that govern the position of the stressed syllable, and explaining such rules in detail is beyond the scope and purpose of this book. However, some hints and practice are provided here to help you start exploring this aspect of English.

(*Note*: In the following examples in this chapter, the main stress in a word is shown above the syllable by a blue line ▬.)

The word 'present' could be pronounced either present (n) or present (v). When the word 'present' is used as a noun, the stress lies on the first syllable, but the stress is shifted to the second syllable to indicate that the word is used as a verb. Here are some further examples:

Noun	**Verb**
convict	convict
progress	progress
suspect	suspect
address	address

Try to think of other words in which the stress is shifted from the first to the second syllable to indicate the difference in using the word as a noun or a verb. Identifying on which syllable the main stress lies will help you to pronounce the word correctly and clearly. For instance, in the word 'compensation' the main stress lies on the third syllable.

For learning purposes, we write each syllable separately as follows:

com-pen-sa-tion

Alternatively, we can put the syllables in a table:

com	pen	sa	tion

Exercise 6.1

Listen to the pronunciation of the following words on the companion website and insert a mark to show on which syllable the main stress lies:

advocacy	arbitration	certificate
competition	distribution	investigation
jurisdiction	legislation	litigated
litigation	obligation	remuneration

If you wish to know more details about vowel sounds and word stress, there are some very useful language books with CDs for pronunciation practice available. Have a look at some of these resources and choose the level that suits you. You may also find some other useful resources provided by the British Council and the BBC, so visit their websites.

Additional pronunciation practice is also available on the companion website for this book.

Intonation

Do not read from a prepared talk. A professional presenter only refers to notes and does not read from a prepared text. If you read a text aloud, your voice becomes flat and the audience will find your talk very boring.

When giving a talk, you should raise and lower the pitch of your voice. Intonation will help you show the important points you are raising in your talk. In addition, the right intonation will portray your enthusiasm and show that you are interested in the audience.

Non-verbal elements in presentation

When you deliver an oral presentation, you should be aware of the effect of the non-verbal communication on conveying your message to the audience.

Whether making a presentation to prospective clients or employers, making a speech, mooting or representing a client in court, your posture and general appearance are important. Your posture, mannerisms and body movements are called **body language**. You should try to be relaxed and let your body stand naturally. Do your best to show that you are interested in your audience. Make sure that any body movement you make is not misinterpreted in any way which might offend other people. Also keep in mind that most people are influenced to some extent by appearance, so remember to dress smartly and tidily.

An important part of making eye contact with your audience is recognising how your presentation is being received. If you are addressing someone who will make a final decision or judgement on your presentation (such as a judge), make frequent eye contact with that person. Then you will be able to gauge whether what you are saying is making an impact and either elaborate further on your point or move on to something else.

Timing of each part of the presentation

Keep an eye on the timing of each part of your presentation and make sure you do not go beyond the time limit you set during the preparation stage.

At the preparation stage, remember to allow time for questions from the audience, if appropriate.

Stage three: feedback and reflection

Reflection is a vital aspect in every profession, including the legal profession. When we finish a task, we examine the outcome of our work and identify areas of strength and areas of weakness. Once we have identified strengths and weaknesses, we look for the factors that led to success and the causes of failure. This in turn helps us to improve our performance and plan for further development.

You should apply the same process to your presentation. Once you have received feedback from your tutor, look at the good aspects of your presentation, i.e. your areas of strength, and make sure you maintain that level. Then, look at the areas which need attention, i.e. your areas of weakness. Think carefully and try to identify the causes, then decide what you need to do to improve.

MOCK TRIALS AND MOOTING

Before addressing the skills required for mock trials and moots, we need to look at the structure of the courts of law.

Here are two diagrams: Figure 6.1 shows the system of courts exercising criminal jurisdiction; Figure 6.2 shows the system of courts exercising civil jurisdiction.

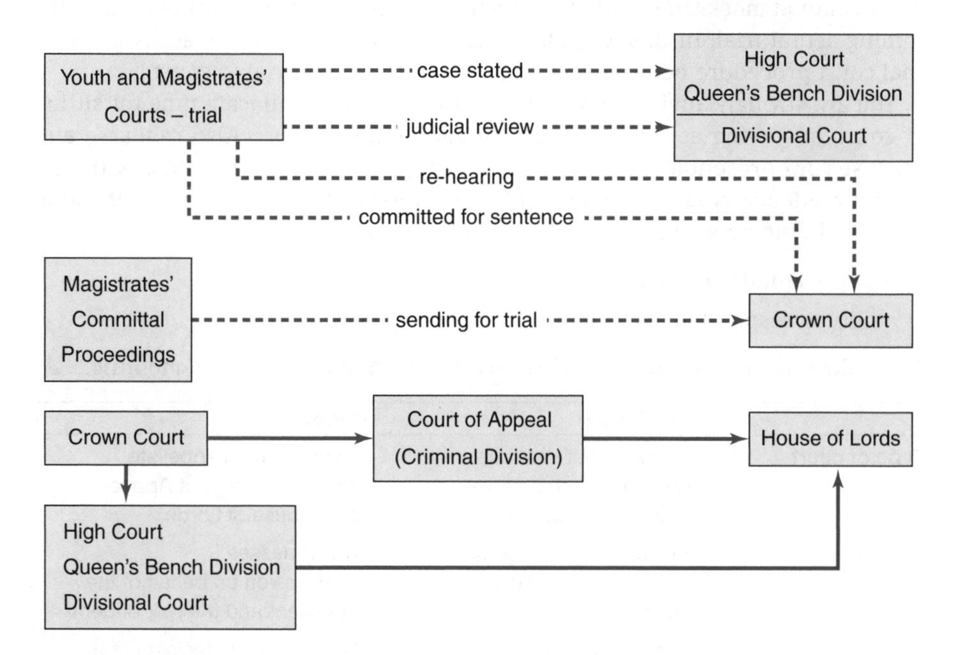

Figure 6.1 Structure of courts exercising criminal jurisdiction

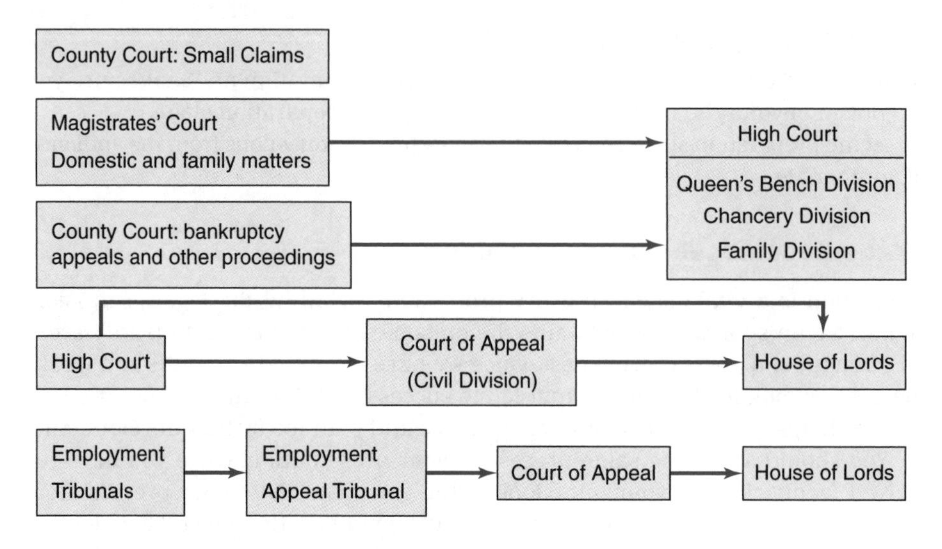

Figure 6.2 Structure of courts exercising civil jurisdiction

(Note: For modes of addressing judges and other adjudicators, see Chapter 9 on Advocacy.)

While studying law at university, you may be asked to take part in a mock trial or to participate in a moot. Both mock trials and moots are based on imaginary cases intended to represent and reflect, as realistically as possible, for training and assessment purposes, what actually happens in court. (Mock trials are also, however, conducted in actual practice on occasion. In particular, lawyers sometimes conduct mock trials with clients when practising and preparing for a forthcoming actual trial. In this way, clients can practise and become accustomed to trial court procedure before becoming involved in a real trial in court.)

You are strongly advised to visit your local courts and allocate time for sitting in court, observing at least one case in each type of court. Also rehearse and practise your presentations on your own or with a friend. If someone is with you, ask for feedback (you will find the advocacy feedback form in Chapter 9 useful for this). Remember that you are likely to be assessed on your:

- oral presentation skills;
- ability to respond to and effectively answer questions.

The following table shows the difference between mock trials and mooting:

	Mock trial	**Moot**
Type of court	Trial at a first instance court, e.g. county and magistrates' courts	High Court (in appellate capacity), Court of Appeal and House of Lords
Hearing	Evidence and witnesses examination and cross-examination	No witnesses Submission on behalf of the appellant and the respondent
Argument	Facts of the case	Reversing the decision of the lower court

Mooting

A moot is a competition in which entrants ('mooters') play the roles of advocates ('counsel'). The background facts and circumstances for the moot are typically based on a real case already decided in the higher courts (such as the Court of Appeal or the Supreme Court). A moot is usually a mock appeal hearing which has been based on existing case law ('authorities'). In other words it is a court hearing in which one party (the 'appellant') is seeking to persuade the court to reverse (overturn) an earlier court decision.

Research carefully therefore in readiness for taking part in a moot. Look for relevant existing case law on which the facts of the moot (sometimes referred to as the 'facts pattern') may have been based. (Further guidance on legal research is provided elsewhere in this book.) Look for cases to refer to and rely upon in support of arguments you plan to present. Also look carefully for relevant cases with contrasting decisions ('conflicting authorities'). Be ready to distinguish existing authorities and to explain clearly why the legal authorities should be interpreted in favour of the case or argument you are presenting. You will be provided with the moot case in advance, so read it carefully and ensure that you are familiar with the facts. Identify and keep in mind the particular points or legal test(s) which the appellant will need to establish to win the appeal. If you are representing the appellant then you will need to establish those grounds to win. If you are acting for the respondent then you will need to satisfy the judge that the appellant does not have sufficient grounds for the appeal to succeed. As with advocacy (see Chapter 9), emphasise your strong points and address the other party's valid arguments by 'countering' them rather than simply ignoring them.

Good practice tip

The judge may ask you to provide further explanation of any point you make, so read relevant cases thoroughly rather than just reading a short summary from the 'headnote' of the case or from a textbook.

Check whether a practice round of the moot is to take place at which feedback and advice will be provided without any formal assessment at that stage. This can be very helpful in identifying which main aspects of your mooting skills you should focus on developing and strengthening. During the competition rounds (there are typically several rounds and a final), judges often provide guidance and feedback. Take a careful note of and reflect on that feedback. Don't worry too much about a wider audience initially as you start mooting. An audience is often not allowed to observe until the final stages.

Since a moot is usually a mock appeal, when mooting you are likely to play the role of either counsel for the appellant or for the respondent (the appellant being the party appealing and the respondent the party against whom the appeal is being made). If there are two in each team then one team member plays the role of senior counsel and the other the role of junior counsel.

Purpose

Apart from assessment on your law course, you will gain valuable benefits when you participate in mooting. Since the moot problem addresses an appeal case, mooting will help you develop your advocacy skills (see Chapter 9).

Mooting can offer you the opportunity to build up your confidence. This will in turn help you to start applying for your first position in the legal profession.

When you take part in mooting you will also develop your skills in consulting primary sources and identifying the point of law in support of your submission.

Participants

As you have seen, there are typically four participants: two counsel (a senior and a junior) for the appellant and two counsel (a senior and a junior) for the respondent. You will know your role when you receive the moot case.

The moot case

You will be given the facts of the case, together with the decision made by the court. Reasoning for reaching the decision and the legal authorities upon which the judgment was based will also be given. In addition, you will be given the grounds of the appeal and details of the court.

Preparation for the hearing

When a party intends to use legal arguments and authorities, they inform the other side and the judges in advance in order to avoid the element of surprise. Check therefore whether you are to send a list of all the authorities you intend to use in the moot to other participants and the judges. The moot organiser will tell you the maximum number of authorities you may use.

You may also be asked to submit a skeleton argument before the hearing.

You will, of course, need to study the decision made by the court of first instant, carry out the necessary research and prepare your arguments. As with advocacy (see Chapter 9) *do not* read out an entire script.

The hearing

At the beginning of this chapter we discussed 'oral presentation at university'. It would be useful if you looked again at the advice given for the 'delivery' of a presentation. Since the submission in a moot 'role-play' is addressing the judges at the Court of Appeal or the Supreme Court there are usually no witnesses, defendants or juries. So, *do not* use informal English when addressing the court (for more information about informal, semi-formal and formal English, refer to Chapter 1).

If you are the first to speak (sometimes referred to as being 'the first up'), introduce yourself, any team members and your opponent(s):

> 'My Lord, I am Miss ... and I represent the appellant together with my learned friend (or 'Junior') Mr ... My learned friends, Mrs ... and Mr ..., represent the respondent.'

Address Court of Appeal and Supreme Court judges as 'My Lord/Lady' in place of their actual names and as 'Your Lordship/Ladyship' in place of 'you'. If you wish to express gratitude to the judge, for example for being helpful, it is preferable to say, 'I am obliged My Lord/Lady' rather than 'thank you'.

Winning the moot

Successful mooting requires the development of presentation and advocacy skills as well as acquiring knowledge of the law for the moot problem. If you are well prepared, you will be able to respond to judicial questions and interact with the judge and opponents.

Winning the moot depends mainly on your presentation of persuasive arguments and advocacy skills. (See Chapter 9 for further details.)

Well developed oral communication skills are essential for legal professional practice. Such skills are needed, for instance, for advocacy, interviewing, and advising and negotiation (see following chapters).

Good practice tips

- Many moots are based on an actual case already decided by a senior court, so research thoroughly.
- Identify the points each party needs to establish to win.
- Recognise the weak points in your case, anticipate your opponent's arguments and prepare your responses to them.
- Ensure you emphasise your strong points.
- Be aware of how long you have to speak and keep your eye on the time, ensuring that you cover all important issues in the time allocated to you.

SUMMARY

- There are three stages for oral presentation: preparation, delivery and feedback/reflection.
- At the preparation stage, carry out research and collect information and plan your talk in a logical order.
- Well-prepared notes and visual aids will contribute to the success of your delivery.
- You must be prepared for questions from the audience and allow time for them.
- When you give a talk, remember that your appearance demonstrates your professional attitude towards the audience.
- To boost your confidence, remember that you have studied the topic in depth and you have prepared well for your talk.
- Do not speak very fast or very slowly, nor very loudly or very softly.
- If you speak at a slower pace, your voice will be much clearer.
- Pay attention to the syllable where the main stress lies in a word.
- Reading from a prepared text is not professional and is boring for your audience.
- Remember that intonation is an important tool to show that you are enthusiastic.

- In oral presentation there are non-verbal elements: body language, body movement and eye contact.
- Reflection is very important: when you receive feedback from your tutor, make a plan to improve your areas of weakness of your oral presentation skills.
- Mooting is different from a mock trial.
- Mooting typically deals with appeal cases.
- To win a moot you have to demonstrate your advocacy skills and provide persuasive arguments.

Visit **www.mylawchamber.co.uk/mckay** to access further resources for practising legal language skills including additional exercises, listening activities and live weblinks for online research.

Chapter 7

Interviewing and advising

Learning objectives

This chapter will help you to:

- conduct an interview using appropriate questioning techniques;
- develop listening skills and vocabulary for checking understanding;
- advise clients using appropriate vocabulary and grammar.

INTRODUCTION

This chapter covers language skills for interviewing and advising a client. The same principles can, however, be applied when interviewing others, such as witnesses. Lawyers must be competent in conducting an effective interview. An interview is a conversation for a particular purpose, such as for providing advice. An effective interview structure is important in ensuring that all necessary information is conveyed and understood during the interview.

INTRODUCTORY STAGE: 'ICE-BREAKING'

When you initially meet the client, talk to him or her in a manner which sets them at ease. This is sometimes termed 'ice-breaking'. It is the stage where you introduce yourself and perhaps exchange a few friendly remarks ('small talk'). For instance:

> 'Good morning, Mr Burgoyne, thank you for coming in to see me this morning. My name is Arthur Montague and I am a solicitor with this firm. Please take a seat.'

FACT-GATHERING STAGE

This is the stage for obtaining information about the particular matter the client wishes to discuss with you and obtain advice about. It involves identifying the client's concerns and obtaining all relevant information. So much of what you say as an interviewer will be in the form of questions. Questioning technique is therefore very important.

Note taking

Try to take selective notes during the interview. You won't have time to write everything down. Too much writing will distract you from listening attentively. So make brief and clear notes of the main points and facts. If you sit looking down at your notes and writing constantly, you will not appear to be paying full attention to your client. Write down keywords and phrases instead. Underline or circle what needs further information or details. Remember you do not need to write down what is already recorded elsewhere (such as in correspondence or documents). You should also keep a detailed file note of what was discussed and agreed, what you advised and what further action is to be taken by you and your client. This can be prepared after the interview. You will also usually send your client a 'follow-up' letter. This is to confirm your advice and instructions, i.e. what legal work your client has asked you to carry out. (See Chapter 3 regarding file notes and letter writing.)

Interview questions

Open questions

Open questions are often used early on in an interview. They leave a good deal of freedom or 'leeway' as to how the question can be answered. The person being asked has freedom to choose what to talk about or what to tell you. Such questions can be used to prompt a client to indicate the type of matter or problem they seek advice on. For example,

> 'Thank you for coming to see me, Mr Abbott. How can I help you?'

If you already have some idea of what the client wants to discuss, open questions can then be used to get the client to 'tell the story' in their own words:

> 'The note I have from my secretary says you want advice concerning a dispute with your business partner. Can you tell me what the dispute is about?'

As you get more information in this way you can then obtain more specific details by using further open questions. For example:

> 'Could you now tell me how this accident you've mentioned occurred?' or 'What happened next?' or 'Please tell me more about...'

Verbs such as 'explain' and 'tell' can be used effectively at this stage.

Having obtained an understanding of your client's goals and concerns, you will want to focus on particular matters you identify as important. You can now take more control of your questioning to get more detailed and specific information by using closed (or 'narrow') questions.

Closed questions

If you only ask open questions you are unlikely to obtain all information necessary to advise your client. Closed questions are more specific questions for getting further information on important matters. Closed questions exert more control over the answer than open questions. They are often short questions and limit the range of likely responses.

The following are examples of closed questions:

> 'You say there was another car involved in the accident. What was the make of the other car?'
>
> 'Was there anyone else in your car when the accident happened?'
>
> 'How many other partners are in the business?'

'What did the other director of the company say when you told her you wanted the company to merge with one of your competitors?'

'For what period of time do you want the contract with Computer Support Services to last?

Notice how these questions are asking for specific information.

Leading questions

Leading questions are a type of closed question and imply or suggest the answer. They can be used to:

- get someone to agree or disagree with what you are saying, often leading to a 'yes' or 'no' answer;
- imply or suggest the answer, by 'feeding' or 'putting the words into the person's mouth'.

For example:

'You were not responsible for ordering stock for the company, were you?'

'So the managing director didn't give you a chance to explain?'

These questions further restrict the answer which can be provided. (Leading questions are also therefore used when cross-examining a witness in court as will be seen in Chapter 9 on advocacy, e.g. 'Isn't it true that you stole the money from the company?')

In interviewing, leading questions can be useful when you want to confirm particular details or facts. For example:

'So the other vehicle drove into the rear of your car?'

Similarly, for clarification:

'So you got authority from the directors before signing the contract on behalf of the company?'

They can also be used to express sympathy or empathy. For instance:

'Am I right in saying you want to make a claim for unfair dismissal because you have made a lot of money for the company and done nothing wrong?'

Further interviewing and questioning techniques

Appropriate use of vocabulary is vitally important during an interview. It can determine the effectiveness of the interview. If, for instance, you are interviewing and advising a lay person (someone who is not a trained lawyer), avoid using terms which only other lawyers are familiar with, otherwise you will hinder the person's level of understanding. It will also do little to endear you to the client. Use language which both you and the interviewee share. You will then avoid alienating them. If you do need to use any legal jargon, make sure that you explain the meaning of such terms to your client.

Clarification

Clarification is used to check that you fully understand what the client is saying. This involves referring to something the client has said and getting the client to provide further specific information about it. For instance:

> 'What exactly did she say when you accused her of that?'
>
> 'What exactly was he doing when you say he appeared angry?'
>
> 'In what way was he behaving strangely?'
>
> 'Please tell me more about...'

Paraphrasing

Paraphrasing involves restating main points or issues in different words to achieve clarity. It can be used to check that you correctly and fully understand what the other person is saying. A paraphrase refers to the crucial or essential points of what the person whose words you are paraphrasing has said. Paraphrasing can be introduced by using a short 'lead-in' phrase. For instance:

> 'In other words, Mrs Herbert (lead-in phrase), do you wish to be advised on what legal action you can take to recover the money owing to you?'

Other suitable lead-in phrases which could have been used here include,

> 'As I understand it, Mrs Herbert, the situation is that...' or 'As I see it...' or 'Let me check that I have the details correct...'

Summarising

Lawyers regularly summarise statements and documents. The court also commonly asks the lawyers acting for the parties in a court case to summarise the main events or legal issues. Summarising (sometimes called recapitulation) involves identifying the essential aspects of information and details provided to you and recapping those main points. Summarising can also be used to check that you understood the client correctly, with phrases such as:

> 'Let me just make sure I understand what you are saying, Mrs Herbert...' or 'In other words, does that mean...?'

Summarising and paraphrasing also help to indicate that you are interested in and paying attention to your client.

Transitions

To keep effective control of an interview it is sometimes necessary to 'move the interview along', in other words to direct the interview towards a new issue or topic. Otherwise, important matters may be given insufficient time and emphasis, possibly resulting in some crucial information being missed. An interviewer therefore sometimes has to change the topic or subject being discussed, to 'move the interview along' to some other more important matter. A transition therefore involves introducing a different topic or issue to discuss.

Bridging the discussion

You can keep the conversation focused on relevant matters by building on what the client has said. For example:

> 'That's very helpful, Mrs Thomas. You say there was another vehicle involved in the accident. Can you give me more information about that vehicle?'

Discourse markers or sequencers can also be used to assist, such as shown below:

> '*Firstly* (or *First of all*), Mrs Wagner, how did the accident happen?'
>
> '*Secondly*, were there any witnesses?'
>
> '*Right*, I understand that, now let me ask you, were any other vehicles involved?'
>
> '*In other words*, is it right to say you were not to blame?'

Other useful words and terms include 'in addition', 'however' and 'on the other hand'.

Elaboration

If you need to obtain more information on a particular matter, the client can be directed to providing this by getting them to elaborate. For instance: 'Then what happened?'; 'What happened after that?'; 'What was the result of that?'

Forming questions

In the above guidance on open, closed and leading questions different styles of techniques are used to ask questions.

> ***Open question:*** How can I help you? (A question word is used and then the usual structure of subject and verb is inverted to form a question)
>
> ***Closed question:*** Was anyone else in the car? (This time the auxiliary verb 'to be' is used and again the normal order of subject verb is inverted)
>
> ***Leading question:*** So you got authority from the directors before signing the contract on behalf of the company? (In this case there is no inversion but the question is inferred and also intonation can be used to indicate it is a question)

Most questions are formed by using either the verbs 'to do', 'to be' or 'to have' at the beginning of the sentence or a question word. The question words 'who', 'which', 'what', 'why', 'when' and 'where' can be used in both open or closed questions but are often used in the latter to get specific information.

> 'Where were you when this happened?'
>
> 'Who said that?'

The verb 'to do' is used when the question word is the object of the sentence but not when it is the subject except for emphasis.

> 'What happened after the crash?'
>
> 'What *did* happen after the crash?'

Negative questions can be used to check details.

> 'Didn't you call the police?'
>
> 'Don't you like coffee?'

Intonation

In 'yes/no' questions the intonation usually rises at the end, while in 'wh' questions it usually falls:

'Did you go to the meeting?' (Voice rises)

'What did you talk about?' (Voice falls)

If the situation is possible but unlikely, stress the modal verb and use a rising intonation:

'We *might* have the conference in London.'

If the situation is more probable, use a falling intonation:

'She may be flying back tonight.'

Question tags

Question tags are frequently used in leading questions to force an answer:

'You saw him drive into her car, didn't you?'

A positive statement can be turned into a question by using a negative question tag and similarly a negative statement can be turned into a positive one with a positive question tag. The same auxiliary verb should be used as the verb in the main clause ('do' is used where there is no other auxiliary):

'You were using your mobile phone, weren't you?'

The negative structures for the above two questions would be:

'You didn't see him drive into her car, did you?'

'You weren't using your mobile phone, were you?'

By using rising intonation while asking a question you can give an impression that you are sure of the answer of what you are alleging. Asking the question using falling intonation will, however, provide an impression of uncertainty.

Exercise 7.1

Try to complete the following questions with the correct question tag. The first one is done for you.

1. You were wearing a seat belt, ***weren't you***?
2. He wasn't keeping to the speed limit, ______?
3. You have a no claims bonus, ______?
4. He wasn't keeping a safe braking distance, ______?

ADVICE STAGE

This is the stage to tell the client what the legal situation is and what his options are. Your advice should help your client to make an informed decision about what to do next.

Verbs of advice and probability

When advising a client, verbs of advice and probability can be used to express your view, assessment or attitude. For instance, 'You ought to' or 'They will try to' or 'You should'.

Other verbs can be used to convey the extent to which something is possible, preferable or necessary. For instance, 'can', 'could', 'may', 'must', 'shall', 'should'.

Grammar notes

The above verbs do not add an 's' in the third person and have no tense forms. They invert with the subject to form questions so there is no 'do'. 'Shall' is frequently used and can mean 'must' and 'will'. For instance:

The agent shall make credit checks.

You shall not murder.

When giving advice as a lawyer the verb 'should' is often used

You should sign this document if you want to complete the transactions.

Exercise 7.2

Try to complete the following sentences with the most appropriate verb: 'shall', 'will', 'can', or 'should'. (More than one answer may be possible.)

1. If you wish to accept this offer you ______ reply in writing.
2. You ______ start an action for breach of contract by completing a claim form.
3. This agreement ______ be governed by English law.
4. It ______ be an offence to spit or leave litter in this public area.
5. He ______ apply to the Home Office for an extension of his visa.

Vocabulary

Useful phrases for the advice stage:

Firstly you could...

Secondly...

Turning to the other option you could...

It is up to you, but I would recommend...

My advice would be to...

I would suggest that you consider...

Conditional sentences in advice sessions

Conditional sentences are covered more fully in Chapter 8, but the following may assist in advising a client.

'I'll act for you if you wish.'

'I'll call your witness if the defendant denies liability.'

These are examples of the first conditional in English which is formed by using the present tense in the 'if' clause and the future in the other clause. It is more positive than the second conditional.

'I'd act for you if you wished.'

'I'd call your witness if the defendant denied liability.'

This is formed by using the past tense in the 'if' clause and would with the infinitive without 'to' in the other clause. 'Were' can be used in more formal situations.

'If I were you I would accept that offer.'

For hypothetical situations a third conditional is used.

'If she had not called that witness she would not have won the case.'

'Might' or 'could' can also be used as alternatives to 'would'.

'If you tell me more about the dispute, I might be able to suggest a legal remedy.'

'If we get all the documents drafted today, we could complete the sale of the business by the end of the week.'

Exercise 7.3

Read the following pairs of sentences and identify which one in each pair is more likely to be accurate and/or less hypothetical when speaking to a client.

1. **(a)** My legal team will work throughout the night if needed to complete the transaction.
(b) My legal team would work throughout the night if needed to complete the transaction.

2. **(a)** I will read the papers tonight if I have time.
(b) I would read the papers tonight if I had time.

Exercise 7.4

Try to complete the following sentences using the correct form of the words in brackets.

1. If your client had offered a reasonable amount of compensation my client ______ (accept) it.
2. If the settlement offer ______ (to be) more reasonable my client would not have gone to court.
3. If they ______ (reduce) prices the company would have stayed in business.
4. If he had worn a safety belt he ______ (not be injured) so seriously.

Conjunctions

A range of conjunctions can be useful when using conditional sentences, including: 'provided', 'supposing', and 'on condition (that)'. For instance:

'I would advise you to provide contracts of employment to your workers, *provided* that [or as long as] you want them to be permanent employees.'

'We could agree to pay him the amount he has asked for *provided* he agrees not to work for a competitor for two years.'

CLOSING STAGE

The concluding stage of an interview should clarify what you are going to do for the client and what further action is to be taken (as well as providing an indication of how much you are going to charge). Finally, check that you have covered everything, e.g. 'Is there anything else?'

Direct speech and reported speech

When interviewing it is sometimes essential to convey precisely what a person said, such as when considering the evidence in a case. Direct speech needs to be used by a client when telling you exactly what was said. Remember that it should be indicated by being placed in inverted commas (' ') when written. For example:

Direct speech: She said, 'I've got authority.'

Reported speech: She said (that) she had authority.

Note how the reporting verb 'said' is used. When using indirect speech avoid casual or 'slang' terms such as 'I says…' or 'He went like…'

In conclusion, a competently conducted interview usually involves the stages summarised in the following checklist.

Interviewing and advising checklist

Stage 1: Introduction ('ICE-BREAKING')

- Set the client at ease to begin with. Exchange 'pleasantries' and establish a good 'rapport' with the client. Show your client you are interested by maintaining appropriate eye contact, asking logical 'follow-up' questions and sitting up straight.
- Be aware of cultural considerations. In some cultures, for instance, sustained eye contact is not regarded as polite.
- Ask your client how to pronounce his/her name correctly if you are unsure.

Stage 2: Fact gathering

- Gather the basic information and identify the client's concerns. Invite him/her to explain the facts, problems, concerns and wishes. Start with open questions, using closed questions later to obtain further specific information. Listen carefully. It is important to obtain all relevant information.
- The Solicitors Code of Conduct of the Law Society of England and Wales states: 'You should take the time to understand what your client really wants and needs.'

Stage 3: Advising

- Address the client's specific questions and concerns by applying the relevant law to the facts and advising.
- Explain your advice clearly and accurately.
- If it is not a straightforward matter then you may have to undertake legal research before providing detailed advice.

Stage 4: Closing

- Check that the client understands clearly what has been discussed and the advice provided. This can often be achieved by providing a short 'recap' of your advice and what future action has been agreed.

Exercise 7.5

Questioning

Place the following questions in order, by following the interviewing and advising checklist above. Also classify each question as an open or closed question.

1. I understand you were in a car accident. Can you give me more details?
2. Would you like some coffee?
3. What treatment are you receiving for the injuries?
4. Is there anything else you wish to discuss?

Exercise 7.6

Interviewing and advising practice

Read the following memorandum from your secretary at law firm Stringwood & Evans. Then, if you are working on your own, undertake the 'Individual exercise' below or if working in a group, undertake the 'Group exercise'.

STRINGWOOD & EVANS

Solicitors

Client: Reinhard Solarin — Date: 29 June 2011

File reference: RS001

Matter: Partnership Dispute

This new client, Reinhard Solarin, telephoned this afternoon. I have made an appointment for him to see you in your office tomorrow at 11.00 a.m. He is a partner in a firm of consulting engineers and is involved in a dispute with the other partners in the business. He told me that the other partners are trying to force him out of the partnership. They are alleging that Mr Solarin has been running his own consultancy engineering business without telling them while continuing to be in partnership with them.

Mr Solarin wants to discuss the details with you and to obtain your advice on his legal rights and possible courses of action.

Regards,

Tracey

→

Individual exercise

Prepare for the interview with your client by writing out a short list of questions to ask him when you meet him. Think of questions which will obtain more information and details of the issues your secretary has mentioned in the memo.

Begin your questions with a friendly introduction. For example:

'Did you have a good journey here?'

'Would you like tea or coffee?'

Group exercise

Role-play the interview with Reinhard Solarin as follows. Pair up with a colleague. One of you plays the role of the client, Reinhard Solarin, while the other plays the lawyer. The client should explain to the lawyer the matters he seeks advice on, based on the information in the memorandum above. If you are playing the lawyer, take brief notes of the information provided by the client. The lawyer should then provide imaginary advice to the client, addressing the matters set out in the memorandum above. The client should take brief notes of the advice. Keep in mind the 'Interviewing and Advising Checklist' as you role-play the interview.

Finally, provide feedback to your partner on his or her performance in interviewing and advising by grading them under each of the four criteria in the 'Interview and Advising Checklist'. Grade from 1 to 5 as follows:

1 = unsatisfactory
2 = poor
3 = average
4 = very good
5 = outstanding

Ask your partner to similarly provide feedback to you on your performance.

SUMMARY

- Prepare adequately in advance of the interview with your client.
- 'Set the scene' by making the client feel at ease, maintaining suitable eye contact.
- Use language appropriate to the client.
- Establish rapport with the client, starting off with open questions to identify the issues and the client's concerns (this is largely a 'listening stage').
- Establish rapport with the client, maintaining appropriate eye contact and using suitable 'follow-up' questions.
- Obtain more detailed information by using narrow and closed questions (this is largely a 'questioning stage').
- Verify and clarify all relevant details, goals and concerns.
- Consider all information carefully before advising the client by applying relevant law to the facts.

- Close the interview by explaining to the client what further steps will now be taken.
- Take notes of the main points which were discussed and of what further action has been agreed.

Visit **www.mylawchamber.co.uk/mckay** to access further resources for practising legal language skills including additional exercises, listening activities and live weblinks for online research.

Chapter 8

Negotiation

Learning objectives

This chapter will help you to:

- speak, question and listen effectively when negotiating;
- make proposals and offers in negotiation;
- obtain information and respond professionally to your opponent when negotiating;
- construct effective arguments and offers during negotiation.

INTRODUCTION

Negotiation involves communicating with another party to try to reach agreement over something. Most legal disputes are settled by negotiation before a court hearing (sometimes referred to as 'settling out of court'). Negotiation also commonly occurs between parties (such as two companies or individuals) when they want to jointly enter into a business deal or arrangement. Many kinds of business agreements are negotiated, including the types of agreement looked at in Chapter 4 (agency agreements, partnership agreements, etc.). These negotiations are often conducted by lawyers on behalf of their clients. Further examples of the matters lawyers negotiate on behalf of their clients include contracts for: the sale or purchase of property; the buying and selling of goods and services; joint venture agreements between companies.

It is the terms of such contracts in particular which the lawyers for the parties will negotiate. We all negotiate regularly in the course of our daily lives, whether with a friend over which film to go to see or the price when buying a car from a car dealership. Whether it is individuals, organisations or nation states negotiating in the field of international relations, the principles of negotiation are basically the same.

Negotiation can be conducted by correspondence, telephone or by electronic communication such as e-mail. Often, however, it is by a personal meeting between the parties and their lawyers. The means chosen for negotiating is sometimes referred to as the 'forum' for the negotiation.

WHY NEGOTIATE?

'Let us never negotiate out of fear. But let us never fear to negotiate.'

John F. Kennedy, inaugural address 20 January 1961

A negotiated settlement can preserve a commercial relationship between the parties as well as saving legal costs, anxiety, time and stress. A negotiated settlement can also ensure privacy concerning what has been agreed and so avoid adverse publicity.

THE NEGOTIATION PROCESS

Opening stage

At this stage the parties:

- introduce themselves to each other;
- set out their initial positions or 'standpoints';
- state what they want to achieve from the negotiation.

At the start of a negotiation the language used will usually be similar to that used when 'meeting and greeting' a client during an interview (Chapter 7). For instance:

> 'Good afternoon, I am . . . and my colleague here is Mr/Miss/Ms/Mrs . . . Shall we firstly discuss . . . ?'

Discussion and bargaining stage

This is when the parties discuss the issues and begin bargaining. Offers or proposals are made at this stage to try to reach agreement.

Making offers

An offer might sound something like this:

> 'Having taken my client's instructions, I can offer the sum of £5,000 in full and final settlement. Would you accept £5,000?'

An initial offer is known as an opening offer, or bid. It should be credible and sensible. Otherwise you risk alienating and offending the other party as well as losing credibility. (A ridiculous proposal is sometimes termed as being in the 'insult zone'.) Your opening offer should therefore be the most favourable and justifiable outcome for your client, with regard to the law and facts of the case (i.e. your client's 'best case scenario'). If your opening offer is at or near to the least you can accept then you severely limit your scope for further negotiation.

As you make further offers, try not to make a range of offers, avoiding for instance: 'If my client was to make an offer in the range of £8,000 to £10,000 would your client accept it?'

This does not make your offer clear and can lead to misunderstanding. Your client will hope that the other party will accept £8,000. The other party will want £10,000 (and know that your client is willing to negotiate up to that amount). It is better to stage your offers:

> 'My client is willing to offer £8,000 in settlement of your client's claim.'

If this offer is rejected then you can move to the next stage (perhaps offering £8,500) and so on:

> 'We consider £8,000 to be a good offer. However, in order to try to resolve this matter amicably I am authorised to increase the offer to £8,500.'

Notice how prepositions are used:

'We are entitled to compensation *for* breach of contract.'

'My client's work performance was poor due *to* personal problems.'

'We hope to arrive *at* an agreement today to avoid the need to proceed to trial.'

Prepositions can also be used immediately before a relative pronoun:

'We are hoping to negotiate a settlement *from which* both parties will benefit.'

Exercise 8.1

Complete the following statements by inserting the appropriate prepositions or conjunctions in the blank spaces from the selection below. (You may need to select some words more than once.)

for by because of due to owing to

1. Your client has no legal grounds ________ insisting on a confidentiality clause.
2. My client has lost profit ________ your client's trade mark infringement.
3. We could settle this ________ mutually agreeing to withdraw our claims.

The list below contains more prepositions and phrases which can be useful when negotiating.

despite in terms of regarding since until except
apart from according to in the event of assuming concerning
because of due to owing to as a result of although

Persuading your opponent

Justifying your proposal

It is important to argue persuasively when negotiating. Provide reasons for your proposals. Your opponent is then more likely to accept what you say. For instance:

'Your client should accept £95,000 *because* the court awarded only £89,000 in a similar case last week.'

You can also state the reason why your opponent should accept your proposal before actually making the proposal. People often continue listening more attentively when you do this. Putting the proposal first causes many people to instinctively stop listening to the rest of the sentence. This is because they are already starting to think instead of how they are going to respond to your proposal.

Here is an example of the reason being stated prior to the actual proposal:

'The court awarded only £89,000 in a similar case last week, so your client should accept the offer of £95,000.'

Exercise 8.2

Rewrite the following proposal by placing the reason before the proposal. Also try to rewrite as concisely as possible.

'I am authorised to offer your client £235,000 compensation for loss of profit. It is a generous offer since your client does not have any evidence to prove that she has lost anything like that amount in lost profit.'

Use clear arguments and explanations to justify your standpoint or offer.

> 'My client has increased the company's turnover by two hundred per cent in the last year. The price that my client is offering to sell his shareholding in the company to your client for is therefore a generous offer which your client should accept.'

The following words can be used to emphasise why your proposal is justified. These words can also be used to enhance or 'add weight' to the persuasiveness of your argument.

naturally	besides	what is more
so	consequently	thus
in addition	therefore	

For example:

> 'Your offer does not take any account of the damage to our company's reputation, *so* we cannot accept your offer.'
>
> 'Your offer is not sufficient for us to accept it, *besides* which there are very good prospects of my client succeeding at trial.'

Similarly, ask your opponent to justify and verify her arguments and proposals. For instance:

> 'On what possible basis are you entitled to that?'
>
> 'Why should my client agree to that?'
>
> 'Why does your client believe he is entitled to that?'
>
> 'What evidence have you got to support that claim?'

Appropriate use of language

You can make your points more clearly and persuasively by selecting appropriate language. Legal terminology is only likely to be appropriate if you are negotiating with a fellow lawyer. 'Your client is clearly in breach of an express term of the contract' would only be appropriate when speaking to another lawyer. If speaking to a client, therefore, language such as, 'Their client has not complied with what the contract requires him to do' would be more appropriate.

You can also demonstrate confidence or conviction in what you are saying by using language which is precise instead of vague. This makes your arguments more persuasive. For instance, 'The court will decide in my client's favour . . .' is better than 'I think maybe the court will decide in my client's favour . . .' The former uses more objective language and is more categorical.

If you don't have your client's authority to confirm agreement to what is being proposed by your opponent then consider agreeing subject to your client's approval:

'Subject to taking further instructions from my client I provisionally accept your offer.'

'Subject to receiving confirmation from my client that she would be agreeable to that, your offer is accepted.'

Alternatively you can postpone your reply until you've taken further instructions from your client:

'I will put that offer to my client . . .'

Exchanging information and responding to your opponent

When negotiating, keep in mind the least you are prepared to accept (your 'bottom line') as well as the best likely outcome.

This exchange of information and views typically involves comparatives and superlatives. Comparatives typically end in 'er', such as 'bigger, or 'ier' for adjectives ending in 'y', such as 'easier'. Superlatives typically end in 'est', such as 'biggest or 'iest' for adjectives ending in 'y', such as 'easiest' and are used with the article 'the'. For long adjectives 'more' is used with the adjective. For example, 'more successful'; 'more helpful proposal'.

Some comparatives and superlatives have irregular form:

little	less	least
bad	worse	worst
good	better	best

Here are some typical examples:

'Fifty thousand pounds is the least we could accept.'

'That is the most we can offer.'

'That is the least which we would accept.'

'I will need more time to take instructions from my client on your offer.'

'Another hour is the longest we will agree to wait for you to decide whether to accept our offer.'

'The offer would need to be a lot more than that before we would seriously consider it.'

'If you were to offer a little more we could reach agreement.'

'The easiest way to settle this claim is to pay him what he is asking for.'

Checking understanding

Ensure that you fully and correctly understand exactly what your opponent is proposing.

'If I understand you correctly, you are proposing that my client accepts delivery of the consignment of furniture at a reduced price of £145,000 including delivery.'

'Let me check that I understand you correctly. What you are saying is that your client will accept £145,000 inclusive of delivery costs if my client agrees to accept the consignment.'

Making qualified responses

Situations often arise where you do not want to reject outright what your opponent is proposing, but equally you may not want to fully agree. Instead you may want to try to agree subject to your opponent agreeing to something else in return, so consider using 'Yes, but . . .', signalling that a negative aspect of your answer is forthcoming.

Here are some further examples:

'We could move on the price, but only if you could move on the delivery time.'

'If my client offered to pay a further £5,000, would your client be prepared to deliver the goods a week earlier?'

Words known as discourse markers or linking words can be used to indicate additional information when making a qualified response. 'However' is commonly used in this way. For instance,

'My client would be prepared to leave the company, however, he would require a good reference.'

Exercise 8.3

Complete the following statements by selecting the most appropriate word(s) from the box section below and inserting them in the blank spaces.

however	in addition	further	anyway	as well
also	furthermore	similarly	for instance	preferably
alternatively	instead	for instance	nevertheless	

1. My client would accept the quantity of carpets your client proposes to supply. _______ that would have to be on condition that the total price is reduced by £100,000.
2. I can only accept that offer for compensation for the pain and suffering resulting from your client's negligence if, _______ , an amount of £50,000 is paid for loss of earnings.

Similarly, conjunctions can be used to indicate that you are expressing some reservation or condition to what is being proposed. For instance:

'We will purchase the entire consignment *as long as* you deliver free of charge within seven days.'

The list below contains more conjunctions which can be used in this way.

although	if	until	as soon as
as long as	in order that	even if	just as soon as
provided	on condition (that)	unless	

Conjunctions or 'linkers' can also be useful when presenting arguments. For example:

'The offer is reasonable *because of/due to/owing to/as a result of . . .*'

Making conditional or hypothetical offers and concessions

Sometimes you will want to suggest possible solutions without committing your client to a binding agreement. In this way you can discuss and investigate creative options.

> 'If my client were to offer . . . would your client . . .'
>
> 'If you agree to keep the goods which have been delivered we will give you a ten per cent discount on the price.'
>
> 'We will give you a ten per cent discount on the price if you agree to keep the goods which have been delivered.'

Note from the last two examples how you can usually change the order of the clauses with such conditional sentences.

Conditional sentences are regularly used when negotiating, to indicate that you are not agreeing to something unreservedly. For example:

> 'If you give me six months salary I will settle.'
>
> 'If you settle today I will accept £35,000.'
>
> 'I will settle today only if you pay £35,000.'

Similar use can be made of conditional sentences by the other party:

> 'If my client offered you six months salary would you accept?'
>
> 'If we agreed to you keeping the company car and offered you £35,000 would you accept?'

'Should', 'would', 'could', 'may' and 'might' are commonly used with such offers. Sometimes the passive structure is used to convey the impression that the offer is hypothetical or that it is merely a suggestion: 'If an offer of £20,000 were to be made, would your client accept it?'

Legal English also uses conjunctions in conditional sentences, such as:

> until although provided that unless in order that on condition that

For example:

> We wouldn't make an offer *unless* there was an assurance that this would be kept secret.

Exercise 8.4

Complete the following conditional sentences.

1. If you were to offer a little more we ________ reach agreement.
2. We ________ definitely move on the price if you could move on the delivery time.
3. If my client agreed to a later delivery ________ your client agree to a discount?

Such questions can help to resolve deadlock in negotiation. Deadlock is a situation where one party refuses to increase its offer to meet the lowest offer which the other party would accept (sometimes referred to as the 'bottom line'). Typical phrases which signal that deadlock is being reached include:

> 'This is the lowest we are prepared to go to.'
>
> 'This is our final offer.'

Deadlock can sometimes be overcome by moving on to another topic and returning later to the issue on which the parties are deadlocked. Expressions which can assist in doing this include 'Why don't we move on to . . .' or 'Let's step away for a moment from . . .' (e.g. considering liability). 'Turning to the issue of . . . (e.g. damages), my client is prepared to offer . . .'

CONCLUDING STAGE

At the conclusion of successful negotiation it is important to confirm exactly what terms have been agreed. Remember that discourse markers and conjunctions can be used to indicate additional information. The following list contains further examples of such words which can be used to clarify and confirm what is being proposed or agreed.

Firstly	to begin with	finally	as a result
therefore	consequently	with reference to	regarding
as regards	lastly	last of all	in summary
to summarise	in conclusion	to conclude	to sum up

For instance:

'Okay, *to summarise*, we *firstly* agreed that Miss Bashorun will be paid the sum of £45,000 within fourteen days.'

Exercise 8.5

Now complete the following by selecting the appropriate words from the table above and inserting them in the blank spaces (more than one choice may be possible).

1. ____________________, my client will deliver the consignment of television sets to Beresford Limited. After that, all other terms of the contract will be complied with.
2. ____________________, the defendant will make payment of the agreed amount once all the other terms of the contract have been complied with.

WITHOUT PREJUDICE NEGOTIATION

If you negotiate on a 'without prejudice' basis, then what you discuss cannot be revealed later in court to assist the court in reaching a decision.

NEGOTIATING STYLES AND STRATEGIES

Consider the following two statements:

'I don't understand how you can possibly say that.'

'I didn't know that. Please explain why you say that.'

Both statements basically say the same thing. However, they differ in manner and attitude. The second one is more conciliatory in tone and facilitates further dialogue. In contrast, the first one is rather confrontational.

Your attitude can therefore encourage or hinder progress during negotiation. By ending with a positive tone instead of a negative one you can assist the successful progress of the negotiation.

Exercise 8.6

Rewrite the following sentences so that the positive aspect (e.g. your client being prepared to accept the amount being offered in the first example) comes at the end of the statement. The first few words of each answer are provided for you. Be careful to use the correct verb tense.

1. My client would accept the amount being offered but only if payment is made within two weeks.

   If you agreed to ______________________________

2. We would pay a further £5,000 if you were to make delivery within five days.

   If you ______________________________

3. The workforce will work extra hours to complete the order if management agrees to a further day's holiday.

   If management ______________________________

4. The firm will employ a further twenty lawyers if Global Enterprises awards the firm with the contract to provide legal services to it.

   If ______________________________

Words which can be used to express your agreement, disagreement or attitude include:

obviously	of course	clearly	preferably	sorry
(un)fortunately	regrettably	frankly	honestly	

For example:

'*Frankly* we are not interested in such an unrealistic offer' (displaying a strong point of view).

'*Sorry*, but we have no interest in accepting such an unrealistic offer.'

There are therefore different styles or strategies of negotiation. Your own style of negotiating will to some extent depend on your personality. You may for instance take a co-operative, conciliatory or competitive approach when negotiating. A competitive approach uses more 'aggressive' vocabulary, whereas a co-operative or conciliatory approach uses more 'diplomatic' vocabulary. Consider the following expressions:

- 'Your offer is ridiculous'.
- 'I wonder if you could reconsider your offer'.

The first of these expressions uses aggressive vocabulary, whereas the second uses conciliatory or diplomatic vocabulary.

Exercise 8.7

Indicate which phrase in each of the following pairs is the diplomatic form of expression and which is the aggressive form. (Write the letter 'D' alongside the diplomatic form and 'A' alongside the aggressive form.)

1. If payment is not received immediately, we will issue legal proceedings without delay. ____
2. We would prefer to reach an early settlement in order to avoid a tribunal hearing. ____
3. We demand that our client is provided with a reference. ____
4. We respectfully request a reference. ____

Exercise 8.8

Place each of the following expressions into either the left-hand or right-hand column of the table depending on whether it describes conciliatory or confrontational conduct when negotiating (the list of terms at the end of this chapter may assist you). The first one is done for you.

being argumentative
behaving aggressively
being condescending
being offensive
negotiating competitively
negotiating collaboratively
being deliberately obstructive
negotiating in bad faith
using conciliatory language
using adversarial language

Conciliatory	Confrontational
	being argumentative

RECORDING THE AGREEMENT

It is important to record details accurately of what has been agreed. If settlement has been reached before legal proceedings have been commenced in court then the court's approval or 'sanction' is unlikely to be necessary. The settlement agreement can then be recorded in correspondence between the parties or their lawyers (e.g. see the letter in Chapter 3 p. 64 concerning Nicholas Tiessen's case).

If a court is involved in the matter, however, then a court order may have to be prepared. This sets out the terms of settlement. Such an order is sometimes referred to as a consent order (e.g., see the order in Chapter 5 p. 125). Regardless of how the agreement is recorded, the terms of settlement should be clear, sufficiently detailed and workable.

Good practice tips

To get a favourable outcome for your client remember to:

- familiarise yourself with the history and details of the case and the governing law;
- identify the issues or topics to be negotiated and the order in which you wish to negotiate them (draft an agenda);
- evaluate strengths and weaknesses of your case;
- consider what your client wants to achieve, his priorities, concerns and objectives;
- decide on your opening position (what your opening offer will be);
- decide on your bottom line on each issue;
- determine what is the best result you can reasonably expect (the best case scenario);
- know what the least is that your client will accept;
- be honest – don't invent facts.

Exercise 8.9

Negotiation

You can develop your negotiation skills with practice. Imagine that your client Kadir Salleh has been offered a position with Marko Enterprises Limited ('Marko') as a sales director. Marko is a multi-national manufacturer of personal computers. Kadir has asked you to negotiate terms of employment on his behalf with this company. He has provided you with the following instructions:

He would accept an annual salary of £45,000 but would like you to try to negotiate a salary of £60,000 for him. He believes that, since he has more experience than others in the company earning £45,000, he deserves more. He would also like 30 days annual holiday, though he tells you that Marko Enterprises Limited usually only provides 20 days holiday per year. Since, however, he will be working some weekends he feels he should be entitled to more than 20 days. He also tells you confidentially that he only plans to work with Marko for about two years, although he doesn't want Marko to know that. But he does want you to obtain Marko's agreement to him being able to work for any other computer manufacturer as soon as he leaves Marko's employment. He has mentioned, though, that Marko usually impose a restriction (known as a 'restrictive covenant') in their contracts of employment. In particular, they usually have a term in their contracts prohibiting a departing employee from working for a competitor for a year after leaving Marko. Kadir would, if necessary, agree to such a restriction for 6 months. In his view the company should agree to that since he has very good contacts in the industry and is therefore able to bring in a lot of business for Marko.

Task 1
Write down what your opening offer is going to be regarding:

- salary;
- holiday entitlement;
- the duration of the restrictive covenant.

Task 2
Taking account of what you have learnt in this chapter about how to make offers, write out exactly what you will say to Marko's representative when making your opening offer →

regarding the above issues. (As well as indicating what you are proposing, remember to provide a reason as to why Marko should accept your offer.)

Task 3
Still taking account of what you have learnt in this chapter, write out how you would respond (i.e. what you will say) if Marko's representative:

- offers Kadir a salary of £40,000 per annum;
- offers Kadir a salary of £45,000 per annum;
- offers Kadir 15 days annual holiday.

Task 4 (Group exercise)
If you are working in a group, now role-play the negotiation. One or two members of the group should play the role(s) of Marko's representative(s) and another one or two from the group should play the role(s) of Kadir's representative in the negotiation. Try to reach an amicable settlement. Take notes of any terms you agree with your opponent(s). Compare these notes with your opponent(s) notes when you have completed the negotiation. Check that you have both accurately recorded the same details of what has been agreed!

Finally, taking account of the good practice tips for negotiation provided earlier in this chapter, discuss constructively with each other your thoughts and opinions on both your own and your opponent's negotiating performance. Consider for instance: what were your strongest arguments? What would you have done differently?

The following is a list provides a list of words and expressions commonly used in negotiation. By learning them you will become more familiar with the language of negotiation and their meanings.

Vocabulary

adjudication: settlement terms being determined by a court

agenda: a list which itemises the issues in dispute and the order in which they will be negotiated

bargaining zone: the range of difference or 'space' between the bottom lines (see below) of the parties

BATNA: best alternative to a negotiated agreement

bottom line: terms (on price, etc.) below which a party is not prepared to reach agreement (deadlock is reached at this point if the other party does not concede further)

bridging solution: an agreement which meets everyone's requirements without compromise (a rare outcome)

brinkmanship: practice of raising another issue just at or close to final agreement being reached between the parties, the idea being that the other party will feel pressured into agreeing to the new proposal on the brink of settlement so as to prevent the agreement falling through

collaborative negotiation strategy: an approach taken by a negotiator seeking to achieve a fair settlement which meets the interests and needs of all parties (this approach is sometimes taken when the parties wish to preserve a working business relationship)

competitive negotiation: negotiation in which each party seeks to 'win' at the expense of the other party (sometimes also referred to as 'zero sum' negotiation)

competitive negotiation strategy: approaching negotiation as a game to be won or lost (sometimes referred to as the a 'zero sum' game), focusing on one's own position rather than taking account of the interests of all parties and considering settlement options which could be mutually beneficial (this strategy is also sometimes termed a positional or distributive strategy)

conditional agreement: agreement subject to the other matters under negotiation also being agreed (or subject to confirmation from your client)

conditional offer: making an offer subject to receiving something in return

co-operative negotiation: negotiation where the parties collectively try to compromise with each other in order to reach agreement

co-operative negotiation strategy: approach towards negotiation taken by a negotiator seeking to find common ground between the parties (sometimes also called a compromising or integrative strategy)

court door negotiation: negotiation conducted just before a court hearing or trial is about to start

deadlock: a situation where the parties cannot progress the negotiation due to neither party being prepared to make a concession which could facilitate an agreement

deal-breaker: an item or matter which a party insists must be agreed to if a settlement is to be reached and on which the other party will not agree

disclosure: process of revealing the existence of evidence (often documents in the possession of a party)

dispute resolution negotiation: negotiation over a claim (such as for compensation)

explicit/agreed agenda: an agenda (see above) which has been agreed between the parties as to content

face-to-face negotiation: negotiation in person (rather than by correspondence, etc.)

final offer: the last offer a party is prepared to make in an effort to agree settlement

forum: the means by which the negotiation is conducted (e.g. by mail, telephone or in person)

full and final settlement: agreement which takes account of and exhausts all claims which the parties may have against each other concerning that particular matter

going below the line: taking account of the parties' underlying concerns and issues to ascertain what the real interests of the parties are, which can assist in reaching an agreement that meets those needs

implicit agenda: an agenda (see above) which one party wants to use in the course of negotiation

information exchange: both parties providing further details of their cases

log-rolling solution: where a party makes a concession on an issue of relatively minor importance to it in return for receiving a concession from another party on something more important (also sometimes referred to as 'trading concessions' or 'trading-off items')

multiple issue negotiation: negotiation involving more than one issue

multiple party negotiation: negotiation involving more than two parties

mutual gain/mutual benefit: a proposal or agreement which addresses the requirements of all parties

opening position/statement: setting out a party's expectations and standpoint in a negotiation

principled negotiation strategy: another term for collaborative negotiation strategy (see above)

problem-solving strategy: another term for collaborative negotiation strategy (see above)

provisional offer: agreeing conditionally to something subject to all other items also being agreed

reality check: making a party (often a client) take a realistic view of his case by setting out to them the reality of the situation (typically with regard to prospects of success at trial and likely value)

resistance point: point below which a party will receive less by negotiating than can be obtained by pursuing an alternative course of action (such as court action)

roadblocks: issues which are a barrier to a settlement being reached (such as emotional issues preventing one party from agreeing to anything the other party suggests)

settlement agreement: details of the agreement negotiated and agreed by the parties (usually recorded in writing)

settlement range/zone: the common ground in which all parties are prepared to reach a settlement. For example, if one party is prepared to offer between £5,000 to £6,500 to settle a claim and the other party is prepared to accept between £6,000 and £7,500 then the settlement range/zone is £6,000 to £6,500. (It is more difficult to negotiate an agreement when the settlement zone is narrow)

splitting the difference: reaching agreement by 'meeting halfway' between what each party is prepared to offer

subject to contract: an agreement which will not be legally binding until a written contract setting out those terms has been signed by the parties

subsidiary/peripheral issues: less important issues in a negotiation

take it or leave it offer: an offer implying that if it is not accepted it will not be improved upon (if the offeree rejects it, that will be the end of the negotiation)

target point: point in the settlement range/zone at which one party aims to reach agreement (e.g. the claimant may have a target point of £6,500 on the settlement range/zone mentioned above)

transactional/deal-making negotiation: negotiation over business terms (e.g. concerning a mergers and acquisition agreement

unconditional agreement: all items being negotiated have been conclusively agreed upon

without prejudice: means that what is said and written during the negotiation cannot be referred to subsequently in court

SUMMARY

- Remember it is not only what you say but how you say it – use an appropriate tone and volume when speaking and maintain reasonable eye contact.
- Avoid being hesitant in manner or speech – maintain a conversational tone.
- Stay calm and avoid being rude, insulting or overly aggressive – skilful lawyers argue persuasively without being argumentative (remember you can be competitive and assertive without being rude). Politeness conveys authority – 'politeness is powerful'.
- Pronounce your words carefully and at an appropriate pace.
- 'Open' the negotiation by asking for more than you are actually prepared to settle for ('open high') but keep your proposals plausible.
- Only start off by offering your bottom line for settlement if that is in keeping with the tradition or culture in which you are negotiating or your bargaining position is a very strong one.
- Keep in mind professional conduct:
  - don't agree to something without having your client's authority to do so;
  - be honest with the other party and don't mislead;
  - respect client confidentiality (you shouldn't disclose information which your client doesn't wish you to reveal during a negotiation).

Visit **www.mylawchamber.co.uk/mckay** to access further resources for practising legal language skills including additional exercises, listening activities and live weblinks for online research.

Chapter 9

Advocacy

Learning objectives

This chapter will help you to:

- acquire vocabulary and grammar for questioning witnesses and presenting a case in court;
- develop questioning techniques and use of persuasive language;
- conduct witness questioning and make submissions to court.

INTRODUCTION

Anyone training or practising as a lawyer must be a competent advocate. Effective advocacy involves presenting information clearly and presenting arguments persuasively in support of a client's case. Good advocacy therefore involves language skills, a good range of vocabulary and a sound grasp of grammar. Clear pronunciation is also important. Remember that you are speaking in public on behalf of someone else. The purpose of advocacy is to persuade a court to accept your arguments and your client's version of events. This applies to both civil proceedings (such as breach of contract claims, etc.) and criminal proceedings (where criminal charges are being brought against someone in court).

COMMENCEMENT

An advocate firstly introduces himself to the court and indicates what the case is about. For example:

> 'Your Honour, my name is Joel Aslam of Carter and Company and I represent the claimant, Mr Harold Lewis. My friend (if a solicitor)/learned friend (if a barrister), Mr John Manders of Francesco Chambers, represents the defendant. This is a breach of contract case …'

TRIAL ADVOCACY

Examination-in-chief

A trial lawyer (advocate) obtains evidence from his or her own witnesses in court by examination-in-chief. They introduce a witness (termed 'calling the witness') with words such as, 'Your Honour, I call first Mrs (name of witness)' or for subsequent witnesses, 'Your Honour, I now call (name of witness)'.

Remember that as the lawyer you cannot give evidence. That is the role of the witness. The advocate's job is to get each witness to provide his/her evidence in support of the client's case. This is done by asking each witness a series of questions to develop your client's case by letting the witness explain in his/her own words.

These questions should be non-leading questions as opposed to leading questions (unless the evidence is not in dispute or the witness is 'hostile'). Unlike leading questions, a non-leading question does not suggest the answer. They are therefore open questions (see Chapter 7 for further details of open questions). Non-leading questions usually start with:

- question words such as: 'who', 'what', 'where', 'when', 'why', 'how';
- words or phrases such as: 'please explain', 'describe', 'tell (the court about ...)'.

For example:

What happened next?

Who was there?

Where were you going?

Was the restaurant busy?

What did you see?

Please explain how that happened.

The relative pronoun or phrase is combined with a verb (such as 'did', 'has' or 'was') to request information. The question is created by inverting the subject and auxiliary verb. Note, however, that when the question word is the subject then the auxiliary 'do' should not be used, e.g. 'Who said that?' ('Do' is used when the question word is the object of the sentence, e.g. 'Who *did* you see?')

Grammar for forming questions

Questions can be formed by altering the order of the subject and verb. The present simple and past simple tenses are typically used when questioning a witness. Words such as 'see', 'saw', 'lie', 'lied' are introduced to form questions and negative statements. Note how 'do', 'does', 'don't' and 'doesn't' are used in the present simple and 'did', 'didn't' in the past simple. For example:

Do you like tennis?

Did they play tennis?

He doesn't ski.

He didn't ski that day.

Correct use of grammar is important to distinguish between questions and statements. To form a question, it's common in English to reverse the usual order of the subject and verb. For instance:

Are you lying? Is Jack violent?

Was there anyone else in the vehicle? Were you present when this happened?

Had you been drinking? Did you drink that evening?

Do you ski? Where do you ski?

One fact at a time

Use a separate question for each fact you want the witness to address. You will find this easier if you deal with the evidence chronologically (in date order). Use straightforward and unemotional language (so no jokes or personal remarks). Imagine for instance that you want to get the witness to provide the following evidence:

> At 6 p.m. on Saturday 23 July 2011 John was taking Jenny in his car to Wilbow's restaurant for dinner.

Using one question for each fact, the evidence can be obtained effectively by asking John the following questions:

> ***Advocate:*** 'What were you doing at 6 p.m. on Saturday 23 July 2011?'
>
> ***John:*** 'I was travelling to Wilbow's restaurant.'
>
> ***Advocate:*** 'How did you get there?'
>
> ***John:*** 'In my car.'

Piggy-back questions

This is a questioning technique of including information just obtained from the witness in the next question. For instance, John has just confirmed that he was travelling to Wilbow's restaurant in his car. So, continuing the above examination-in-chief, you can get more information by piggy-back questions such as:

> ***Advocate:*** 'Was anyone else in the car with you or were you alone?'
>
> ***John:*** 'Someone else was with me.'
>
> ***Advocate:*** 'You say someone was with you in your car. Who was with you?'
>
> ***John:*** 'Jenny.'

Note how such 'piggy-back' questioning enables you to:

- keep control of what the witness says;
- provide a clear structure for your questions which is easy for the witness to follow;
- convey a thorough and memorable impression or 'picture' to the court of the evidence being provided.

You can then continue with short, non-leading questions to get the further information you require:

> ***Advocate:*** 'Why were you going there?'
>
> ***John:*** 'For dinner with Jenny.'

Keep your questions open but focused on what information you are aiming to get the witness to provide. Open questions provide the witness with the opportunity to describe what happened or some other evidence in their own words, e.g. 'What happened as you entered the room?' Closed questions ask the witness to provide a specific fact, e.g. 'Who was driving the car?' or 'What colour was the car?' (See Chapter 7 for further details of closed questions.)

If you want to refer to evidence already provided orally or in documents such as witness statements (see Chapter 5 for court documents), refer to the document, page number and paragraph number. For example:

> 'Mrs Vilmart states in paragraph five of page one of her witness statement that the red car was being driven very fast. What do you say about that?'

By asking short, simple questions you will avoid multiple (compound) questions. These are questions which ask more than one question or address more than one issue at a time. They can lead to misunderstanding. For instance, 'Did you see Edward Archer, what was he doing and what time was this?' This is really three questions and the witness will be unsure which part of the question to answer. Break the question down into separate questions, one fact at a time.

Cross-examination

Once a witness has provided his or her examination-in-chief, the advocate for the other party can then cross-examine the witness. It is a lawyer's professional duty to put his or her client's case and to challenge the other party's case when cross-examining. This means putting your client's version of events to the witness. A witness's reliability or credibility can also be attacked and undermined in cross-examination. For instance, by showing that the witness is uncertain about what he actually saw, or is an unreliable witness because of her character (e.g. the witness has a criminal conviction), or that he is biased (e.g. the witness has a personal interest in the outcome of the proceedings).

Ask leading questions in cross-examination. A leading question is one which suggests or implies the answer. They usually prompt a short answer 'yes' or 'no' type of answer. For instance:

> 'You saw your colleague Henry Hodson steal the money, didn't you, Mrs Smith?'

Leading questions often begin with words such as 'did', 'was' and 'were'.

Notice how leading questions are assertive questions and in effect worded like statements. Tell, don't ask. So rather than say, 'Is it right to say that the man was angry,' frame the question as,

> 'The man was angry, wasn't he?'

Similarly, to put it to a witness that your client, Mr Mendoza, did not assault Mr Anders, the question should be phrased as an assertive question. So rather than 'Did Mr Mendoza assault Mr Anders?' the question is better phrased by leading the witness. For example, 'Mr Mendoza didn't assault Mr Anders, did he?' Alternatively the question 'tag' can be placed at the beginning of the sentence, e.g.

> 'Isn't it correct to say that Mr Mendoza didn't assault Mr Anders?'

Avoid the 'w' questions such as 'who', 'what' and 'where' used in examination-in-chief. Instead, use questions which result in the specific answers you want from the witness. To help you do this, start your questions with words such as 'did', 'was' and 'were'.

Also, remember that a question sentence can be ended with a preposition: 'Where was the defendant coming from?' By raising the tone of your voice towards the end of a question you can also 'signal' a leading question, e.g.

> 'You saw the Ford collide with the Honda, *didn't you*?'

So as you can see, by using closed questions you can control the witness and get the answer you want. Use short questions, addressing one point at a time. This will also help you to avoid asking compound (multiple) questions (referred to above).

As with examination-in-chief, piggy-back questions can also be used effectively for clarifying and obtaining more detailed evidence. So for instance:

> 'You say that the vehicle that was ahead of you was driving fast. How fast was it travelling?'
>
> 'So you say you thought about signing the contract to buy the company. Did you in fact sign it?'

Remember to listen carefully to the answer to each question. Do not be so focused on thinking of or finding the next question from your notes that you do not listen attentively to the witness's answer to your last question. Otherwise you are likely to miss something important that the witness says which you should pursue further (such as by piggy-back questioning – see above).

Laying a foundation for challenging a witness

You can put your client's case and challenge a witness more effectively by laying a foundation before challenging the witness. This means leading up to the challenging question with questions which the witness is unlikely to dispute. Consider the following question:

> 'Mr Kammer, you didn't see if the car driver was driving dangerously when his car struck Miss Peters, did you?'

Now consider the following:

> 'You're good friends with Miss Peters, aren't you, Mr Kammer?'
>
> 'You were talking to her when the car struck her, weren't you?'
>
> 'So you weren't paying attention to what was happening on the road, were you?'
>
> 'You want to help your friend Miss Peters with her claim for the injuries she received, don't you?'
>
> 'Mr Kammer, I suggest you have simply assumed that the car driver was driving dangerously and that you didn't actually see how he was driving, isn't that correct?'

The witness may still deny the allegation in the final question that he didn't see the driver driving dangerously. Your suggestion, that he didn't see how the driver was driving, is, however, more likely to influence the judge when the foundation is first laid in this way. (Practice exercises in cross-examining are available at the end of this chapter and in the corresponding website materials for this chapter.)

Finally, don't ask one question too many. Consider the following example:

> ***Question:*** 'Did you see my client bite off Mr Tyrell's left ear?'
>
> ***Answer:*** 'No.'

The advocate has presented the evidence to the court which is required in support of his client's case and he should now sit down. Note, however, how he continues and asks one question too many:

> ***Question:*** 'So why have you told this court my client bit off Mr Tyrell's left ear when you did not see my client do that?'
>
> ***Answer:*** 'Because I saw him spit it out!'

Good practice tips

- Don't quarrel with the witness – don't cross-examine crossly!
- Avoid the phrase commonly used in films, 'I put it to you' – it adds nothing and provides the witness with advance warning that you are about to say something he should get ready to deny.
- First, think of the answer you want to obtain then phrase your question to get that answer (as a general rule, don't ask a question in cross-examination that you don't already know the answer to).

Re-examination

When re-examining a witness you are getting the witness to give further details, explanation or clarification of their earlier answers in cross-examination. So if, for instance, you think a witness did not completely answer a question in cross-examination, re-examination provides an opportunity for clarification. Leading questions are generally not permitted. You can, however, preface your question with a phrase such as: 'In cross-examination you said...' or 'You said in cross-examination...' or 'You told the court you were watching the man in the black coat because he was shouting. How long did you watch him for?' For example:

> 'You told the court that you watched the defendant standing outside the jeweller's shop looking suspicious. How long were you watching him for?'

Making a closing speech

The closing speech provides the opportunity to comment and present arguments to persuade the court to find in favour of your client. This is sometimes referred to as 'making final submissions'. Your role as advocate is to present arguments and to speak on behalf of your client, not to state your personal opinions. So avoid words such as 'I believe' or 'I think'. Instead use words and phrases such as:

> 'In my submission...'
>
> 'I suggest that...'

'It is my submission that...'

'I submit that...'

'I (respectfully) contend that...'

'I invite you/the court to accept that...'

Keep your statements short and use plain English. Say only what is needed – then sit down.

Ending your case

When you have finished making your case, you can end with a simple phrase such as:

'That is the case for the (claimant/defendant), Your Honour.'

APPLICATION ADVOCACY: MAKING AN APPLICATION TO COURT

Introduction

It is standard practice when applying to court for any order or decision to introduce yourself, your opponent and then to say what the application is for. For example:

'This is an application on behalf of the claimant for summary judgment, Your Honour'

or

'Your Honour, this is an application for summary judgment'.

Explain the background to the case and what it is you are applying for (i.e. why you are applying to the court, and what court order you want the judge to provide). Give clear arguments and reasons as to why the judge should provide that order.

For practice, refer to the application notice for summary judgment in Chapter 5 and try making that application orally. (Making an application in court and closing speech also involve building on the skills involved in making a presentation, for which see Chapter 6.)

Good practice tips

- Introduce yourself and the person acting for the other party (your opponent).
- State what your application is about.
- Briefly indicate the background to the case (i.e. what the case is about).
- Explain why you are making your application.
- Explain the effect on your client if your application is refused.
- Address potential objections to your application.
- Conclude.

A CIVIL CASE: CHOOSING THE CORRECT PART OF SPEECH

Adjectives, nouns, verbs, prepositions and so on are known as **parts of speech** (or **grammatical classes**). Each has a different function in the structure of an English sentence:

The oil company employed (verb) Jack Rossini as Chief Executive.

Jack Rossini was an employee (noun) of the oil company.

As a result of his injuries in the accident, Alan Johnson is no longer considered employable (adjective).

Exercise 9.1

Choose the most appropriate word or phrase from the table below to complete the following sentences. The words in brackets in each sentence indicate the intended meaning for which you should choose the associated word or phrase from the list below. You therefore need to think about the meaning and the part of speech required in each case. (Note: you will not need to use all of the words given below.)

I refer you to	**denies that**
call	**admits owing to the claimant**
based on the evidence	**summary judgment**
version of events	**established the legal grounds**
is more credible	**that concludes my submission, Your Honour**

Example: I *now call* [introduce witness] Mrs Harper.

1. My client ____________ [does not admit] he is liable for breach of contract.
2. The evidence of the independent witness supports the claimant's ____________ [view of what happened].
3. Your Honour, I submit that the claimant has ____________ [met the legal test] for granting this application for an injunction.
4. I submit, Your Honour, that, ____________ [on the basis of what the court has seen and heard], liability has been established in this case.
5. Your Honour, ____________ [please look at] exhibit 2, the letter dated 14th October 2011.
6. In that letter, Your Honour, you will see that the defendant ____________ [confirms the debt] the sum of £10,000.
7. Your Honour, this application is for ____________ [an order for immediate judgment without a full trial] against the defendant.
8. Your Honour, I contend that Mrs Harper's evidence ____________ [is more believable] than that of the other witness.

LANGUAGE PRACTICE FOR A CRIMINAL CASE

Words followed by prepositions

Words ending in '-ed' used as past participles are often followed by prepositions (e.g. 'by', 'of', 'for'). For example: 'I'm tired of waiting.'

Exercise 9.2

Put the correct preposition from the list in each space below:

of to with for

Example: accused *of*

1. prosecuted ______
2. charged ______
3. convicted ______
4. acquitted ______

Prepositions are also used in the following phrases:

on bail   on trial (for)   (not) guilty of/innocent of   in mitigation of

Exercise 9.3

Now rewrite these sentences using the appropriate phrases from the list above:

Example: He was put on trial for burglary. = He was *prosecuted for* burglary.

1. She was convicted of blackmail. = She was found ________ blackmail.
2. In mitigation, the barrister explained that his client had stolen the money to feed his sick children. = ________ the charge, the barrister explained that his client had stolen the money to feed his sick children.
3. The footballer was prosecuted for a public order offence. = The footballer was put ________ a public order offence.

Exercise 9.4

Put the appropriate word from the box in each space in the following text. You need to consider both the meaning of the sentence and the part of speech required in each case. (Note: you will not use all the words.)

sentence/sentenced	**acquittal/acquitted**	**bail/bailed**	**convicted/conviction**
charge/charged	**trial/tried**	**mitigate/mitigation**	

Eric Jones, 23, unemployed, was arrested at home and (**1**)________ with firearms offences and fraud. He was not remanded in custody but was released on (**2**) ________ to appear at Kingston Crown Court for the (**3**) ________. At the court he was (**4**) ________ of the firearms charge, but was found guilty of fraud and (**5**) ________ to 2 years in prison, despite his counsel arguing in (**6**) ________ of his client that he had been forced into the crime by his business partners. Mr Jones appealed against the (**7**) ________. The appeal was unsuccessful, but the (**8**) ________ was reduced to 18 months in prison.

ADDRESSING THE COURT: SPEAKING TECHNIQUES

Volume and pace

If your speech is not heard and understood you will not present your case effectively. Worse still, you may be misunderstood and misinterpreted. Speak at a volume appropriate to the surroundings. The volume of your voice when speaking to a friend at home, for instance, will not be the appropriate volume when addressing a large courtroom. Such a venue requires you to project your voice with increased volume to deliver your case clearly over a greater distance than normal. Be careful not to keep your head down when addressing a judge, a jury or a witness. So don't constantly stare at your notes. (Your voice is then projected downwards rather than towards the judge or jury, which can result in them not hearing or understanding you clearly.)

Another common mistake is to speak too fast or too slowly. Nervous advocates and public speakers typically speak too fast (often to get the ordeal of speaking in public over with as fast as possible). Nervous, inexperienced advocates also often combine this with speaking incessantly and without pausing. This results in 'ums' and 'ers', etc., known as 'fillers'. The use of fillers is usually an anxious attempt to subconsciously try to conceal the fact that the advocate is trying to think what to say next. Fillers add nothing to what you are saying and can be very distracting. Try to replace such fillers by pausing and taking a breath of air.

Deliberate pauses can be used to good effect:

- to indicate a change or transition from one topic or point to another;
- to emphasise the point you are making (try this by stopping what you are saying and watch how your listeners suddenly look up from their notes to see why you've suddenly stopped);
- to give the listener time to consider, understand and take note of what you are saying. By continuously speaking rapidly the listener is likely to miss some of what you are saying, potentially a vital part of your argument or application.
- to simply give you a chance to draw breath.

Skilful advocates vary their pace of speech, for instance increasing their pace to emphasise an important point and increase the persuasiveness of what they are saying. Altering the pace and volume of your voice can also help to maintain the listener's attention.

Body language

Advocacy also involves certain inter-personal skills, including non-verbal communication (NVC) or 'body language'. Much advocacy in court is conducted standing up. Your posture and general appearance are therefore important. Most people are influenced to some extent by appearance. Avoid distracting mannerisms or gestures such as playing with your hair, twirling a pen, using hand gestures or putting your hands in your pockets. Such gestures can detract from what you are saying by distracting the listener's attention. If you tend to 'fidget' in this way, try putting your hands behind your back as you speak or gently grip your notes or a lectern.

Maintain regular eye contact with your audience. This does not mean 'staring out' the person you are addressing. Keep in mind, however, that within Western culture avoiding eye contact generally suggests lack of sincerity or belief in what you are saying. So try to keep regular eye contact, glancing down at your notes occasionally rather than continuously staring at them.

Try to avoid detailed and lengthy notes. They are usually more of a hindrance, resulting in poor eye contact and monotonous delivery. If, for instance, you are making a closing speech, it is usually preferable to rely on a list of no more than one page which sets out the main points you need to make. You can use this as a checklist to ensure that you mention everything which is important. By not reading out a fully prepared speech your presentation will convey a more natural and spontaneous impression. This will also make your presentation more flexible to deal with interruptions or unexpected questions (such as from the judge).

Also, staring at notes while the witness is answering a question you have asked may result in you missing any facial expressions or mannerisms the witness displays which may indicate or suggest evasiveness or lack of honesty. If you'd been watching the witness, you might have 'picked up' on such behaviour which would potentially have alerted you to pursuing a point further.

Alter the rhythm and intonation of your voice to maintain the listeners' interest and place emphasis on important points.

Good practice tips

- Speak clearly and with sufficient volume.
- Modulate the tone, pace and pitch of your voice to maintain the judge's interest.
- Use the correct mode of address to the judge, i.e. 'Your Honour', 'Your Lordship', etc. (see below for correct modes of address).
- Adopt a suitable posture (for instance do not slouch or put your hands in your pockets).
- Use appropriately formal language (neither pompous nor too colloquial).
- Demonstrate courtesy, a professional manner and ensure a smart appearance (do not make personal comments for instance about the opposing advocate).
- Avoid distracting mannerisms (such as hand or arm movements).
- Maintain reasonable eye contact with the judge.
- Avoid over-reliance on notes.

Modes of address

The correct mode of address to a circuit judge and a judge in the County Court is 'Your Honour'. Here there is no difference in expression between using the vocative case (i.e. addressing the judge as if by name) and the accusative case (i.e. instead of 'you').

Higher value cases are heard in the High Court, where a judge should be referred to as 'My Lord/Lady' or 'Your Lordship/Ladyship'. Here there is a difference between the vocative and the accusative case. In particular, 'My Lord/Lady' is the equivalent of the judge's name (i.e. the vocative case), whereas 'Your Lordship/

Ladyship' is the equivalent of 'you' (i.e. the accusative case). It is, however, permissible to combine both modes of address in one statement or sentence. For example:

'My Lady, my client has appeared before your ladyship previously.'

In addition, when referring to the judge in the third person the expressions 'His Lordship/Her Ladyship' and 'His Honour/Her Honour' are used. Thus an advocate would say to a witness:

'Please indicate to His Honour using this diagram where you were standing when you witnessed the assault.'

However, the term 'judge' is often used when speaking to a judge of any status in private or in his or her own chambers. District judges in England and Wales and tribunal judges (such as employment tribunal judges, etc.) are addressed as 'sir' or 'madam'.

A barrister addresses or refers to a fellow barrister in court as 'My learned friend' and to a solicitor as 'My friend' (vocative case).

The table below summarises these modes of address:

Audience	**Mode of address**
High Court judge	My Lord/Lady *or* Your Lordship/Ladyship
Members of the jury	Ladies and gentlemen of the jury
Barrister	My learned friend
Solicitor	My friend

NOTE TAKING IN COURT

It is important to take an accurate note of what is said in court. Your notes may later be relied upon as a record of the evidence (such as if there is a subsequent appeal).

- Write only on one side of each page.
- Divide each page with a vertical line about a quarter of the way in from the left edge of the page. You can then write your notes on what is said in evidence on the right side of the line and use the left side for 'reminder' notes and references. For instance, if you want to refer to a specific part of a witness's evidence given in examination-in-chief, you can take a note on the left side of the page (opposite that part of the evidence) of what you want to mention later. This will then be a useful reminder and reference for finding what you are looking for when you need it.
- Note main points briefly and clearly.
- Only write down everything that is said when a witness is answering a question and it is important to record exactly what he says (e.g. for later cross-examination).
- When preparing to examine or cross-examine a witness, take a note of the main points you need to put to them. Use this as a checklist when asking the questions. This ensures that you cover all important points. As a general rule do *not* write out every question in advance of examining the witness.

- You will need to write quickly so use shorthand (a system of writing by shortening words) and abbreviations. For instance, prefixes and suffixes (i.e. word endings) can be easily abbreviated, often by simply using the first letter. A word like 'profession' can be written 'p/fession' and 'confession' as 'c/fession.' Names can be shortened to initials, e.g. 'EP' for Emma Peters. (Do not, however, abbreviate names of individuals in this way in court documents.)

Some further examples of abbreviations typically used in practice include:

acknowledgement	**ackt**	examination-in-chief	**XIC**
affidavit	**afftt**	cross-examination	**XX**
claimant	**cl**	application	**appln**
defendant	**deft** (or **D**)	witness statement	**ws**

Finally, remember that in court the judge will also be taking notes. When you are 'on your feet' in court addressing the court, therefore, keep in mind that the judge needs time to write down important phrases and actual words stated in evidence. Always ensure that the judge has sufficient time to note down the important information you are providing to the court.

Good practice tips

- Prioritise your points by make your strongest points first – this is more persuasive.
- Speak clearly and maintain the listener's interest by varying your tone and pace of speech.
- Maintain reasonable eye contact – this provides a more confident and sincere impression.
- Avoid over-reliance on your notes – this will make your advocacy more spontaneous and interesting.
- Don't speak too quickly and pause when necessary (such as to let the listener take notes or for effect).
- Cases are usually written as '*Hadley* v *Baxendale* (1854)', etc. If it is a civil case the 'v' is pronounced 'and'. If it is a criminal case, however, the 'v' is expressed orally as 'against'. Do not say 'versus' or 'vee'!

ADVOCACY PRACTICE

Your performance and competency in advocacy can be developed and refined with practice.

Exercise 9.5

Look at the court papers in Chapter 5 concerning the motor vehicle accident on 20 October 2011 between Nicholas Tiessen, Matthew Gluck and the Londinium Delivery Company Limited (the witness statement of Jason Garfinkle and the particulars of claim). Imagine that you are Nicholas Tiessen's lawyer. Use the following diagram of the accident to assist you with these exercises.

→

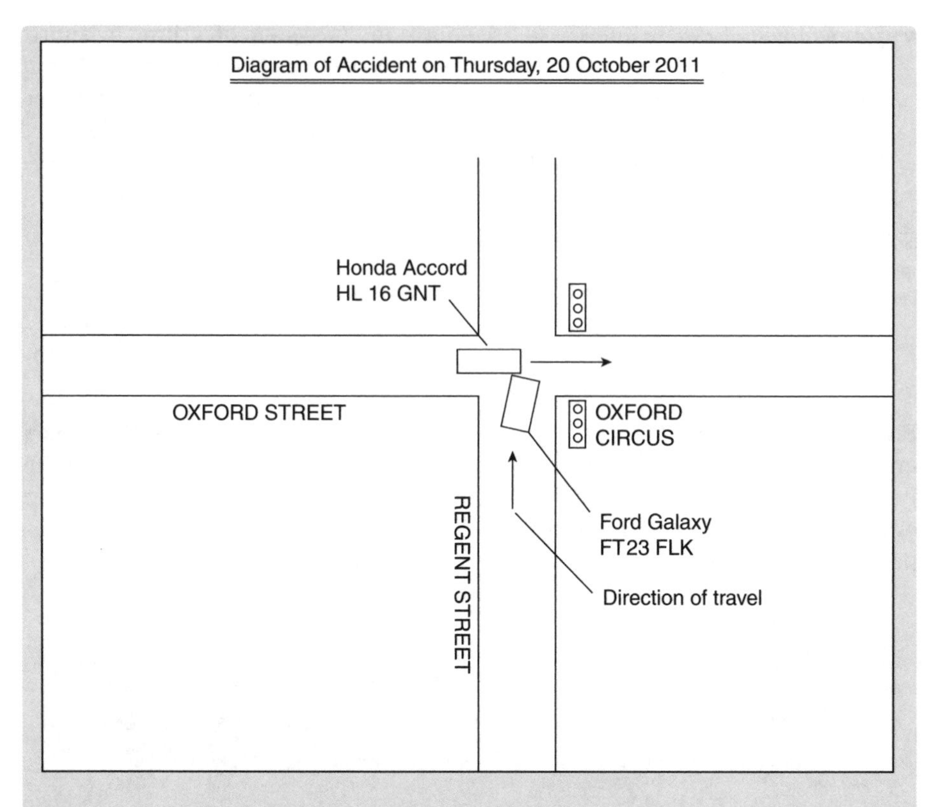

Task 1
Prepare examination-in-chief questions to ask your client Nicholas Tiessen (the claimant) concerning:

- Your client's description of the accident
- Your client's allegations as to why Matthew Gluck was responsible for the accident
- Details of your client's injuries

Task 2
Write out leading questions to ask Matthew Gluck in cross-examination which put your client's case concerning:

- The allegation that Matthew Gluck drove through a red traffic light
- The allegation that Matthew Gluck was using a mobile telephone while driving
- The allegation that Matthew Gluck was arguing with his passenger
- (The following is an example to get you started: 'The accident occurred because you drove through a red traffic light, didn't it, Mr Gluck?')

Task 3
Prepare a short closing speech on behalf of your client, setting out your arguments and referring to the evidence in support of your client's claim.

Task 4
Read out loud the closing speech you prepared in Task 3. Ask a friend or colleague to listen to you and fill in the feedback form below. Alternatively, assess yourself by filling

→

in the feedback form. Keep these criteria and feedback in mind as you further practise and develop your advocacy skills.

ADVOCACY FEEDBACK FORM

Provide feedback by grading the advocate's performance under each of the following criteria on a scale of 1 to 5 (1 = unsatisfactory; 2 = poor; 3 = average; 4 = very good; 5 = outstanding).

- Advocate enunciated words clearly ☐
- Advocate spoke at sufficient volume ☐
- Advocate spoke clearly, avoiding long silences and hesitations ☐
- Advocate used language persuasively and expressed herself/himself clearly ☐
- Advocate avoided distracting mannerisms ☐
- Advocate varied his/her tone and pace in order to retain court's interest ☐

(For further materials and practise in advocacy see the accompanying website materials for this chapter.)

ALTERNATIVE DISPUTE RESOLUTION (ADR)

In addition to court proceedings (litigation), which involves advocacy in court, there are several other recognised ways of resolving legal disputes. Known collectively as alternative dispute resolution, these processes include:

Negotiation

We considered this in Chapter 8. It is a communication process which is voluntary and non-binding until the parties reach agreement between themselves.

Mediation

This involves an independent person (a 'third party') assisting the parties to reach agreement. The independent person, known as a mediator (or 'neutral'), is chosen by the parties. The mediator cannot make binding decisions so cannot impose a decision or settlement like a judge or jury can in court. Mediation is also private and less formal than litigation, which has formal court rules.

Arbitration

A neutral person also intervenes here but with arbitration that person has power to make a decision. Like litigation, therefore, arbitration is an adjudicatory process, but it does not take place within the formal court system. Neither is it usually governed by conventional court rules or procedure.

Exercise 9.6

Vocabulary for ADR

Taking account of the information above concerning ADR, place the following words and terms in the correct column(s) in the grid below to indicate which ADR process(es) they apply to. Some words and expressions may apply to more than one of the ADR processes.

voluntary
highly formal
imposes a binding decision
parties control the process
governed by rules of court
usually private
usually public
can save time and costs
arbitrator
enables more creative solutions than a court
neutral chosen by the parties
judge
mediator
neutral
this process is often specified in contracts
an adjudicatory process

Negotiation	Mediation	Arbitration	Litigation

SUMMARY

- Use non-leading questions in examination-in-chief, with words such as ‘who’, ‘what’, ‘where’ and ‘why’, etc.
- Avoid compound questions – deal with one fact at a time.
- Put your client’s case to the other party’s witnesses in cross-examination by using leading questions.
- Control the witness in cross-examination to get the answer you want, starting questions with words such as ‘did’, ‘was’ and ‘were’, etc. Tell, don’t ask!
- Address the court by speaking clearly, fluently and at an appropriate volume and pace.
- Make appropriate use of notes (don’t be a ‘prisoner to your notes’ by constantly staring down at them).
- Use pauses as appropriate for emphasis.

- Be careful to avoid distracting mannerisms.
- Maintain the judge's interest by varying the tone and pace of your voice.
- When applying to court for a court order, state clearly what your application is for (e.g. an order for a specific sum of money to be paid by the other party to your client) and why your client is entitled to the order.
- When making an application to court or making a closing submission, prioritise your points, making your strongest points first.

Visit **www.mylawchamber.co.uk/mckay** to access further resources for practising legal language skills including additional exercises, listening activities and live weblinks for online research.

Appendix: Legal study and research guide

OVERVIEW

Throughout this book you have been presented with legal and linguistic skills practice in reading, writing, drafting and advocacy among others. Such practice should assist in developing your competence in using legal English both in legal study and in legal practice. The purpose of this section of the book is to provide you with a further appreciation of the *sources* of law and their relative importance.

SOURCES OF UNITED KINGDOM LAW

Legislation

United Kingdom (UK) law is primarily created by legislation. The sources of legislation are:

- European Union legislation;
- legislation enacted by or delegated by the UK Parliament.

The ultimate source of UK law is now legislation created by the European Union. The UK largely lost 'sovereignty' over its law-making process as a result of becoming a signatory to the European Union (EU) on 1 January 1973. In particular, the UK Parliament granted overriding law-making authority to the EU by enacting the European Communities Act 1972. The EU has its own Parliament, with a Secretariat in Luxembourg, and committee meetings usually held in Brussels.

European Union (EU) law

Primary European Union (EU) law consists mainly of treaties. The primary source of EU law is the Treaty on the Functioning of the European Union (TFEU).

Secondary EU law takes the form of:

- *Regulations:* a Regulation is entirely binding upon the UK as a member state of the EU. It is directly applicable in UK law without the need for the UK Parliament to enact the regulation through domestic legislation. Regulations are directly applicable, both against the state (known as being 'directly applicable') and against individuals and companies (known as being 'horizontally applicable'). An example of a Regulation is the free movement of workers within the European Community Regulation.
- *Directives:* a Directive imposes a binding duty on member states to implement the provisions contained within the Directive. A Directive, however, is not directly imposed. Instead, the member state is responsible for determining the form and method by which to implement the provisions of the Directive into

its domestic law. A Directive is said to have 'vertical effect' since it 'directs' a member state to incorporate the Directive into its own law.

- *Decisions:* these are binding and include Decisions from:
  (a) the European Commission (primarily based in Brussels, but also in Luxembourg, consisting of 'commissioners', and which represents the EU as a whole);
  (b) Decisions of the European Court of Justice (ECJ) based in Luxembourg (e.g. decisions in competition law cases).
- *Recommendations and Opinions:* issued by the Commission or the Council (consisting of Ministers from member states and which adopt legislation proposed by the Commission). Such Recommendations and Opinions are persuasive in nature rather than binding. (The ECJ adjudicates on disputes between member states relating to alleged violations of treaties as well as making rulings on the correct interpretation of EU legislation.)

English (UK) law

UK legislation is created by the UK Parliament (Parliament). This legislation is in the form of 'statutes', also known as 'Acts of Parliament'. There is in addition a subordinate source of law which is drawn up under powers specifically delegated by particular statutes (for instance 'statutory instruments', which are a main source of this 'secondary' legislation, often containing the 'small print' of a statute).

There is no written constitution in England (i.e. no definitive document in existence) to provide a specific text to refer to as the source of England's constitution (such as exists in the USA.) (Note that in the USA each state has its own law-making powers and justice system. There is, however, an overriding system of 'Federal law' as well as a more centralised appeal court system consisting of an Appeals Court and ultimately the Supreme Court.)

Case law

There is a general principle in English law (and in the law operating in other parts of the UK) that courts must interpret the wording of legislation literally (i.e. by attributing the literal meaning to each word, regardless of how perverse an interpretation that may lead to). Courts are provided with some assistance in interpreting the meaning and intended purpose of legislation. For example:

- the statute may provide definitions of words or clauses used within the statute;
- the Interpretation Act 1978 (which provides definitions for a range of standard words and phrases commonly used in statutes);
- English dictionaries;
- Hansard (transcripts of the actual debates by members of both Houses of Parliament concerning the particular legislation and its enactment).

English courts are required to interpret legislation in accordance with the Human Rights Act 1998. They are also required to interpret statutes in accordance with EU law. This means that UK courts are now adopting the European approach to interpretation (i.e. by interpreting legislation in light of the intended purpose of the legislation as opposed to purely on a literal interpretation).

There are many instances, however, in which the intended purpose or specific meaning of legislation is in doubt and has to be further interpreted. Similarly, the law often has to be interpreted in relation to specific circumstances. It is the courts which then interpret the law. In doing so, an English court adheres to the doctrine of *binding precedent*. This is a concept whereby a judge is bound to rule consistently with previous decisions by a higher court on similar points of law and circumstances when making a finding in a particular case. It is very unusual, however, for two cases to be exactly the same in terms of facts and circumstances and lawyers will often try, therefore, to *distinguish* a previous court decision which is adverse to their particular case. If a particular case can be distinguished from an earlier case (i.e. a precedent) then the precedent need not bind the court in determining its decision regarding the present case.

AREAS OF LAW

In broad terms, English law can be classified into *civil law* and *criminal law*.

Civil law

Civil law is concerned with the legal rights and obligations of individuals and organisations in relation to each other and includes a wide range of law, including (with examples from previous chapters):

- tort law (e.g. Nicholas Tiessen's car crash case);
- contract law (e.g. the Travelgraph case);
- employment law (e.g. Charles Scoville's case);
- land law;
- company and commercial law.

The remedy in civil law usually involves monetary compensation, i.e. damages and/or some remedy such as an injunction (see Chapter 5 for an example of an injunction order).

Criminal law

Criminal law addresses law enforcement in the sense of the state or police authority prosecuting individuals or organisations for having committed crimes. Crimes can involve violence, for instance grievous bodily harm (GBH) or murder. A crime can also be committed in the course of commercial activity, however, such as fraud. In criminal law a defendant is charged with a crime and prosecuted, as you will have seen in previous parts of this book. The prosecution is brought by a prosecutor. The defendant pleads guilty or not guilty and will then be found guilty or not guilty by the court. The defendant will be convicted if found guilty and acquitted if found not guilty. Rather than damages being awarded, the defendant will then be sentenced by way of punishment (though the court may also make a compensation order, requiring the convicted person to pay some monetary compensation to his victim).

THE COURT SYSTEM

Civil courts

The High Court

The High Court of England and Wales consists of three divisions:

- Chancery (Ch) Division;
- Family Division;
- Queen's Bench (QB) Division.

The Chancery Division hears actions such as bankruptcy, copyright and mortgage cases. The Family Division deals with matrimonial cases, e.g. divorce, etc. The Queen's Bench Division deals with higher value and more complex civil cases (such as tort cases for personal injury worth over £50,000) and breach of contract cases (such as the case of *Travelgraph* v *Matrix Printers* which you considered earlier).

The County Court

There are approximately 250 county courts throughout England and Wales. They generally handle lesser value civil claims (e.g. personal injury cases valued under £50,000 and breach of contract claims up to £15,000).

Tribunals

There are a range of tribunals for various matters such as immigration, rent reviews and employment law cases. The latter are known as Employment Tribunals (you considered an Employment Tribunal case earlier).

Court of Appeal (Civil Division)

Hears appeals from the lower courts, i.e. county courts and High Courts.

The Supreme Court

Ultimate UK appeal court, formerly known as the House of Lords (HL). Appeals to this court are only possible on a point of law.

European Court of Justice

A court or tribunal may refer a case to the European Court of Justice (ECJ) for clarification of any aspect of EU law if necessary in order to deliver its judgment.

Criminal courts

Magistrates' Courts

These generally hear less serious criminal cases.

Crown Courts

Crown Court cases are heard in front of a judge and jury, the judge adjudicating and directing on the law and a jury deciding on the facts of the case. Crown courts also hear appeals from magistrates' courts.

Court of Appeal (Criminal Division)

Hears appeals from Crown courts.

The Supreme Court

Final appeal venue (the appeal must be on a point of law).

FINDING THE LAW

UK statutes are published by Her Majesty's Stationery Office (HMSO) as well as in publications such as *Halsbury's Statutes* (which summarises and explains English law in straightforward English). There are also various series of law reports including the *All England Law Reports* (All ER) and the *Weekly Law Reports* (WLR). (A law report is a transcript of the court's decision in a particular case.) Quality newspapers such as *The Times* and *Financial Times* regularly report cases in abbreviated form. Developing the habit of reading law reports will assist you in further developing your vocabulary. Electronic sources via the internet are increasingly an effective way of conducting legal research. Some of the most useful of these sources are therefore provided in the following section.

Electronic sources

A number of 'on-line' resources are fee-paying subscription services, although a wide range of on-line legal databases are available free. The following is a non-exhaustive list of the latter (a more detailed list is contained in the online research resources guidance below). You should, however, always satisfy yourself of the suitability of the sources you access.

www.curia.eu.int (ECJ judgments)

www.hmso.gov.uk

www.parliament.uk

www.lawreports.co.uk

www.courtservice.gov.uk (Court forms and judgments, etc.)

www.companieshouse.org.uk

www.thelawyer.com

There are also a number of 'link sites' and 'gateways' which may assist in locating useful legal websites. For instance:

www.ials.sas.ac.uk/eagle-i.htm (Institute of Advanced Legal Studies)

www.venables.co.uk/legal

www.bailii.org

www.barcouncil.org.uk (the Bar Council)

www.lawsociety.org.uk/home.law (the Law Society)

www.law.cam.ac.uk/jurist/index.htm

LAW ANALYSIS AND STUDY

When researching law or undertaking the study of law (whether at undergraduate or post-graduate level) you will obviously encounter statutes and case law.

Reading statutes

The excerpt on page 200 shows the first page of a typical statute, the Human Rights Act 1998. Most statutes are referred to by their 'short title' in this way. The longer title which follows then describes in more detail the purpose and aims of the statute.

Reading case law

Note carefully the name of the case. This includes the names of the parties (the Claimant's name followed by the Defendant's name) followed by what is known as the 'citation'. This normally includes the year of the case report along with details of the volume/page number of the law report series where the report can be located. When referring to a case it is necessary to cite the case, in other words provide the case citation, for example: *Series 5 Software Ltd* v *Clarke* (1996) 1 All ER 853 (indicating the names of the parties and where the case can be found, i.e. in volume 1 of the *All England Law Reports* at page 853).

When reading a case also note carefully the court which decided the case (taking account of its authority, i.e. is it a High Court or a House of Lords decision, etc.?). Many case reports have a 'headnote' which can be very useful since this provides a summary of the facts and decision. It will also set out the fundamental legal principles on which the judgment is based (known as the *ratio decidendi*).

When writing coursework, etc., grammar remains important, as does the need to use plain English which is concise and clear in meaning. As a general rule, however, remember that academic English involves using the 'third person' (e.g. 'he', 'they', 'it' as opposed to 'I' or 'you', etc.) and the 'passive' voice instead of the 'active' voice. (See Chapters 1 and 2 for more guidance on academic writing.)

Finally, keep a written record of your legal research. The form on page 201 may assist you with this.

ELIZABETH II c. **42**

Human Rights Act 1998

Short title of statute

1998 CHAPTER 42

An Act to give further effect to rights and freedoms guaranteed under the European Convention on Human Rights; to make provision with respect to holders of certain judicial offices who become judges of the European Court of Human Rights; and for connected purposes. [9th November 1998]

Long title of statute, describing the purpose and aims of the statute

BE IT ENACTED by the Queen's most Excellent Majesty, by and with the advice and consent of the Lords Spiritual and Temporal, and Commons, in this present Parliament assembled, and by the authority of the same, as follows:—

Introduction

The Convention Rights.

1.—(1) In this Act "the Convention rights" means the rights and fundamental freedoms set out in—

(a) Articles 2 to 12 and 14 of the Convention,

(b) Articles 1 to 3 of the First Protocol, and

(c) Articles 1 and 2 of the Sixth Protocol,

as read with Articles 16 to 18 of the Convention.

(2) Those Articles are to have effect for the purposes of this Act subject to any designated derogation or reservation (as to which see sections 14 and 15).

(3) The Articles are set out in Schedule 1.

(4) The Secretary of State may by order make such amendments to this Act as he considers appropriate to reflect the effect, in relation to the United Kingdom, of a protocol.

(5) In subsection (4) "protocol" means a protocol to the Convention—

(a) which the United Kingdom has ratified; or

(b) which the United Kingdom has signed with a view to ratification.

(6) No amendment may be made by an order under subsection (4) so as to come into force before the protocol concerned is in force in relation to the United Kingdom.

RESEARCH SHEET

Summary of the purpose of the research

Search words (identify here the main area of law or subject of the problem, e.g. if researching law concerning car crashes, words such as 'personal injury', 'tort', 'negligence' and 'accident' would be relevant search words)

Research trail (details of cases read and other legal materials read such as statutes and their sources)

Details of research findings and conclusions

RESEARCHING FOR STUDY AND PRACTICE

This section provides more detailed guidance on how to research competently and professionally.

As with reading, keep in mind why you are researching the law. What matter is to be resolved or question answered? First, establish the particular area(s) of law involved. If you are unsure, *Halsbury's Laws of England* (or the on-line version called *Halsbury's Laws Direct*) is a resource which can assist you. *Halsbury's* has an extensive index containing a variety of areas of law from which you can select the subject headings relevant to your research task. Then refer to the relevant volume of *Halsbury's* which relates to those subject headings as indicated in the index. Also look for *Halsbury's Laws Direct*'s updating facility, which incorporates the *Cumulative Supplement* and the monthly *Noter-Up*.

If you know the name of a statute, *Halsbury's Statutes* (and its up-dating supplements) is a useful starting point. Similarly if you know the name of a specific case, *Current Law Case Citator* is a helpful source of reference. The Daily Law Reports Index lists cases by subject which have been reported in newspapers since 1988.

When starting your research, first, plan a research strategy as follows:

- consider and analyse the facts and circumstances carefully – identify the problem and your objective;
- identify the specific issues and legal subject areas you need to research;
- compile keywords of relevant terms (e.g. 'employment law', 'unfair dismissal', etc.)
- use appropriate research resources (see below) to look for relevant statutes and case law (which may help you clarify the law), etc., focusing your research by using the keywords you have selected.

To ensure that your search results are as relevant and precise as possible, think carefully about the topics and subjects involved. (Relevant keywords can also often be found in the question or your research instructions.) Then consider which sources are most suitable for you to search.

Good practice tips

- You can restrict your internet search by using 'AND' between two keywords to avoid searching every source relating generally to the two separate words, (e.g. 'negligence AND accident').
- You can widen your search with 'OR' between two keywords to make a general search of both words (e.g. 'negligence OR accident').
- Where your keywords are generally associated with each other and you do not want your search to include those common word associations, you can avoid those associations by placing 'NOT' between the words. (This will result in a search of the first word without common associations being made with the second word.) Be careful when using this technique, however, that you do not narrow your search to the extent that you exclude information from your search results which you require.
- In addition, these techniques can be combined (e.g. 'negligence AND collisions OR accidents').

If you are unsure of the correct spelling of a word you wish to use as a keyword, try placing '*' where you are unsure of the exact spelling. Many electronic databases will then search for permutations of words to help you, e.g. by entering 'neglig*' many databases will come up with results for 'negligence', 'negligent', etc. Note that some databases use an exclamation mark (!) rather than an asterisk (*) for this.

If you only want your search to come up with results relating to two search words being associated with each other, put the two (or more) words in inverted commas, e.g. 'wrongful dismissal'. Your selection of keywords and phrases (for looking up indexes and electronic sources) must be sufficiently precise to access the particular information you require. Consider using combinations of keywords, but do so carefully.

Keep a record of your research trail by noting details of every publication, statute, case, website, etc. you search. You will then be able to show the research route you took to your final answer. The following is a suggested list of things to note when researching:

- A brief statement of the problem and relevant facts.
- Key words and phrases.
- Research trail (including titles of publications referred to, volumes, page numbers and paragraph references, internet web page references, statutes and section number references, case names and references, journal references).
- Conclusions.

Take notes of your findings before writing your final answer. This will ensure that you have considered all relevant areas for research before reaching conclusions. When setting out your answer, explain why the law you are citing is relevant. For instance, what principle or legal concept does the statute or case you are referring to address? Apply this to the facts and circumstances of your research task. How, for instance, are the circumstances you are considering similar or distinguishable from the statute or case, etc. you are referring to? Based on this analysis, set out your conclusions.

SOURCES OF LEGAL INFORMATION

As mentioned earlier in this appendix, English legal resources basically consist of the following:

- statutes (Acts of Parliament);
- law reports;
- legal journals and publications;
- textbooks;
- reference works such as legal encyclopaedias and information websites.

The first two of these, statutes and law reports, are known as **primary sources** and consist of the actual law. The others are **secondary sources**, which are not the text of actual law but discussion, interpretation and explanation of it.

For locating Acts of Parliament (Acts) from 1950, *Current Law Statutes Annotated* is useful. The annual volumes contain useful comment and guidance on statutes. *Halsbury's Statutes* is another core reference work. It has a useful index volume which is arranged in alphabetical order by subject headings. Ensure that you check the following volumes for any changes to the statute you are researching:

- the loose-leaf *Noter-Up*;
- the *Annual Cumulative Supplement*;
- *Is It In Force?*;
- *Halsbury's Statute Citator.*

An electronic version of these resources is available on the Butterworths website under 'Legislation Direct'.

Acts dating from 1947 can also be located in *Current Law Legislation Citator*, which lists statutes alphabetically. An alphabetical listing of statutes from 1235 can be accessed at *Jurists UK Statutes*. English law reports divide into two historical periods – before (pre) and after (post) 1865. Many important cases before 1865 have been reprinted in a series called the 'All England Law Reports Reprint (All ER Rep)'.

For cases after 1865, there are the following main sources of law reports. The *Law Reports* by the Incorporated Council of Law Reporting, which divides into four main categories:

- Queen's (and King's) Bench Reports (QB)
- Chancery (Ch)
- Family (Fam)
- Appeal Cases (AC)

The *Weekly Law Reports* (WLR) along with the *All England Law Reports* (All ER) are additional valuable sources and both are published weekly. A source of English case law commonly used by the legal profession is *The Law Reports*, published by the Incorporated Council of Law Reporting, which uses the following abbreviations to refer to the different types of cases it reports:

- AC – Appeal case reports of the House of Lords and Judicial Committee of the Privy Council;
- Ch – Chancery case reports of the Chancery Division and appeal decisions from that division;
- QB – Queen's Bench Division of the High Court case reports and decisions of the civil and Criminal Divisions of the Court of Appeal;
- Fam – Family law reports of the Family Division and decisions of the Court of Appeal from that division.

When using *The Law Reports* look for the *Cumulative Index* to help you locate cases relevant to your research task. Check the 'headnotes' at the beginning of the text of each case for a useful summary of the legal arguments and decision reached in the case. Also look for the *Weekly Law Reports* (WLR) for reports of recent cases. The *All England Law Reports* (All ER) are also extensively used by legal professionals. The All ER can be accessed on-line through *All England Direct*.

Very old law reports (from around the twelfth to the sixteenth century) are not usually required for current legal study or practice but can be accessed on-line for personal interest and research on the free website: **www.bu.edu/law/seipp**.

English statutes are published by Her Majesty's Stationery Office (HMSO) and are available on-line at **http://www.hmso.gov.uk/acts.htm**.

Statutory instruments (delegated legislation which contains more detailed and specific law in some areas) are available at **http://www.hmso.gov.uk/stat.htm**.

Halsbury's Statutory Instruments lists all statutory instruments in force alphabetically by subject matter in its *Consolidated Index*.

If you have the name of a case but are unsure where to find it, the *Current Law Cases Citator* provides a useful index of cases since 1947. It is available in printed form and on-line and will refer you to the corresponding *Current Law Year Book* containing details of the case.

For thorough research of case law concerning a particular subject, *The Digest* is a valuable resource. This is a set of volumes set out by subject headings, in alphabetical order. This work includes cases from virtually every country with a common law system except the USA. Start your search of *The Digest* by looking for the index volumes.

It is also good practice to get into the habit of referring to regular legal journals such as the *Law Society Gazette*, *New Law Journal* and the *Solicitors Journal*, which regularly summarise important new cases and legal issues. The *Legal Journals Index* is useful for information on the range of legal journals published in the UK which are available on a variety of specific legal subjects. For information on a wider range of legal journals available internationally refer to the US publication entitled *Index to Legal Periodicals*.

SOURCES OF EUROPEAN UNION (EU) LAW

European Union (EU) law is now of central importance in English law and must therefore be taken into account when researching. The EU has set up some libraries in its member states as **European Documentation Centres**. The nearest of these libraries to you can be found in the *Directory of EU Information Sources*.

Primary EU legislation consists of 'treaties', which can be found in the EU publication *Consolidated Treaties*. The treaties can be freely accessed via the Europa website: **http://eur-les.europa.eu/en/treaties/index.htm.** *Sweet and Maxwell's Encyclopedia of European Union Law* can also be found in the average library.

EU secondary legislation consists of Regulations and Directives. This law can be found in the *EU Official Journal*. The index of this journal is useful if you have the name or reference for what you are searching for. You can check that the EU law you are concerned with is up to date by checking the EU *Directory of Community Legislation in Force*.

EU Regulations are directly binding in the law courts of member states and have direct effect (being intended to confer rights on individuals). Remember that Directives, however, require member states to implement particular laws within their own legal systems (by a specified date). It is therefore important to be sure that the Directive you are interested in has actually been implemented in UK law. For this, consult Butterworth's *EC Legislation Implementer*.

If you are unsure which area of law to search under, try starting your research with *Eurovac Thesaurus* (an official EU publication), which lists subject areas, or try the subject index of *Halsbury's Laws*.

EU regulations and EU law reports

The *European Court Reports* (ECR) is the official series of EU law reports and cover decisions of the European Court of Justice (ECJ) and the General Court. Cases since June 1997 can also be located the ECJ's *Curia* website (**http://curia.europa.eu/en/content/juris/ondex.htm**). To help you find particular EU cases you may find Butterworth's *EC Case Citator* useful.

Depending on the size of library available to you, you are also likely to find a range of EU periodicals and journals which can assist you. For instance, look for: *Bulletin of the European Union*, *European Current Law* and *European Law Review*.

Some EU organisations recognise and conduct their business in several European languages, English virtually always being one of those languages. A combined terminology is therefore developing and appearing in community law decisions and policies. This terminology is sometimes referred to as 'Eurospeak'. For translation of Eurospeak terms into the languages of various EU member states, refer to *Eurovac Thesaurus*.

Glossary

The following is a glossary (guide) of legal terminology. Please note, however, that this glossary is for guidance only and is not intended as an exhaustive or comprehensive source of definitions. The meanings provided are those commonly associated with the words and phrases in a legal context and it should be borne in mind that those same words and phrases may have a different meaning in a different context.

acknowledgement of service Court form used by a party to legal proceedings to confirm receipt of a statement of case (such as a claim form).

acquittal A finding by a court of not guilty to a criminal charge.

action Legal proceedings/claim (see also 'cause of action').

ad hoc For a specific purpose, typically for a temporary period.

ad infinitum For ever.

adjourn Postpone or keep court case or application on the court file.

admissability Degree to which the law of evidence permits particular evidence to be taken into account.

advocacy Representing a party by means of spoken submission to a court or tribunal.

advocate A court lawyer (see barrister and solicitor).

affidavit A written statement sworn on oath.

agenda An itinerary or list of matters for discussion at a meeting.

aggravated damages Additional compensation awarded by a court to compensate for particularly objectionable conduct on the part of the defendant.

agreement Contract or arrangement agreed orally or in writing between different parties.

alibi A defence to a criminal charge based on the contention that the accused was elsewhere when the crime is alleged to have been committed.

appeal Challenge to the validity or correctness of a decision of a court or tribunal (usually based on the contention that the law was incorrectly interpreted).

appellant Term used to describe a party appealing against a court or tribunal decision.

applicant Person or organisation making an application to court for a specific remedy prior to trial.

arrest The physical seizure of an individual (normally by a policeman) on suspicion of a crime having been committed by that individual or to prevent a crime being committed.

attorney (US) A qualified lawyer who has the rights of audience in court; **(Br)** a person appointed to act for or represent another for certain purposes.

bail The release of an individual from police custody pending further appearance by that person in court or at a police station.

bailiff An officer appointed to carry out court orders and execute writs.

balance of probabilities Usual standard of proof required in a civil case (more probable than not).

Bar, the Collective term for barristers.

barrister A lawyer who is a specialist court advocate and referred to as 'counsel' (often being instructed by a solicitor to appear in court on behalf of a client) or the 'prosecution'.

beneficiary Individual benefitting from a legal document (e.g. from a will).

bias Situation of someone (such as a witness) having a personal interest in the outcome of legal proceedings.

boilerplate clause A clause in a contract intended to cover eventualities which could occur (e.g. specifying the governing law in the event of a dispute).

bona fide In good faith; legal; without taking part in wrongdoing.

brief (to counsel) Set of instructions prepared by a solicitor and provided to a barrister, setting out details of a case (including relevant facts, law, etc.) to enable the barrister to provide representation in court on behalf of a client.

burden of proof Term used to indicate which party the onus is placed on to establish or prove a case and to what degree, e.g. in a civil case the burden of proof is on the claimant to establish the case on the 'balance of probabilities' (whereas in a criminal case the prosecution must normally establish the case beyond all reasonable doubt).

case A legal dispute between specific parties.

case law Law created by court decisions, i.e. law created by cases which provide precedents of relevance for future legal disputes (see 'precedent' below).

case theory A party's interpretation of and approach to the legal issues and evidence in a case.

cause of action The legal grounds or basis of a claim or 'action' commenced in court (e.g. breach of contract).

certificate of incorporation Certificate issued by the Registrar of Companies confirming that a company has been incorporated (i.e. legally recognised as having been created).

chambers Has two main meanings: (1) to refer to a hearing in private as opposed to in open court (referred to as being 'in chambers') and (2) to refer to a barrister's place of work ('counsel's chambers').

charge Allegation (usually in writing) of specific criminal conduct against an individual. (That individual is then said to have been 'charged' – such as with theft, for instance.)

chronological In date order.

circa Latin term commonly used in English to mean 'approximately'.

circumstantial evidence Evidence other than evidence by direct testimony or physical (real) evidence.

civil action/proceedings Legal action based on a civil right (as opposed to a criminal action), such as breach of contract, for instance.

claim form Court form used to commence legal proceedings in court.

claimant Party commencing civil legal proceedings.

class action A legal action commenced in the name of one or a few named claimants on behalf of a class of claimants.

client Term used by lawyers to refer to their 'customers'.

common law Legal rules and principles founded on court decisions as opposed to statutes or similar written laws or regulations.

conference with counsel Meeting between a barrister and a client (usually in the presence of a solicitor).

confidentiality clause A clause in an agreement providing that the agreed terms will be kept secret.

consideration (contract law) The price for which the promise of the other is bought. The definition given by Sir Frederick Pollock is: 'An act or forbearance of one party or the promise thereof is the price for which the promise of the other is bought and the promise thus given for value is enforceable.'

contempt of court Refusal or failure to comply with a court order or requirement.

contingency fees Fees charged by a lawyer for legal work which are based on a percentage of the damages recovered on behalf of that client (generally only permissible in the USA, albeit contingency fees can be charged in Employment Tribunal cases in the UK).

contract A legally enforceable agreement.

contributory negligence Degree to which a claimant is deemed to have contributed to or caused the accident or degree of injury for which damages are being claimed. (Damages can be reduced to reflect this degree of contributory negligence.)

conviction A finding by a court or tribunal that an individual is guilty of the offence charged. (That person is then said to have been 'convicted' of the offence charged – e.g. of a theft.)

corroboration Evidence from an independent source which substantiates a party's version of events.

costs Term used to refer to legal costs or expenses of legal work conducted by lawyers on behalf of clients.

counsel Term used to refer to a barrister. Also a term in the US for an attorney.

counsel's opinion Legal advice proposed by a barrister.

counterclaim A claim by a defendant in legal proceedings who in turn alleges that he has a legal claim against the claimant.

county court Civil court which usually deals with lower value civil cases.

court list List or schedule prepared by a court which provides details of the date and time that each trial or hearing is scheduled for.

Crown Prosecution Service (CPS) The organisation which prosecutes criminal cases in court in England.

Criminal Injuries Compensation Authority (CICA) A government scheme to provide monetary compensation to victims of crimes of violence.

cross-examination Questioning of a witness in court by a party other than the party calling that particular witness to provide evidence.

Crown court Criminal court of the Supreme Court of England and Wales with jurisdiction over the most serious criminal cases. (There are a number of Crown courts located throughout England and Wales.)

culprit A person who has done something wrong or been accused of an offence.

custodial sentence A sentence of imprisonment by a court or tribunal.

damages Monetary compensation (such as for personal injury).

de facto In fact, whether by right or not.

defamation Making of false statement.

default judgment Order made administratively by a court when a party fails to comply with some act required by the court (e.g. failing to file a document with the court in time).

defence Statement of case setting out the legal grounds and details on which a defendant is defending legal proceedings being pursued against that defendant.

defendant The party to legal proceedings against whom the claim is being made by the claimant.

deposition A written or recorded witness statement taken on oath.

directions A list of steps or instructions, usually issued by a court, setting out the specific actions which each party in a legal action is required to comply with prior to the case being heard in court. This is in order to ensure that the legal proceedings concerned proceed efficiently and that the parties in the case have properly prepared their cases in readiness for trial.

director Individual with management responsibilities within a company. (All directors of a company are collectively referred to as the 'board of directors'.)

disbursements Costs incurred in the course of legal work other than a solicitor's fees (e.g. travelling expenses and fees payable to expert witnesses).

discontinue Notifying the court that proceedings are no longer being pursued (i.e. are being discontinued) so that those proceedings are closed.

disclosure Revealing to another party to legal proceedings the past or present existence of evidential material (usually documents) which may be relevant to the case.

discovery The process whereby each party to legal proceedings reveals details of documentation and information in their possession which may be relevant to the case, thereby providing another party in the case with the opportunity to inspect or obtain copies of such material. The court usually orders that discovery should take place simultaneously between the parties.

district judge A judicial officer of the county court who acts as judge in many county court cases.

dock Box where accused stands in criminal court.

documentary evidence Evidence in written form (e.g. letters, contracts, etc.).

e.g. For example or for instance.

either way offence A category of criminal offence triable either in a magistrates' court or a Crown court.

estoppel Prevented by law.

et al. And others.

etcetera (etc.) And so on.

et seq. And the following pages.

evidence Information and material (such as witness testimony and documentation) on which a court or tribunal bases its deliberations and findings.

evidence-in-chief Evidence elicited from a witness by the party calling that witness.

examination-in-chief Questioning of a witness in court by the party calling that particular witness to give evidence.

exemplary damages Additional compensation awarded by a court amounting to more than the actual losses sustained by a party and intended as a penalty to reflect the court's particular disapproval of the defendant's conduct. (Usually only awarded in US courts, where some exemplary damages awards have amounted to hundreds of millions of dollars.)

ex parte A hearing in court which takes place with one of the parties to the proceedings being absent and unaware of the hearing. (A more modern equivalent phrase now commonly used is 'without notice'.)

expert witness Witness who gives evidence on a subject he or she has professional expertise in (e.g. a doctor).

express term Term or provision in an agreement which is specifically (i.e. expressly) stated or written.

extraordinary general meeting Any general (shareholders') meeting of a company other than its annual general meeting (AGM).

facts in issue Disputed facts which need to be proved to win the case.

force majeure Event(s) or occurrence caused by events outwith the control of the parties (e.g. parties to an insurance contract), such as natural disasters (sometimes referred to as 'Acts of God').

freezing order Court order preventing access to assets or money (sometimes termed 'freezing' the assets).

further and better particulars More specific detail or information of a specific aspect of the case referred to in the statements of case (court documents). (Such further detail or information will usually be provided in response to a request by a party for such further detail or information in order to clarify the claim being made.)

general damages Term usually used to mean compensation (damages) which is assessed by the court (typically damages for pain and suffering).

habeas corpus order requiring person detaining another to justify detention to court.

hearing The process of being heard in court.

High Court Civil court which deals with higher value civil cases.

i.e. Abbreviation for Latin phrase '*id est*' and meaning 'that is to say' or 'in other words'.

ibid. In the same source (Latin word used in referencing), i.e. the last source referenced. (Note: in numbered notes, it cannot be used if the previous note contains more than one source *unless* you intend to reference all the sources.)

illegal Against the law (e.g. stealing is illegal).

implied term Term of an agreement not expressly stated but recognised in law by virtue of the obvious understanding between the parties or by their conduct or the circumstances of the agreement. (An implied term can also be imposed by statute, e.g. implied term of satisfactory quality.)

in camera In private (e.g. a court hearing closed to the public is sometimes referred to as being 'in camera').

indictment Statement and particulars of a criminal charge.

inference Process of taking into account surrounding circumstances in deciding upon which evidence to prefer when conflicting evidence is presented.

injunction A court order compelling a person to do or refrain from doing something.

indictable offence Includes the more serious criminal offences (e.g. murder), such offences being triable only in the Crown court in England.

in open court A trial or court hearing in public.

instructions Details from a client to his or her lawyer setting out what the client wants the lawyer to achieve for the client.

instructions to counsel Written information prepared by a solicitor and provided to a barrister to enable that barrister to provide advice to a client or to draft legal documentation on behalf of a client. Such 'instructions to counsel' usually include a summary of the facts of the case, relevant law and any relevant supporting documentation.

intellectual property Law relating to copyright, rights to inventions (patents) and trademarks, etc.

inter alia Among other things.

interim order An order made by a court prior to the final trial or hearing of a particular case (e.g. an order for directions setting out the further steps each party is required to take prior to trial).

interlocutory application/hearing/order An application to court, court hearing or court order made prior to trial.

inter partes Term used to refer to a court hearing at which all parties are present (as opposed to an '*exparte*' hearing at which at least one party is absent).

interim order Temporary court order effective until trial or further court order.

interrogatory A request for further information.

issue (of proceedings) To commence legal proceedings by lodging relevant papers at court (such as a claim form). (This is referred to as 'issuing proceedings'.)

judge Trier or adjudicator of a case responsible for making findings of law (and sometimes of fact, but see also 'jury', below).

judg(e)ment A decision or declaration of the court, usually setting out the court's findings and details of any damages (compensation) or other remedy which the court has decided to grant to any party in the case.

jurisdiction The authority to decide and enforce the law (e.g. the county court and the High Courts have jurisdiction to try breach of contract cases in England and Wales).

jurisprudence Legal theory.

jury Group of individuals (usually 12) who make findings of fact in the serious criminal cases (in the Crown court in England and Wales).

law A system of rules and regulations governing and determining permissible conduct within society.

leading question A question which suggests the answer or which implies the existence of some particular fact(s) or circumstances.

lease Record of details of interest in land conveyed between a landlord and tenant.

leave Permission (e.g. to seek 'leave of the court' is to seek permission of the court).

legal action Court proceedings.

legal privilege A legal right to refuse to disclose or produce documentation or other evidence on the basis of some special interest recognised by law. (This typically relates to the legally recognised right for discussions and correspondence between lawyer and client to remain 'privileged' and thus protected from disclosure.)

letter before action Correspondence sent by a prospective claimant or their legal adviser intimating to another party an intention to commence legal action against that other party along with brief details of the proposed legal action. (Note that a more modern equivalent is a 'letter of claim'.)

letter of claim Modern term for 'letter before action' (see above).

liability Legal responsibility to comply with or discharge a legal obligation or indebtedness.

libel Written statement damaging another's reputation.

limitation period The time limit prescribed by law in which a claimant must commence a claim in court. Failure to issue the claim in court within this time limit will usually result in the claimant losing the legal right to pursue that particular claim (e.g. the limitation period for a personal injury claim is three years in the UK).

liquidated damages A term used to refer to a specifically quantifiable amount of monetary compensation which a claimant is seeking from another party (i.e. a sum which can be precisely calculated as opposed to an amount which is variable at the court's discretion).

listing for trial Procedure for providing the court with final documentation and information in order to enable the court to finalise a date for trial.

litigant A party to legal proceedings (i.e. to litigation).

litigation Legal action/proceedings involving a dispute between parties.

locus Location of an incident, particularly of an accident.

Magistrates' Court Criminal court in England and Wales which tries the relatively less serious criminal cases. (Usually conducted by a **magistrate**.)

member A shareholder (i.e. holder of shares in a company).

mens rea 'Guilty mind': thought/state of mind/intentions required for a finding of guilt in certain criminal offences.

minor An individual under 18 years of age.

minutes Record of matters discussed and decided in the course of a meeting (e.g. a directors' or shareholders' meeting).

mitigation A term used in criminal law to refer to submissions seeking to justify or at least provide some explanation for a party's conduct and aimed at persuading a court or tribunal to show some sympathy towards that party.

mitigation of damages A term used in civil law to refer to efforts made by a claimant to minimise or alleviate loss and damage sustained.

mode of trial hearing A court hearing to determine whether a criminal trial should proceed in a magistrates' court or a Crown court.

mortgage Term for security provided by a borrower to purchase property.

NB Latin for '*nota bene*' and meaning 'note carefully'.

negligence Used in a legal sense to refer to a failure to comply with a duty of care towards others imposed by law or by generally accepted standards.

non sequitur A conclusion or statement which does not logically follow from the previous statement.

null and void Not legally enforceable.

Old Bailey Central London criminal court.

oral evidence Spoken (as opposed to documentary) evidence.

party Person or organisation entering into an agreement or engaged in legal proceedings.

per se By itself (formal).

plaintiff Person or party commencing a legal action. Note that the term 'claimant' is now used in English courts in place of 'plaintiff' (the term 'plaintiff' still being in general use, however, in American courts).

pleadings A term previously used to refer to the court documents setting out each party's case and now largely superseded by the term 'statements of case'.

poll Means of voting at shareholders' meetings whereby votes on a particular resolution are counted on the basis of the number of voting shares held by each person voting (as opposed to 'on a show of hands').

post-mortem An examination of a dead body to establish the cause of death. Literally 'after death'.

practice Term often used to mean a law firm, e.g. Jonathan's legal practice. (The verb is 'practise', e.g. Jonathan practises law.)

precedent Existing document, draft or court decision which is relevant to and used as the basis for subsequent legal drafting or decisions. (The 'doctrine of precedent' refers to a concept whereby previous court decisions establish the general legal position for subsequent legal disputes involving similar circumstances.)

prima facie Appears on the face of it or from a first impression.

privilege (See 'legal privilege' above.)

probability Degree of inclination to believe a version of events based upon a particular state of affairs and the evidence presented.

proceedings Term used to refer to an ongoing court action (known as court or legal proceedings).

proof Evidence.

proxy An individual appointed to represent a shareholder at a shareholders' meeting.

PTO Abbreviation typically placed at the end of a document meaning 'please turn over'.

quantum (of damages) The level or amount of monetary compensation (damages) awarded by a court or agreed between the parties to a case by negotiation.

quash Overrule or annul a previous court decision.

Queen's Counsel A title bestowed on barristers who have demonstrated a high level of professional expertise and competence. Barristers appointed as 'Queen's Counsel' may use the letters 'QC' after their names and are sometimes referred to as 'silks' or 'leading counsel'.

quorum Minimum number required to be present at a meeting in order for decisions taken at that meeting to be valid.

ratio decidendi Fundamental legal principles on which a court judgment on a court case is based.

registered office Official address of a company as recorded with the Registrar of Companies at which official documents and legal proceedings can be served on a company.

registrar of companies Official responsible for maintaining the 'Company Registry' recording details of incorporated companies.

remedy The specific means by which a party receives restitution or satisfaction for loss caused by another (e.g. the usual remedy for personal injury is damages).

resolution A decision made by members of a company.

respondent Person defending an application to court for a specific order or defending employment tribunal proceedings.

res ipsa loquitor 'The thing speaks for itself' – term sometimes used when cause of something (e.g. an accident) is evident from the circumstances and so therefore is the person responsible.

res judicata Settled and binding (decision), e.g. the matter is *res judicata*.

restrictive covenant A contract in which a party agrees to be restricted in some manner as to future conduct, e.g. clause to prevent an employee competing with his or her employer.

return date Date when a case will be considered further by a court.

rights of audience Right to appear in and address a particular court or tribunal.

search order Court order requiring access to premises or production of documents or property.

service Provision or delivery of court documentation (such as a claim form, notice of a forthcoming court hearing, etc.). A person receiving such documentation is referred to as having been 'served'.

set aside A subsequent order or direction from a court cancelling a previous judgment or order (referred to as 'setting aside' the previous order or direction).

setting down for trial Now usually referred to as 'listing for trial' (see above).

settlement An agreement reached between parties to a legal dispute which concludes that dispute.

shareholder Owner of shares in a company (i.e. someone who is a 'member' of that company).

skeleton argument Written summary of a party's case and legal arguments.

slander Malicious or false statement spoken about another.

solicitor A lawyer who prepares cases and legal transactions on behalf of a client (often instructing a barrister to provide representation in court).

special damages Actual financial losses which can be specifically ascertained as having been incurred between the date the cause of action arose and the date of trial (e.g. loss of earnings up to trial, property damage sustained, etc.).

standard of proof The criterion or degree of proof required in order for a party to establish its case (e.g. in civil cases the standard of proof is 'on the balance of probabilities' whereas in a criminal case it is usually 'beyond all reasonable doubt').

statement of truth Statement at the end of a court document certifying that the contents are true.

statute Legislation in the form of written laws and regulations (such as Acts of Parliament created by the UK Parliament).

stay A halt to or suspension of court proceedings (those proceedings then being 'stayed').

striking out Court decision to refuse to further entertain a party's claim or part of it (that claim or part of the claim then being 'struck out').

subpoena Witness summons requiring a witness to attend court to give evidence.

sue Informal term meaning to issue legal proceedings.

summary dismissal Immediate dismissal of an empolyee by an employer (i.e. without notice).

summary judgment Procedure by which a court decides a claim or issue without a trial.

summary offence Category of criminal offence triable in a magistrates' court (e.g. common assault).

supra Used in a legal text to refer to a source already referred to somewhere other than in the immediately preceding note.

testimony Statement or assertion made to a court by a witness.

title Person's right of ownership of property.

tort Norman-French word meaning 'wrong' and now commonly used to mean a breach of a duty imposed by civil law (e.g. negligence).

unless order Court order providing that unless a party does something by a certain date (e.g. file its defence) a further order will be made (such as striking out that party's claim).

unliquidated damages Damages (monetary compensation) which cannot be precisely quantified upon commencement of legal proceedings (as opposed to liquidated damages which can; see above).

vicarious liability A legal concept whereby a person or entity can be held liable for the fault or wrongdoing of another. (A typical example of this is an employer being liable for the negligence of an employee acting in the course of his employment, i.e. 'vicariously liable').

vice versa The opposite is true; the other way round.

warranty A guarantee in a contract.

will Document providing details of a person's (testator's) wishes for the disposal of his or her estate on death.

withdraw Term used where a party removes (withdraws) legal proceedings already started.

without prejudice A legal concept whereby oral or written communication can be entered into between parties with a view to reaching a negotiated settlement, i.e. on the basis that the details of such communication cannot be disclosed to the court or relied upon in court in the event that a settlement is not achieved.

writ Court form traditionally used to commence legal proceedings in court. (Note that claim forms are now used far more commonly for commencing legal proceedings.)

Suggested answers to exercises

CHAPTER 1

Exercise 1.1

1. Unfortunately, we are unable to offer you a place on this course.
   or
   We regret to inform you that we are unable to offer you a place on this course.
2. University fees have substantially increased lately.
3. This department was established to support students.
4. I think I have some typing errors in my essay.
5. Prices have been reduced.
6. Many small businesses went bankrupt last year.
7. They have to postpone the meeting until our colleague returns from the conference.

Exercise 1.2

1. a 12-day trial
2. a five-member committee
3. a four-hour deliberation
4. a well-made point
5. the 12-men and women jury
6. the judge-made law

Exercise 1.3

In 1972 the Parliament passed the European Communities Act 1972 (ECA) in order to enable the UK to become a member of the European Community, thus avoiding further legislation. One of the many impacts of European legislation was the introduction of laws written for a civil law interpretation. Subsequently, the introduction of the Human Rights Act 1998 (HRA) required all statutes to be compatible whenever possible. As a result of these two Acts, we have seen a change in statutory interpretation.

Exercise 1.4

A full-time law degree lasts for three years and you are expected to study, on average, four modules each semester; some modules are compulsory, while others are optional.

It is useful for academic study to look at one way of classification of law. Under such classification there is a distinction between public and private law. The main focus of public law is the role of law and government in society, in other words it deals with the relationship between the state and its citizens, and so this includes constitutional law, administrative law and criminal law. You might find that constitutional and administrative law is counted as one module. Private law is mainly concerned with the relationship between individuals and business as well as the duties and rights of individuals towards each other. Thus, private law covers a wide range of modules, such as law of contract, low of tort, land law, family law, company law, employment law, etc.

In addition to the above classification, when you study the English legal system, you will find that law is divided into two main areas, namely civil law and criminal law.

Exercise 1.5

1. Addition: additionally, as well as, besides, furthermore, in addition, moreover
2. Cause (reason) and effect (result): accordingly, as a result, because, because of, consequently, due to, for this reason, hence, owing to, since, therefore, thus
3. Conditional clauses: as long as, assuming, even if, if, in case of, on condition that, provided that, unless

Exercise 1.6

1. A person who was not a party to this contract cannot be bound by it.
2. A mother who had injected her brain-damaged son with a lethal dose of heroin to end his suffering was found guilty of murder.
3. The directors of those hospitals in which patients have died from superbug infections because of failures by senior management will be prosecuted under new manslaughter laws.
4. Lord Judge, the Lord Chief of Justice, who comes from the ranks of criminal barristers and judges, said that he was commuting Carlos Khumala's 30-month prison term to a suspended sentence as an 'act of mercy'.
5. The Limitation Act 1980 imposes time limits within which an action for breach of contract must be brought.
   or
   An action for breach of contract must be brought within the time limits imposed by the Limitation Act 1980.
6. An ex-world championship bridge contestant, who constantly belittled his wife's card-playing abilities, was jailed for life for killing her.

Exercise 1.7

The Clearstream trial in France had five defendants, who were accused of involvement in a smear campaign, and some forty civil claimants, whose names had been linked to fake bank accounts supposedly holding the proceeds of bribes from an arms deal.

Exercise 1.8

1. It is **apparent** from the facts provided that John drove his car negligently.
2. Jennifer is the sole **beneficiary** of her uncle's will.
3. The judgment of the court was that the **defendant** was liable for having caused the accident.
4. The client **received** a cheque from her solicitor this morning.
5. My legal **practice** does not include providing advice on corporation tax and I therefore **referred** Mr Anderson to another lawyer who does **specialise** in that area of work.

Exercise 1.9

The right order of the sentences is: 2 5 4 1 3

Exercise 1.10

The correct order of the paragraphs is: 5 7 2 4 8 6 1 3

CHAPTER 2

Exercise 2.1

A heading could be: 'The relationship between the rules of conduct and the mental element in crime' *or* 'The interrelationship of "actus reus" and "mens rea" '.

Exercise 2.2

The element of *mens rea* exists in voluntary manslaughter, but there is no *mens rea* in involuntary manslaughter.

Exercise 2.3

Note: The '0' in the answers to 2.3 means that no article is needed. The text for 2.3 has two paragraphs, 18 gaps in the first paragraph and eight gaps in the second paragraph.

the 0 a a a the the the 0 the 0 the the 0 an a 0 the.
the the 0 the the the 0 0.

Exercise 2.4

There are 14 gaps in this paragraph.

the a a the the the a the a the the a an the.

CHAPTER 3

Exercise 3.1

1. call for the witness
2. draw up a court order
3. make progress
4. was found in
5. take down a statement
6. take over

Exercise 3.2

1. strongly suggest
2. extremely generous
3. solemnly declare
4. successfully defended
5. extremely fruitful
6. substantially increase
7. severely injured
8. totally objective
9. deliberately mislead
10. refrain from
11. dismissed without notice
12. settle out of court

Exercise 3.3

1. applicant
2. employment tribunal
3. instructions
4. unfairly dismissed
5. dismissal
6. disciplinary hearing
7. misconduct
8. notice period
9. contract of employment
10. legal grounds
11. prospects of success
12. mitigate
13. award
14. damages
15. settlement

Exercise 3.4

ir	un	dis	im	in	il	mis
irrelevant	unreliable	disobedient	immature	invalid	illegal	misrepresent
irresponsible	unfair	dishonour	impossible	inaccurate	illiterate	
	uncertain	discomfort		indirect	illegible	
	unease	disable			illogical	
	unavoidable					

Exercise 3.5

able	al	ate	ion	ful
personable	personal		suggestion	hopeful
usable				lawful
				useful
				restful

ive	less	ous	some	ist
suggestive	worthless		awesome	
	lawless			
	useless			
	restless			

Exercise 3.6

ir	un	dis	im	il	mis
irresponsible	unable	disable	impossible	illegal	misrepresent
		discomfort		illogical	
		dissatisfaction			
	unavoidable				

Exercise 3.7

1. will accept
2. is received I will

Exercise 3.8

1. act on behalf of
2. contract
3. our instructions
4. express term
5. breach of contract
6. proposals to compensate
7. satisfactory proposals
8. legal proceedings

Exercise 3.9

1. Mrs Matthews who *has had an accident remains in hospital.*
2. Instead of visiting her *in hospital, she would like you to meet with her at her home once she is released from hospital.*

Exercise 3.10

The Occupiers Liability Act 1957 provides that an occupier will owe a common law duty of care to visitors regardless of:

(i) whether a specific contract has been entered into: and
(ii) whether any independent contractual duty of care also exists.

Exercise 3.11

1. appeal against **2.** contract for **3.** decide against **4.** enter into **5.** negotiate with **6.** act for

Exercise 3.12

set out above
otherwise

Exercise 3.13

1. begin **2.** after **3.** end **4.** before **5.** If **6.** about/concerning

Exercise 3.14

Compound construction	Simple form
in the event that	if
at a later date	later
as a consequence of/for the reason that	because
until such time as	until
similar to	like
at that particular time	then
prior to	before
in close proximity to	near

Exercise 3.15

Suggested answer: American courts award higher damages in personal injury cases than English courts.

Exercise 3.16

1. referred to
2. obtain a statement
3. independent witness
4. award damages
5. are instructed
6. full and final settlement

Exercise 3.17

1. Took their client's instructions.
2. To pay £25,000 to Nicholas Tiessen in settlement of his claim.
3. Within 28 days.
4. Nicholas Tiessen's legal costs and date of birth.

Exercise 3.18

1. of
2. to
3. of
4. to
5. by
6. within
7. in good time
8. In terms of

Exercise 3.19

1. For advice concerning an agency agreement his firm is considering entering into with MacFadyen Aviation Limited.
2. MacFadyen Aviation Limited.
3. Whether the principal (Cadmium Aerospace Limited) can also continue selling to customers in Europe and North America while the agency agreement is in force. Also, whether Cadmium Aerospace can appoint other agents in these areas.
4. How the agent's (MacFadyen Aviation Limited) commission is to be calculated and what minimum level of sales it is required to achieve.

Exercise 3.20

1. I asked Mr Anderson what his job was.
2. I said to Mrs Kennedy that we'd meet again next week.
3. I said that an employee would usually agree to provide a reference.

Exercise 3.21

The two irrelevant sentences are: 'This client turned up 20 minutes late for our meeting' and 'She also told me that one of the decorators was wearing a dirty old shirt.'

CHAPTER 4

Exercise 4.1

1. d **2.** f **3.** g **4.** b **5.** i **6.** h **7.** a **8.** e **9.** c

Exercise 4.2

1. The report will have been published by the end of next month.
2. The terms and conditions of the agreement are currently being drafted. It is optional to add 'by their lawyer' if you want to specify who is doing it.
3. Your case has been listed for hearing next Wednesday.
4. All the necessary documents have been submitted to court.
5. A new director will be appointed as soon as possible.
6. Last week the reasons for amending some clauses in the draft contract were explained.
7. A director may be disqualified for breach of health and safety law.
8. The terms of the settlement must be contained in a compromise agreement. [In this sentence, the passive is used because the terms of the settlement are important.]
9. The compensatory award is calculated on the basis of net pay.
10. It has been decided to hold a conference to discuss the impact of the new regulations.

Exercise 4.3

1. d **2.** f **3.** l **4.** b **5.** h **6.** k **7.** i **8.** a **9.** j **10.** e **11.** g **12.** c

Exercise 4.4

2. resolved
3. appointed
4. registered
6. presented convened given/provided
7. resolutions
8. declared

Exercise 4.5

1. Convening a meeting means to schedule and hold or conduct a meeting.
2. By using audio-visual conferencing, the board of directors of a company can hold board meetings even if the company's directors are located in different countries around the world.
3. Board meetings (meetings of the directors of a company) are held to conduct business on behalf of the company. A board meeting may therefore be held for instance to approve a loan

from a bank, to appoint another director or to discuss and agree general business decisions on behalf of the company.

4. A quorum is the minimum number of directors or shareholders who require to be present at a meeting for a resolution (decision) to be validly passed at that meeting. Only if that mimimum required number is in attendance is the meeting *quorate*. (The usual quorum for a small private limited company is two and the 'model articles of association' provide that the quorum for a company with those articles is usually two.)

Exercise 4.6

Minutes of General Meeting

MAPLINK LIMITED

Minutes of an extraordinary general meeting of the Company held at 44 Princess Diana Walk, South Kensington, London, W2 3SL on 16 May 2011 at 11.00 a.m.

Present: Thomas Shapiro
Dimitris Yavaprapas

In Attendance: Gisela Wirth

1. NOTICE AND QUORUM

It was noted that due notice of the meeting had been given to all members and that a quorum was present. The meeting was therefore declared open.

2. APPOINTMENT OF FURTHER DIRECTOR OF THE COMPANY

The chairman proposed the following resolution as an ordinary resolution.
'That Kadir Salleh be appointed a director of the Company'. On a show of hands the chairman declared the resolution passed unanimously.

3. CHANGE OF COMPANY NAME

The chairman proposed the following resolution as a special resolution:
'That the name of the Company be changed to Travelgraph Limited'.
On a show of hands, the chairman declared the resolution passed unanimously.

CLOSE OF MEETING

There being no further business, the chairman declared the meeting closed.

____

Chairman

Exercise 4.7

1. An agreement is unanimous when everyone voting is in agreement (i.e. no one dissents).
2. A shareholder is also sometimes referred to as a 'member' of the company.
3. If there is an equal number of either directors or shareholders voting for and against a resolution then the chairman of the meeting sometimes has a casting vote. Someone holding a casting vote when this happens (i.e. when there's deadlock) can then decide whether the resolution is passed or not by exercising his or her deciding casting vote.

4. To requisition a meeting is to call or schedule a meeting.
5. A proxy is someone who attends a shareholders' meeting in place of and to represent a shareholder at that meeting. (A proxy can vote at the meeting on behalf of his or her appointing shareholder.)

Exercise 4.8

1. £75,000 per year (i.e. per annum)
2. Sales director
3. 25 days per annum
4. English law
5. The service contract is for a term of three years, terminable on six months notice thereafter.
6. Kadir cannot terminate his employment with the company under the contract before three years. After that, however, either party can terminate the contract by providing six months notice in writing.

Exercise 4.9

1. He's got to attend the meeting. (informal English)
2. He has to attend the meeting. (semi-formal English)
3. He must attend the meeting. (standard English)
4. He needs to attend the meeting. (standard English)
5. He is to attend the meeting. (formal English)

Exercise 4.10

1. two
2. £90,000 (two machines at £45,000 each)
3. Yes (Matrix Printers will be technically in breach of contract because clause 2 provides for delivery on 15th August 2011)
4. Upon Travelgraph making full payment (as provided by clause 3)
5. Clause 4 provides '... that all risk of loss and damage shall pass to the Buyer upon delivery of the Machines.'

Exercise 4.11

SPONSORSHIP AGREEMENT

Date: 17th October 2011
Parties: (1) Antonio Perez
(2) Bannerman and Law (a firm) of 11 The Strand, London ('the Sponsor')

1. **DEFINITIONS**

'Tennis event' means in this Agreement any and all tennis competitions, events and tournaments anywhere in the world where Antonio Perez plays tennis in his capacity as a professional tennis player. The definition further includes any social or business event(s) which Antonio Perez attends for the purpose of representing the Sponsor and/or promoting the Sponsor. This includes (but is not limited to) exhibition tennis matches.

'Sponsorship fees' means in this Agreement the monies payable by the Sponsor to Antonio Perez in accordance with clause 4.

→

2. **SPONSORSHIP**

In consideration of the Sponsor paying to Antonio Perez the Sponsorship fees, Antonio Perez agrees to provide the Sponsor with the commercial benefits as set out in the provisions contained in clause 3.

3. **SPONSORSHIP BENEFITS TO BE PROVIDED TO THE SPONSOR**

3.1 Antonio Perez shall wear at any and all tennis events a sports shirt displaying the words 'Bannerman and Law – Worldclass Lawyers'.

3.2 Antonio Perez shall attend on four days per annum at events stipulated by the Sponsor to play tennis with commercial clients of the Sponsor and/or to meet with and socialise at events organised by the Sponsor.

4. **SPONSORSHIP FEES**

The Sponsor shall pay Antonio Perez annual fees of £90,000 during the period of this Agreement in equal quarterly instalments (in advance). In addition, the Sponsor shall provide Antonio Perez with the use of a Jaguar XKR motorcar during the course of this Agreement.

5. **TERMINATION OF AGREEMENT AND RENEWAL**

5.1 Subject to earlier termination in accordance with clause 5.2, this Agreement shall continue for a duration of 2 years from the date of signing of the Agreement.

5.2 This Agreement will be terminable by written notice from the Sponsor at any time upon any of the following events occurring:

(a) Antonio Perez failing to comply with his obligations to attend events in accordance with clause 3.2 above;

(b) Antonio Perez having a bankruptcy order made against him;

(c) Antonio Perez's public reputation being detrimentally affected due to adverse national press or media reporting which proves to be accurate and truthful in relation to Antonio Perez's private life.

5.3 Early termination of this Agreement in accordance with this clause shall be entirely without prejudice to the legal rights and duties acquired by any party to the Agreement prior to termination.

6. **GOVERNING LAW**

This Agreement shall be governed by and interpreted in accordance with English law. The parties hereto irrevocably agree to the English courts having exclusive jurisdiction to determine any legal dispute arising between the parties relating to this Agreement.

Signed ______________________ (Antonio Perez)

Signed ______________________ (Bannerman and Law)

Exercise 4.12

1. hereby
2. further
3. moreover
4. furthermore
5. hereby
6. henceforth
7. in addition
8. during
9. within

Exercise 4.13

This agreement shall continue in force/for a period of two years save and except that it may/be terminated by either party providing to the other/three calendar months notice in writing.

Exercise 4.14

In the event that/the Agent fails to achieve a minimum total sales amount of/£750,000 within/ twelve months of the commencement of this Agreement/the Principal shall be entitled/to terminate this Agreement/by notifying the Agent in writing accordingly.

The court staff will not let the administration office not to be opened to the general public by 10.30 a.m. on each and every week day. This can be redrafted to remove the double-negative as, *The court staff will not let the administration office remain unopen to the general public by 10.30 a.m. on each and every week day.*

Exercise 4.15

Suggested draft:

1. The Principal further agrees to pay a bonus to the Agent amounting to 1 per cent of total net sales in the event that: the agent achieves sales exceeding £1,250,000 within the first year from commencement of this Agreement.
2. At the end of clause 4 entitled 'REMUNERATION', possibly adding a further paragraph marked '4.2'.

Exercise 4.16

draft order	bankruptcy order
business interests	board meeting
convene a meeting	pension document
written document	intellectual property
propose a resolution	sponsorship agreement

Exercise 4.17

Compound construction	**Simple form**
for the reason that	due to/since/because
hereinafter	below
aforementioned	set out above
save as aforesaid	otherwise
in the nature of	like
at this point in time	now
by means of	by
in the event that	if
in order to	to
on a monthly basis	monthly
until such time as	until
during the time that	while

Exercise 4.18

Column A (items within same category)	Column B (items not within same category)
Travelgraph's customer lists	Kadir's driving licence
Travelgraph's stock records	Kadir's CD collection
Kadir's desktop computer	Copies of letters written by Kadir applying for employment
Travelgraph's accounting records	Kadir's academic diplomas
Travelgraph's sales records	The motorcar in the garage belonging to Kadir's wife
Computer access codes to	
Travelgraph's computer records	The computer desk in Kadir's study
Travelgraph's expansion plans	Kadir's CV (resumé)
Travelgraph's purchasing policies	
Travelgraph's software programmes	

Exercise 4.19

Column A	Column B
1. ad hoc	(*g*) not permanent
2. bona fide	(*a*) genuine
3. *ex gratia*	(*h*) as a favour/for free
4. *ex parte*	(*b*) without notice
5. *ratio*	(*c*) reason
6. Regina	(*e*) the Queen
7. status quo	(*f*) the existing state of affairs
8. ultra vires	(*d*) beyond the powers

CHAPTER 5

Exercise 5.1

1. damages **2.** contract **3.** claimant **4.** claims **5.** recover

Exercise 5.2

1. of **2.** into **3.** in **4.** to **5.** with **6.** on **7.** with **8.** between

Exercise 5.3

A	B
Particulars of claim	Claimant
Defence	Defendant
Defence and counterclaim	Defendant

Exercise 5.4

Eric Jones was arrested at home and charged with **(1)** fraud. At court he was convicted of **(2)** fraud and sentenced to **(3)** two years in prison

Exercise 5.5

1. He was prosecuted for burglary.
2. The bank manager was convicted of fraud.

Exercise 5.6

Old fashioned/dated language	Equivalent modern language
aforesaid	stated previously
aver/plead	contend/allege
in camera	in private
in open court	in public
save that/save insofar	except that
plaintiff	claimant
pleading	statement of case
prescribed by	provided by/indicated by
undernoted	noted below
writ	claim form

Exercise 5.7

1. Delete 'obliges you to do'. (The order is to prohibit Kadir Salleh from working for Worldlink Limited.)
2. solicitor
3. set aside this order
4. contempt of Court
5. sent to prison
6. Respondent
7. confidential information relating to Travelgraph Limited
8. Respondent shall pay the Applicant
9. to the Court
10. Order
11. Applicant's
12. Stringwood & Evans, 18 Bond Street, London, W1 1KR, tel. no: 020 7538 2892

Exercise 5.8

Column A	Column B
may	it is possible
must	it is compulsory
shall	will

Exercise 5.9

Verb	Noun	Adjective	Negative
advise	adviser advisor advice advisability	advisable advisory	inadvisable

(continued)

Verb	Noun	Adjective	Negative
consult	consultation consultancy consultant	consulting consultative	X
continue	continuation continuity continuance continuum	continuous continual	discontinue discontinuous discontinuation discontinuance
employ	employment employer employee employability	employable	unemployment unemployable unemployed unemployability
obey	obedience	obedient	disobey disobedience disobedient
pay	payment payer payee	payable	non-payment unpaid
prohibit	prohibition	prohibitive	X
respond	response respondent	responsive	irresponsive
vary	variety variation variable variance	variable variant various	invariable invariant

Exercise 5.10

1. I arrived, then they discussed the case
2. They were in the middle of the discussion when I arrived.
3. When I arrived they had already finished the discussion.
4. They had been discussing the case for some time before I arrived.

Exercise 5.11

1. She told us last Thursday that she had already been offered a new job.
2. A meeting was held after we received new instructions.
3. The witness was very nervous when we first talked because he had not appeared in court before.
4. When I saw the motorist, he was holding a mobile telephone.
5. They waited until everyone was ready and then they started the meeting.
6. He was travelling at a speed of over 70 mph when the accident took place.
7. When Phil came to my office, I had been writing a report for three hours.
8. Lucy told us the rationale behind her decision after we had asked her twice.
9. While he was interviewing the witness, Lisa was preparing the documents.
10. We thanked Christine for all that she had done for us.

Exercise 5.12

1. am
2. witnessed
3. was driving
4. was
5. was coming
6. heading
7. was driving
8. was travelling
9. approached
10. could
11. were showing
12. proceeded
13. began
14. caught
15. was heading
16. could
17. was holding
18. appeared
19. came
20. braked

Exercise 5.13

1. that **2.** which/that **3.** whom **4.** who

Exercise 5.14

1. b
2. b

Exercise 5.15

1. Matthew Gluck (1st Defendant) and Londinium Delivery Company Limited (2nd Defendant)
2. Honda
3. Thursday 20 October 2011
4. At the junction between Oxford Street and Regent Street
5. Chelsea and Westminster Hospital
6. Computer programmer
7. £4,000
8. Londinium Delivery Company Limited owns the vehicle driven by Matthew Gluck. It will be vicariously liable for his negligence if he was driving in the course of his employment when the accident happened.

Exercise 5.16

1. the claimant
2. the claimant's bundle of documents
3. witness statements
4. negligence
5. was at fault
6. medical evidence
7. on the balance of probabilities
8. will have to rule on
9. be calling

Exercise 5.17

quantum	noun	compensation	noun	requisite	adjective
quantify	verb	compensate	verb	advise	verb
quantifiable	adjective	compensatory	adjective	advice	noun
claim	noun/verb	require	verb	advisable	adjective
claimant	noun	requirement	noun	inadvisably	adverb

Exercise 5.18

1. quantum
2. advise
3. advisable
4. requirement
5. claimant
6. inadvisably
7. requisite
8. compensation
9. quantifiable
10. advice

Exercise 5.19

IN THE CENTRAL LONDON COUNTY COURT **CASE NO. KR 65739**

BETWEEN :

NICHOLAS TIESSEN	**Claimant**
and	
MATTHEW GLUCK	**1st Defendant**
and	
LONDINIUM DELIVERY COMPANY LTD	**2nd Defendant**

COUNSEL'S ADVICE ON QUANTUM

Background details

1. I am asked to **(1) advise Mr Tiessen on quantum** in regard to **(2) injuries sustained** in a **(3) road traffic accident on 20th October 2011**. The accident occurred when another vehicle collided with the claimant's vehicle. This other vehicle, a Ford Galaxy registration number **(4) FT23 FLK**, drove through a red traffic light, entering the junction between Oxford Street and Regent Street in London from Regent Street.

2. Instructing solicitors have kindly enclosed with **(5) instructions** the **(6) medical report** of Mr Paulo Jarvis, **(7) consultant orthopaedic surgeon**, dated 1st December 2011. This report indicates that Mr Tiessen incurred a moderate hyperextension sprain of the cervical spine, commonly referred to as a 'whiplash' injury. This injury incapacitated him for 5 weeks, during which time he was unable to work. Following a course of physio-therapy, however, Mr Tiessen has now returned to work **(8) as a computer programmer**. He now considers that he has almost completely recovered, save for continuing to suffer occasional **(9) symptoms** of stiffness in the neck and intermittent headaches. According to Mr Jarvis such symptoms are likely to continue for several months and Mr Tiessen is expected to make a complete recovery **(10) from his injuries** within 6 months from the date of the accident.

Damages

3. Mr Tiessen sustained a relatively minor **(11) whiplash injury** resulting in moderate symptoms. There are some continuing symptoms although Mr Jarvis's report has

→

provided an encouraging prognosis in his **(12) report**, indicating that he expects Mr Tiessen to make a full recovery within 6 to 9 months of the **(13) date of the accident**. Mr Tiessen was off work for several weeks but has not had his career prospects adversely affected by the accident.

4. The Guidelines for the Assessment of General Damages provided by the Judicial Studies Board (JSB) indicate that the level of appropriate damages for a whiplash injury of this nature is within the range of £750 to £2,500. The following cases further assist in **(14) assessing** the level of damages a court would be likely to award.

(a) *Evans* v *Morton* 3rd March 1998 (Oxford County Court)
The award for pain, suffering and loss of amenity (PSLA) was £1,675. The facts of this case are fairly similar to those in Mr Tiessen's case. The claimant was involved in a road traffic accident and sustained a whiplash injury. The claimant experienced immediate neck pain and was taken to hospital. He was unable to work for several days as a toolmaker. There were continuous symptoms of neck pain and shoulder pain from which the claimant made a **(15) full recovery** in approximately 7 months. The extent of injury was broadly of the same degree of severity as sustained by Mr Tiessen. Taking account of inflation the award of £1,675 represents an award at today's value of approximately £1,950.

(b) *Sangster* v *Kensington Building Services* 4th April 1997 (Birkenhead County Court)
The claimant sustained a whiplash injury in a road traffic accident and suffered continuing pain and stiffness in the neck as well as headaches, making a full recovery in approximately 6 months. The claimant was off work for 2 days and was unable to play football as a pastime for 2 months. The total award for PSLA was £1,500. Uplifted for inflation this represents **(16) an award** today of approximately £1,800.

5. Taking account of these cases and the JSB Guidelines I am of the of the **(17) opinion** that an award of £2,000 represents the likely value of Mr Tiessen's **(18) claim** for pain, suffering and loss of amenity.

A. LAWYER

Justice Chambers

9th December 2011

Exercise 5.20

IN THE CENTRAL LONDON COUNTY COURT — **Case no. KR 65739**

BETWEEN :

NICHOLAS TIESSEN	**Claimant**
and	
MATTHEW GLUCK	**1st Defendant**
and	
LONDINIUM DELIVERY COMPANY LIMITED	**2nd Defendant**

→

CONSENT ORDER

Upon the parties having agreed terms of settlement of this claim, IT IS HEREBY ORDERED BY CONSENT THAT:

1. The First and Seconds Defendants shall by **(1) 6th January 2012** pay to the **(2) Claimant** the sum of **(3) £14,250**.

2. The Defendants shall jointly pay the **(4) Claimant's costs** of this action, to be taxed on the standard basis in default of agreement.

3. These terms are in **(5) full and final settlement** of this claim and that upon payment of the above mentioned damages and costs the **(6) Defendants shall** be discharged from any further liability to the Claimant in respect of this action.

District Judge Hemmings

Dated this 16th day of December 2011

Exercise 5.21

1. He was seen driving a new Ferrari motorcar.
2. That he had won the lottery.
3. A written statement from the lottery organisers confirming that he had won the lottery.
4. His employers did not investigate properly nor provide Charles with a chance to explain. If they had, then it is likely that they would have discovered that Charles was not at fault.

Exercise 5.22

1. Henry Moore said that he had got the Ferrari-driving swindler.
2. Scoville was told that he was being dismissed immediately.

Exercise 5.23

1. began
2. was employed
3. working
4. having
5. told
6. given
7. arrived
8. driving
9. entering
10. shouting
11. told
12. arrived
13. informed
14. explained
15. dismissed
16. contend
17. denied
18. to provide

Exercise 5.24

The main stress in each word is indicated by a blue line above it.

de-ci-sion
pro-ced-ure
re-pre-sen-ta-tive
al-le-ga-tion
mis-a-pro-pri-a-tion
dis-mis-sal
fair-ness
mis-con-duct
ad-mis-sion
tri-bu-nal
con-duct
in-for-ma-tion
in-ves-ti-ga-tion
em-ploy-er
de-clare
con-si-dered
hear-ing
e-vi-dence
wrong-do-ing
re-spon-dent

Exercise 5.25

The unanimous decision of the tribunal is that: the Applicant was unfairly dismissed.

Charles Scoville, the applicant, was dismissed on 26.4.2011 on the grounds that he had stolen two million pounds.

The tribunal looked at the relevant legislation, s. 98 of the Employment Rights Act 1998. This requires that an employer has reasonable grounds for believing that an employee has acted wrongfully in order to dismiss him/her fairly. The employer must also provide a fair hearing (i.e. fair procedure) before dismissing the employee.

The tribunal also considered the relavant case law, *BHS* v *Burchell* [1980] which established the need for a warning, the opportunity to reply and a proper disciplinary hearing. Also *Icelandic Foods* v *Jones* [1983] ICR 17 sets out the band of reasonable response.

Evidence was given by Mandy Renwick of Chameleon Gaming Systems and DC Clouseau.

The Chair, Charles Rumbelow, awarded £20,000, payable within 14 days.

Exercise 5.26

1. Under no circumstances are they to be disturbed while holding a meeting.
2. Only when the solicitor has finished preparing the case will she submit the documents.
3. No sooner had he started the car engine than the police asked him to produce his driving licence.
4. At no time did the defendant show remorse for his crime.

Exercise 5.27

't'	'd'	'id'
reached	employed	accepted
dismissed	entitled	contended
	considered	carried
	believed	decided

Exercise 5.28

1. Daryl Cosimo
2. Central London County Court
3. Means that there are genuine, realistic prospects for the case to success. Not fanciful.
4. An order for summary judgment.
5. A court judgment without a full court trial. (Sometimes awarded by a court when one party's case is clearly correct, or 'clear cut.')
6. Daryl Cosimo did building work and supplied materials at Antonio Ahman's work premises and has not been paid.

CHAPTER 6

Exercise 6.1

The main stress is indicated by a blue line above it.

li-ti-$\overline{\text{ga}}$-tion   ob-li-$\overline{\text{ga}}$-tion   dis-tri-$\overline{\text{bu}}$-tion

in-ves-ti-$\overline{\text{ga}}$-tion   ju-ris-$\overline{\text{dic}}$-tion   re-mu-ne-$\overline{\text{ra}}$-tion

le-gis-$\overline{\text{la}}$-tion   ar-bi-$\overline{\text{tra}}$-tion   com-pe-$\overline{\text{ti}}$-tion

$\overline{\text{ad}}$-vo-ca-cy   cer-$\overline{\text{ti}}$-fi-ca-te $\overline{\text{li}}$-ti-ga-ted

CHAPTER 7

Exercise 7.1

1. weren't you?
2. was he?
3. don't/haven't you?
4. was he?

Exercise 7.2

1. should **2.** should **3.** shall/will **4.** shall **5.** should

Exercise 7.3

1. (a) is the correct answer. (Answer 2(b) is more hypothetical, not emphasising the likely possibility of there being real need for the legal team to work through the night.)
2. (a) is the correct answer, being more likely to convey the situation accurately.

Exercise 7.4

1. would have accepted
2. had been
3. had reduced
4. would not have been injured

Exercise 7.5

Correct order of questions:

2. Open question
1. Closed question
3. Open question
4. Open question

CHAPTER 8

Exercise 8.1

1. for **2.** because of/due to/owing to **3.** by

Exercise 8.2

Suggested answer: 'Your client does not have any evidence to support her claim for lost profit. My client's offer of £235,000 for loss of profit is therefore a generous one.'

Exercise 8.3

1. However **2.** in addition

Exercise 8.4

1. could/might **2.** would **3.** would

Exercise 8.5

1. Firstly/To begin with **2.** Finally/Lastly/Last of all

Exercise 8.6

1. If you agreed to payment being made within two weeks then my client would accept the amount being offered.
2. If you were to make delivery (or deliver) within five days then we would pay a further £5,000.
3. If management agrees to a further day's holiday then the workforce will work extra hours to complete the order.
4. If Global Enterprises awards the firm with the contract to provide legal services then the firm will employ a further twenty lawyers.

Exercise 8.7

1. A **2.** D **3.** A **4.** D

Exercise 8.8

Conciliatory	Confrontational
negotiating collaboratively using conciliatory language	being argumentative behaving aggressively being condescending being offensive negotiating competitively being deliberately obstructive negotiating in bad faith using adversarial language

CHAPTER 9

Exercise 9.1

1. denies that
2. version of events
3. established the legal grounds
4. based on the evidence
5. I refer you to
6. admits owing to the claimant
7. summary judgment
8. is more credible

Exercise 9.2

1. for **2.** with **3.** of **4.** of

Exercise 9.3

1. guilty of **2.** in mitigation of **3.** on trial for

Exercise 9.4

1. charged **2.** bail **3.** trial **4.** acquitted **5.** sentenced **6.** mitigation **7.** conviction **8.** sentence

Exercise 9.6

Negotiation	**Mediation**	**Arbitration**	**Litigation**
Voluntary	Voluntary	Arbitrator	Highly formal
Parties control the process	Parties control the process	Imposes a binding decision	Imposes a binding decision
Usually in private	Usually in private	Usually in private	Governed by rules of court
Can save time and costs	Can save time and costs	Neutral chosen by the parties	Usually public
Enables more creative solutions than a court	Neutral chosen by the parties	This process is often specified in contracts	Judge
	Mediator	An adjudicatory process	An adjudicatory process
	Neutral		

Index